Writing Proposals

The Allyn and Bacon Series in Technical Communication

Series Editor: Sam Dragga, Texas Tech University

Thomas T. Barker
*Writing Software Documentation:
A Task-Oriented Approach*

Carol M. Barnum
Usability Testing and Research

Deborah S. Bosley
*Global Contexts: Case Studies in
International Technical Communication*

Paul Dombrowski
Ethics in Technical Communication

David Farkas and Jean Farkas
Principles of Web Design

Laura J. Gurak
Oral Presentations for Technical Communication

Sandra W. Harner and Tom G. Zimmerman
Technical Marketing Communication

Richard Johnson-Sheehan
Writing Proposals: A Rhetoric for Managing Change

Dan Jones
Technical Writing Style

Charles Kostelnick and David D. Roberts
*Designing Visual Language:
Strategies for Professional Communicators*

Carolyn Rude
Technical Editing, Third Edition

Gerald J. Savage and Dale L. Sullivan
*Writing a Professional Life:
Stories of Technical Communicators On and Off the Job*

Writing Proposals

A Rhetoric for Managing Change

Richard Johnson-Sheehan

University of New Mexico

Longman

New York   San Francisco   Boston
London   Toronto   Sydney   Tokyo   Singapore   Madrid
Mexico City   Munich   Paris   Cape Town   Hong Kong   Montreal

Vice President and Editor-in Chief: Joseph Opiela
Marketing Manager: Christopher Bennem
Production Manager: Donna DeBenedictis
Project Coordination, Text Design, and Electronic Page Makeup: Elm Street
  Publishing Services, Inc.
Senior Cover Design Manager: Nancy Danahy
Cover Designer: Caryl Silvers
Art Studio: Burmar Technical Corporation
Senior Manufacturing Buyer: Dennis J. Para
Printer and Binder: Hamilton Printing
Cover Printer: Coral Graphic Services

Library of Congress Cataloging-in-Publication Data

Johnson-Sheehan, Richard.
    Writing proposals : rhetoric for managing change / Richard Johnson-Sheehan.
        p. cm.
    Includes bibliographical references and index.
    ISBN 0-205-32689-7
    1. Proposal writing in business. I. Title.

    HF5718.5 .J64 2001
    658.15'224—dc21

                                                                    2001029373

Please visit our website at http://www.ablongman.com

ISBN 0-205-32689-7

1 2 3 4 5 6 7 8 9 10—HT—04 03 02 01

Contents

Chapter Four: Describing the Current Situation   55

Chapter Five: Developing a Plan   76

Chapter Six: Describing Qualifications   98

Chapter Seven: Introductions, Costs, and Benefits   117

Chapter Eight: Developing Budgets   142

Chapter Nine: Writing With Style   161

Chapter Ten: Designing Proposals   185

Chapter Eleven: Using Graphics   208

Chapter Twelve: Putting the Proposal Together   226

References   265

Index   267

Preface

What is a proposal? In the first chapter of this book, proposals are defined as "tools for managing change." The key words in this definition are tools, managing, and change. By *tools*, I mean proposals are devices that help us do our work. They help us to present our ideas, our plans, and our dreams for the future. *Managing* means taking control of a situation. It means directing people and resources in a way that allows us to achieve specific ends. *Change* is really what life is all about. Despite human attempts to find absolute truths, natural laws, or first principles, few things ever stay the same for long. The world is endlessly evolving around us, urging us to continually reinvent ourselves—to keep changing. Proposals are tools for managing these changes. They are tools for taking purposeful action in a world that never seems to stop moving.

So how do we go about using proposals to manage change? The subtitle of this book, "Rhetoric for Managing Change," suggests the fundamental *approach* that grounds this text. The strategies in this book are rooted in rhetorical theory, a discipline going back at least a few thousand years. Put concisely, rhetoric is the study of what *could be* or what *should be,* not necessarily what *is.* It is a forward-thinking discipline, more concerned with what we are going to *do* in the future than what happened in the past. For this reason, the discipline of rhetoric is particularly helpful in illuminating the proposal development process. After all, rhetoric is a discipline that studies change and how humans use communication to mold and shape their social environments.

Indeed, in ancient Greece and Rome, teachers of rhetoric like Gorgias, Protagoras, Aristotle, and Cicero showed their students how to interpret various social situations and then express themselves in ways that shaped those situations to their advantage. In this book, I aimed to do the same—first providing time-tested methods for examining complex rhetorical situations, then offering persuasion strategies that will help you manage people and resources efficiently and effectively. Students of rhetoric will find that I have adapted familiar rhetorical strategies to the proposal writing process. Where possible, I have tried to give credit where credit is due.

Premises of This Book

A few important premises set this book apart from other texts on writing proposals. In my experience, most books about proposals urge writers to approach the task from a "sales" or "winning" point of view. They take a rather narrow bottom-line approach, putting too much emphasis on getting the clients' money rather than understanding the clients' needs.

There are two problems with the sales-oriented approach. First, proposals are often used as planning tools rather than sales tools. People use them as blueprints for planning their future actions and strategies. These kinds of proposals are designed to offer plans, not to sell or win anything. A second problem with the sales-oriented approach is that proposals are really the beginning, rather than the end, of a relationship with a client. Using persuasion to urge, perhaps even to trick, clients into agreeing with an unsound plan may meet the writers' short-term monetary goals, but these kinds of proposals inevitably lead to complications in the future. The challenge is to write a proposal that wins the contract, while also providing a sound strategy for taking action.

An initial premise of this book, therefore, is that writing proposals should be approached from a problem-solving point of view. The proposal-writing process should help you and your team sort out complex situations and devise plans that meet specific goals. Of course, sales are an important purpose of most proposals. However, in this book it is assumed that a thorough understanding of the situation, a sound plan, and solid credentials will ultimately win contracts and funding. Therefore, the emphasis is placed on solving the problem rather than obtaining the money.

A second premise is that you, as a proposal writer, need to pay attention to change as you assess situations and develop plans for improving those situations. Put bluntly, proposals are never written in a social vacuum. Rather, they are written in social, political, and ethical environments that are always mutating and mutable. What was true today or yesterday may not be true tomorrow. Therefore, the key to writing successful proposals is to first identify what changed to create the current problem or opportunity. Then with these elements of change identified, you can use proposals to shape these forces to your advantage. In the end, this book assumes that there are two kinds of truth—absolute truth and dynamic truth. *Absolute truth* is the domain of philosophers and theologians. *Dynamic truth* is the domain of proposal writers and rhetoricians. This is the reality that we are continually inventing and reinventing for ourselves. This book will show you how to use proposals to manage dynamic truth to your advantage.

The third underlying premise of this book is that proposals should be written "visually." In this multimedia age of television and computers, people tend to think in images rather than in words alone. In this book, you will notice that almost all the techniques discussed employ strategies that take advantage of your and your readers' abilities to think visually. Some of the visual techniques are more apparent, such as the use of cognitive maps to invent a proposal's content or the use of design principles to guide the page layout of the text. Other visuals are subtle, such as the use of similes and metaphors (Chapter 9) to create visual images in the readers' minds. Indeed, I believe one of the downfalls of many books on writing is their over-reliance on a "literal" or "linear" approach to thinking and writing. These books assume that writing is a matter of stringing words together. This kind of literal/linear writing restricts a writer's creativity by limiting his or her ability to draw from alternative perspectives. Moreover, literal/linear writing also makes picturing a proposal's ideas harder for the readers to visualize. On the other hand, visual writing allows both writers and readers to develop a strong visual sense of what the proposal is illustrating.

Content and Organization

The ability to write effective proposals is a powerful skill, but the act of writing is only part of the overall proposal development process. In this book, you will also learn the techniques that will—

- **Help you tap into your innate creativity to invent the content of your proposals.** Some of the "invention" techniques in this book, such as logical mapping (Chapter 4), may seem a little strange at first. However, these techniques will help you gain unique insights into problems and opportunities. They will help you devise creative strategic plans that use imagination and foresight.
- **Help you organize your ideas in ways that achieve specific goals.** The organizational pattern of a proposal is much more than a convenient structure for presenting your case to the readers. It is a means for helping you formulate your approach and develop your strategy for success. You will learn how to use the proposal genre to generate new ideas and new ways of understanding your or your clients' needs.
- **Show you techniques for expressing your ideas plainly and persuasively**. The use of good style should be a choice, not an accident. You will learn simple, time-tested techniques for clarifying your message for the readers. You will also learn how to amplify your prose by using stylistic techniques that tap into your readers' motives, values, attitudes, and emotions.
- **Show you how to use visual design to clarify and enhance the arguments in your proposals.** In an increasingly visual age, readers are becoming more reliant than ever on visual cues to help them find the important information in proposals. They also expect proposal to include graphics that illustrate and reinforce the written text. You will learn design principles that will help you devise winning designs for your proposal and include graphics to enhance the text.

This book is organized to lead you through the writing process for composing, revising, designing, and editing proposals. Chapters 1 through 3 offer techniques that will help you prepare to write a proposal by analyzing your readers and the contexts in which they will use your proposal. Chapters 4 through 8 discuss the drafting of various parts of a proposal, helping you generate ideas by "mapping" your thoughts visually. Chapters 9 through 11 discuss style and design in proposals, allowing you to express your ideas clearly and persuasively in ways that will urge readers to say "yes" to your ideas. Finally, Chapter 12 will show you techniques for revising and polishing your proposals into final form. This final chapter also includes two sample proposals for you to study.

Acknowledgments

A book like this one is never the work of just one person, though one person usually takes the credit. So, let me thank the others who helped put this book together. First, I appreciate the help of my colleagues and students at the University of New Mexico who have shaped this text through their direct and indirect suggestions for improvements. Specifically, James Burbank, Karen Schechner, Shannon McCabe, Andrew Flood, Craig Baehr, and Kristi Stewart helped me edit the final draft. Professors Charles Paine and Scott Sanders have offered insightful suggestions to streamline some of the invention techniques described in this book. I also want to thank the reviewers of this book, who offered immeasurably helpful comments to improve the text: Jamie Larsen, North Carolina State University; Diana C. Reep, University of Akron; Deborah Andrews, University of Delaware; Dean Hall, Kansas State University; Roger Munger, James Madison University; and Sam Dragga, Texas Tech University.

Finally, this book is dedicated to Tracey and Emily, who helped me struggle through the rough spots as the book went from thought to page. In their own ways, they provided the motivation to keep going when times were tough.

Richard Johnson-Sheehan

Writing Proposals

1 Introduction to Proposals

Overview

This chapter will provide an overview of the purpose and importance of proposals. The chapter will meet the following learning objectives:

1. Discuss the importance of proposals in an evolving world and workplace.
2. Define the study of rhetoric and its relation to proposals.
3. Define the genre of a proposal and the "areas" of a basic proposal.
4. Identify the "rhetorical elements" of the proposal writing process.
5. Show that a research proposal is a business proposal.

Why Do We Write Proposals?

Put simply, a proposal is a tool for managing change. We write proposals because the world around us is endlessly evolving and shifting, often creating new opportunities and new problems. We write proposals because, as the old proverb says, "the only constant is change." Even the most successful plans, the strongest buildings, and the securest relationships need to be reimagined, reconsidered, and rebuilt to keep up with a world in flux. Proposals are instruments for managing those changes.

Some people resist change. They worry about losing what they have, so they try to ignore the evolutionary forces around them, attempting to hold change back or slow it down. As a proposal writer, you should view change as an ally, not an enemy. You should always recognize that a changing world creates new openings and new opportunities that can be used for growing and advancing your business, organization, or research. You should look forward to change with optimism, not regret or fear. The sooner you realize that change is something to be *managed,* not resisted, the sooner you can start using proposals to capitalize on the openings that are created by change. The victims of change are people who fight the currents of reality, eventually being drowned or swept away by the advancements in their field. Managers of change, on the other hand, are people who learn how to use proposals to steer and shape reality, riding the currents of change rather than fighting them.

The purpose of this book is to help you write effective proposals by using time-tested rhetorical strategies to identify new opportunities and solve problems.

You will learn how to develop plans for action, organize your ideas, improve the clarity of your writing, and persuade your readers to say yes to your ideas. You probably don't need to be told how important proposals are to your career or business. More than likely, you picked up this book in the first place because you have an important proposal to write, or perhaps proposals play a significant role in your working life. As you already know, proposals are important tools in the workplace, whether you are a CEO pitching a multimillion-dollar design to a client, a middle manager proposing a new project for your workgroup, or a scientist looking for research funding from the National Science Foundation.

In short, proposals are about money and power. They are about who is doing what, for whom, and for how much. Learning to write effective proposals can be the basis of your success in the professional world.

Rhetoric

In this book, we will follow a *rhetorical approach* toward developing proposals. Rhetoric, despite its negative undertones in the mainstream media, is more than empty political promises or amplified speech. Rather, rhetoric is the art of persuasive communication, a rich discipline with over two thousand years of tradition to draw from. Aristotle (384–322 B.C.) offered one of the earliest definitions of rhetoric when he wrote, "Let rhetoric be defined as an ability in each case to see the available means of persuasion" (Aristotle 1991, p. 36). In this definition, Aristotle suggests that being persuasive requires you to first "see" or map out the current situation in which you are operating. Then, you can develop a persuasion strategy that suits that particular situation.

Until the late nineteenth century, rhetoric was a central study in universities, but today the word *rhetoric* is usually associated with words like *mere, just,* or *empty.* With this denigration of rhetoric, it is probably no coincidence that most people in our society struggle to express themselves in writing and speech. A quick glance at the documents around you should demonstrate how far communication skills have declined. These documents often lack substance, organization, style, and design. They often don't address their readers' needs, and they regularly lack a purpose and a point. It is ironic that rhetoric is denounced by a society that desperately needs it most. After all, in this information age, those who can write or speak persuasively are well on their way to success. Those who cannot communicate effectively find themselves imprisoned in their own words.

To help you become a stronger communicator, this book will show you how rhetorical strategies can be applied directly to the development of proposals. Rhetoric is often defined as the "art of persuasion," but it is also the study of *change.* Rhetoricians see change as the normal condition of reality. Rhetoric is the study of what could be, what might be, or what should be. It is not necessarily the study of what *is.* Consequently, an understanding of rhetoric helps us anticipate change, react to it, and then use effective communication strategies to shape the changing world to our own advantage. Rhetoric is a means for gaining power in that uncertain reality.

Rhetoric's emphasis on change is reflected in the two elements of rhetoric, which will be addressed in each chapter of this book: interpretation and expression.

Interpretation

Interpretation involves using rhetorical strategies to ask the right questions and then impose mental structures on situations that are evolving, uncertain, or chaotic. For example, imagine that you are a manager who scheduled a staff meeting to help you solve an important problem. As you step into the room, you hear members of your staff arguing, you notice other people walking around the room, and you see papers strewn across the table. Members of your staff seem to be coming at you from all directions, trying to tell you about the "problem."

What would you do? Well, more than likely, your first reaction would be to impose some structure on this chaotic meeting. After telling people to quiet down, you would start questioning each of your staff members to figure out what the current situation really is. As your staff answers your questions, you would find that some of the information they provide is useful. Meanwhile some details and opinions—no matter how emphatically expressed—are not very relevant. In most cases, you would also soon realize that some important facts that you need to make a decision are not available. Eventually, as you gather facts, you would start mentally working out a plan for dealing with the problem that created the chaos in the first place.

When you prepare to write a proposal, the situation is similar to this chaotic meeting. Usually, when you start writing a proposal, there are thousands of confusing facts, opinions, and concerns floating around in your mind. On your desk, you have reports, notes from meetings, clippings from magazines and newspapers, and your own scribbled comments on pads of paper. At this point, ineffective writers—just like ineffective managers—are often overwhelmed by the sheer mass of information that they need to process. And, like ineffective managers, these writers often fail to achieve their goals because they do not know how to organize the available information into a useful form.

Quite the opposite, effective writers, just like effective managers, know from experience that they need to first "interpret" the many available fragments of information. Only then will they be able to grasp the big picture by recognizing what information they already possess and what information they still require before taking action. Experienced writers know that the challenge is not to "discover" order in a chaotic situation, because, frankly, there is no order to be discovered. Rather, effective writers use interpretive strategies to *impose* order on the current situation. A knowledge of rhetoric offers you a basic interpretive structure from which you can take control of chaotic situations and solve problems.

Expression

Expression is the performance side of rhetoric. Once you have properly interpreted the situation you face, then you can begin developing a rhetorical strategy to help you express your ideas persuasively to the readers. Expression involves inventing the content of the proposal by describing the current situation, setting some goals, and promoting the plan. It uses organizational strategies to capitalize on your readers' expectations for the structure of the document. Expression also takes advantage of your readers' psychological tendencies by weaving emotional and authoritative themes into the style of the document. And finally, expression uses visual design to deliver a professional package that will stand above your competitors' efforts. Expression is not simply a means for spinning the facts to your advantage. Rather, it is a way to generate ideas and use the facts effectively to persuade your audience to accept your ideas.

In this book, you will find this interpretation/expression balance used in each chapter to first help you impose order on chaotic writing situations and then use powerful rhetorical strategies to bend each writing situation to your will. In fact, you might find that the strategies you learn in this book go far beyond writing proposals. A knowledge of rhetoric is useful in all situations where communication is important.

The Proposal Genre

One reason proposals are so difficult to write is that they rely on a somewhat difficult genre. Let us imagine that your company wants to bid on a landscaping contract for a new building being constructed in Chicago. Before the proposal is even written, both you (the bidder) and your readers (the clients) can already anticipate the basic pattern of the proposal and what types of questions it will answer. First, your clients know that you, as the bidder, will demonstrate to them that you understand their situation/problem (i.e., their need for some landscaping around a new building in Chicago). Second, the readers also expect your proposal to describe a plan completing the job. Third, your clients will expect you to show them that you are qualified and have the capability to carry out your plan. And finally, because you are bidding for the work, they know you will tell them how much the work will cost.

As this example shows, readers usually expect a proposal, as a genre, to address some fundamental questions:

- What is the current situation?
- What is needed to improve the current situation?
- What is a good plan for improving the current situation?
- Why are you, as the bidders, the best-qualified people to do the work?
- How much will the work cost?
- What are the tangible benefits of the plan?

This list of questions might make proposals sound complicated, but if you think about it, people use these questions to conduct business all the time. Aren't these the same questions you would expect a mechanic to answer before fixing a problem with your car? Wouldn't you expect a surgeon to answer these questions before she puts you on an operating table? Would you want to do business with a mechanic or surgeon who did not, would not, or could not provide answers to these questions up front? Of course not.

FIGURE 1.1
The Proposal Genre

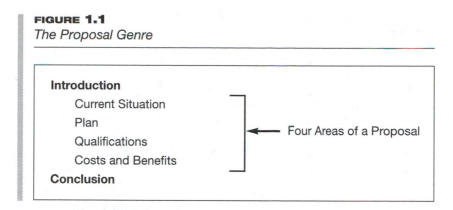

Just like you, your clients expect your proposal to anticipate and answer their questions up front. To address the readers' expectations, a typical proposal will account for four important areas, as shown in Figure 1.1.

Of course, the proposal genre is not a formula into which writers plug and chug content. In fact, many proposals do not follow this pattern in this order. Nor do each of these areas of the proposal genre require a separate section of the proposal. Nevertheless, in almost all cases, if a proposal accounts for these four areas, it will have addressed the readers' expectations.

In this book, we will handle each of these areas separately and in some depth. Once you master the model genre in Figure 1.1, you will find that you can shape this genre to suit each unique proposal writing situation. With practice, you should be able to internalize your own proposal writing process, writing effective proposals for many different projects.

The Writing Process and Four Rhetorical Elements

The best way to write proposals is to follow a repeatable *process* that takes you from your initial ideas to a finished proposal. In this book, you will learn a process for writing proposals that includes four stages:

- **Invention**—putting your ideas on paper and identifying persuasive strategies that will help you convince the clients to say yes
- **Drafting**—writing and designing a rough draft of the proposal
- **Revision**—crafting the organization, style, and design of the draft
- **Editing**—polishing the draft for final submission

These four stages imply a progression from invention to editing, but writers almost always find themselves moving back and forth among the stages. For example, drafting or revision often leads to a need for more invention. Revision often highlights places where more drafting is needed. Editing can sometimes lead you to rethink some of the strategies you invented at the outset. Most good writers of proposals cycle back and forth among these stages as they shape the document.

You will also learn how to address four *rhetorical elements* at each stage of the writing process:

- **Content**—the logical arguments, examples, facts, and data that you will need to make your case to the readers
- **Organization**—the structure that holds your proposal together and highlights you proposal's key points
- **Style**—the use of plain or persuasive styles and the tone/persona projected by your proposal
- **Design**—the visual elements of your proposal, including page layout and the use of graphics to reinforce your points in the written text

These rhetorical elements, based on something called the *Canons of Rhetoric,* are principles that ancient rhetoricians once used to teach their students how to speak persuasively in public. In the following chapters, you will learn how to handle each of these four rhetorical elements as you invent, draft, revise, and edit your proposal.

As you learn to write proposals, you should pay close attention to the process you are following as you write. Mastering the proposal-writing process requires hard work and practice. However, as you master the writing process (invention, drafting, revising, and editing) and the rhetorical elements (content, organization, style, and design), you will gain an intuitive sense of the means of persuasion that are available in any given proposal-writing situation.

A Comment on Research Proposals

What about research proposals? Some scientists and researchers believe that their proposals, especially grant proposals, are something quite different from business and technical proposals. They might point out that a research proposal is not really *selling* a product or service like other proposals. Rather, research proposals are simply asking for funding to conduct a study into a particular area. With some funding, hard work, and a little luck, the research project might yield some new insights, facts, and truths.

Actually, this way of thinking about research proposals can greatly hamper attempts to secure funding for important studies. After all, funding organizations are typically interested in how they or others can use the results of the research. For them, the research *is* providing a service or product, for which the funding organization is paying money. To illustrate, let us say you are a medical researcher writing a grant to the National Institutes of Health (NIH). Your research proposal will be much more attractive to the NIH Board of Directors if it addresses a recognized problem in our society (e.g., cancer, AIDS, trauma) or your community (e.g., drugs, low birth weight, farm safety). Your proposal will also be much more desirable if it shows how your project moves us one step further toward solving the problems that face our society. In other words, the results of the research should be useful in some way.

Are you selling out if you make these kinds of adjustments to fit a funding source? Of course not. Usually foundations and corporations offer funding for research because they believe an important problem needs to be solved. Even the most altruistic foundations have motives for offering their money to researchers, and they would like to see how your research or project advances their causes. If you show that your project addresses the needs of the funding organization, your chances for receiving funds will increase substantially.

In the end, research proposals are simply specialized business proposals. The researcher is proposing to do a service for a funding organization that has identified a problem or need in the community. In Chapter 2, we will discuss more specifically the writing of research proposals. As a researcher, though, you should keep in mind that you need to consider the business side of research when writing a proposal. The sooner you start thinking about research proposals as business proposals, the sooner you will be successful in securing funding.

Last Word

Proposals are written to manage change. To accomplish your goals as a proposal writer, you can use rhetorical strategies to impose intellectual order on chaotic situations. You can then invent the content for your argument, organize your response, craft your text, and deliver a professional document. The remainder of this book is designed to show you how to use effective interpretation and expression strategies to write proposals that succeed.

CASE STUDY **Elmdale Hill**

To help illustrate the proposal writing process, each chapter in this book will be followed by a scene from an ongoing case study. The case study will demonstrate how these strategies can be used to interpret a problem and develop a proposal to solve that problem. Through this case study, you can observe how these somewhat abstract strategies work in a realistic proposal situation.

The case is based on the Elmdale Hill business district, a ten-by-three-block shopping area that includes a variety of retail and grocery stores, restaurants, bars, and theaters. Elmdale Hill has always been a popular district for shopping and entertainment, but several storeowners have experienced a significant drop in sales over the last six months. Most owners blame the drop in sales on the recent opening of the new Wheatmill Mall, just a few miles away.

But other problems in the Elmdale Hill might be turning away the business district's usual customers. For one thing, many people think Elmdale Hill is less safe than it once was. After a rare murder in the area, the local television news has been increasing its coverage of crime in the Elmdale Hill district. Every small incident seems to be making the evening broadcasts, giving viewers the impression that there is a crime wave in the area. Also, the number of panhandlers and street people seems to have increased this year. Elmdale Hill has always been a haven for the "alternative" customer, who is more likely to give change to homeless people. But in the last year, it has almost become impossible to walk a couple blocks in the Elmdale Hill business district without being asked for money. Another reason Elmdale Hill seems less safe is increased amount of graffiti and litter in the area. Graffiti and litter just seem to attract more graffiti and litter.

Elmdale Hill is still a quaint place to shop, and it has loyal customers who patronize the shops for everything from food to clothing to entertainment. However, in discussions with their customers, store managers have found that people seem to hold a less positive image of the district. Words like *less safe, dirtier,* and *more expensive* seem to be regularly used in descriptions of the district. Clearly, the new mall cannot be blamed for all of Elmdale Hill's problems.

Each scene from this case will focus specifically on four business owners in Elmdale Hill who want to improve the district. John Legler owns Milano's, an upscale Italian restaurant. Karen Sanchez owns a clothing store for women called New Fashions. Thomas Lee manages one of the last large-screen theaters in the city, called the Star Catcher. And, Sally Johnson owns the Dust Jacket, a small bookstore. All four of these business owners have noticed a significant drop in their revenues, causing them concern about their future and the future of the Elmdale Hill business district. Recently, they have also noticed more vacant storefronts in the area and heard rumors of more business owners considering closing or relocating out of the district.

The four business owners decide they need to take action before they are forced out of business. But where do they start? After all, the problem is larger than their individual businesses. How can they go about improving the entire district when they only control their small parts?

In each chapter of this book, you will see how John, Karen, Thomas, and Sally use a proposal to help them work toward solving Elmdale Hill's problems.

Questions and Exercises

1. What are some of the problems or opportunities on your campus, in your workplace, or in your community that might be addressed with proposals? List out a few of these problems/opportunities. Under each of these topics, offer some reasons why these problems/opportunities might exist. Then, write down some ways in which you might use proposals to address them.

2. Find a proposal in the library, at your workplace, or on the Internet. Write a memorandum to your instructor in which you study the strengths and weaknesses of the proposal's content, organization, style, and design. Does the proposal address the areas of the proposal genre? Does the proposal include any areas in addition to the proposal genre discussed in this chapter? Are there any areas missing? If so, explain why you think the proposal writer chose to leave out specific areas. Overall, do you think the proposal is effective or ineffective? Why?

3. Using the Internet and e-mail, find and contact a person who writes proposals regularly. Ask what kinds of proposals he or she writes. Ask what kinds of situations require a proposal to be written. Present your findings to your class, highlighting any advice that the proposal writer may have offered to you about writing good proposals.

4. Identify some situations on your campus, in your workplace, or in society where rhetoric is used to manage change. How is persuasion used to first

"identify the available means of persuasion" and then alter that situation to the advantage of the speaker or writer? Who tends to use persuasion in our society? How do they use it?

5. Imagine you have just been assigned to an advisory committee that has been asked to develop ways to reduce the number of cars being driven to your campus or workplace. What information do you have already on this topic? What information would you still need to solve the problem? What are some questions you would need answered before you and your team began writing a proposal to solve this problem?

2 Identifying Problems and Opportunities

Overview

This chapter will show you how to define problems and opportunities by using *stasis* questions. The chapter will meet the following learning objectives:

1. Define solicited, unsolicited, external, and internal proposals.
2. Show how to interpret a Request for Proposals.
3. Illustrate how the Five W and How questions are used to define a problem or opportunity.
4. Explain how the three *stasis* questions are used to answer the *why* question.
5. Discuss how to interact with a Point of Contact.

Two Basic Reasons for Writing Proposals

Proposals are written for two basic reasons: to solve a problem or to take advantage of an opportunity. In either case, the first question that you, as the writer of the proposal, should ask yourself is, "What changed?" That is, what elements in the current situation changed recently to create this problem or opportunity? For example, if your company's computer network is no longer keeping up with your company's accounting needs, what changed to cause that problem? If a client is looking for someone to conduct an environmental impact study, what changed in their situation to cause them to seek out this kind of study? As mentioned in the previous chapter, change is the essence of proposals. So, before you start to develop a proposal, it is critical that you first identify the elements of change that brought about a particular problem or opportunity.

In this chapter, we are going to take our first step toward writing a proposal by discussing how to interpret the *stasis*, or status, of a proposal opportunity. By determining stasis, you can identify the specific problem or opportunity that created the need for a proposal. Essentially, you need to figure out why the readers are looking for someone to help them solve their problem or take advantage of an opportunity.

Unsolicited and Solicited Proposals

Proposals are classified according to how they were initiated, where they will be used, and what purpose they will serve. Depending on how the proposal was initiated, a proposal can be either *solicited* or *unsolicited.*

Solicited Proposals

Solicited proposals are requested by a client to address a need that they have identified. These proposals are often initiated through a Request for Proposals (RFP) or a direct contact from the client. Solicited proposals tend to be used in business-to-business transactions to propose new research, plans, or projects. Grant proposals that seek funding for research are also solicited proposals, because they usually answer a call for grant proposals.

Unsolicited Proposals

Unsolicited proposals are initiated by you or your company when a problem or opportunity needs to be addressed. You can use these proposals to propose changes, improvements, or new products in your own company. Or, as a sales tool, they can be used to pitch existing products or services to another company.

Proposals can also be classified according to whether they are *external* or *internal.* An external proposal is one that will be used to conduct business between two companies or organizations. External proposals tend to be formal, because they are often used as interim contracts between two companies. In other words, if an external proposal is accepted by the client, you cannot go back and change the terms without their approval.

Internal proposals can be formal or informal. They are used within a company or organization to suggest new strategies, new products, or new ideas. Often, internal proposals are used informally to help groups of people plan out new strategies together. Internal proposals can also be used formally to pitch ideas to the company's management.

Reading RFPs

A solicited proposal is born when a business or government agency publishes or sends out a Request for Proposals (RFP). RFPs are called a variety of different names, according to the kind of work or information the client is seeking. An RFP might be referred to as a Call for Proposals (CFP), an Information for Bid (IFB), a Request for Grant Proposals, a Call for Quotes (CFQ), an Advertisement for Bids (AFB), among other names. Whatever it is called, an RFP is essentially an announcement that a client is seeking proposals for a specific project. Some RFPs are simply single paragraphs with a few hundred words describing the project and deadlines. Other RFPs, especially from government agencies, can run on for pages and pages, describing in detail the project, goals, and even the kinds of plans that would be acceptable. Requests for Grant Proposals, such as those from government foundations like the National Science Foundation (NSF) or National Institutes of Health (NIH), might include an entire packet of information with forms and guidelines.

RFPs can be found in a variety of places. The U.S. government publishes its RFPs in the *Commerce Business Daily* and the *Federal Register.* You can subscribe to these periodicals, access them through the Internet, or locate them in a major library in your area. State and local governments often publish RFPs in the classi- fieds section of major local newspapers or on their Web sites. Private corporations usually send their RFPs directly to past bidders or publish RFPs in trade maga- zines. Nonprofit organizations, such as foundations or government agencies that fund scientific research, usually offer application packets that can be requested by mail or phone. To locate these agencies, you can use keyword-searchable grant databases, which are usually available to the public at most major universities. More and more, the government, companies, and foundations are publishing their RFPs online and submitting them to databases, making the Internet an increasingly necessary tool for any proposal writer.

Put simply, an RFP concisely describes the project that an organization wants completed. For example, Figure 2.1 shows a rather typical RFP from the *Commerce Business Daily,* published by the U.S. government.

FIGURE 2.1
A Sample Request for Proposals

Health Care Financing Administration 7500 Security Blvd., Baltimore, MD. 21244-1850

A—RETROSPECTIVE EVALUATION OF LIFESTYLE MODIFICATION PROJECT SOL HCFA-99-0016 POC Paula Kolick, Contract Specialist (410)-786-5165 Pending the availability of funds, the Health Care Financing Administration (HCFA) is seeking to contract with a qualified research contractor to evaluate health outcomes and cost effectiveness of lifestyle modification programs for people with coronary artery disease (CAD). This project, the Retrospective Evaluation of Lifestyle Modification (RELM) Project, will be conducted over 30 months. The Health Care Financing Administration (HCFA) expects the awardee to participate in the design of the RELM Project and coordinate all aspects of the evaluation. The RELM Project is a nonconcurrent cohort study of the cost-effectiveness of risk factor modification programs for patients with demonstrated CAD. HCFA will study patients with a prespecified level of coronary artery occlusion who have participated in a formal lifestyle modification program compared with nonparticipants having comparable demographic characteristics and illness severity. HCFA would like to evaluate a variety of lifestyle modification programs currently operating in the United States to determine if this service would be of benefit to the Medicare population. Requests for the RFP must be in writing and must be received by the above office within 15 days of this notice. No telephone requests will be honored. The RFP will be available on a first-come, first-served basis until supply is exhausted. Please mail requests to Paula Kolick, Health Care Financing Administration, 2-21-15 Central Bldg., 7500 Security Blvd., Baltimore, MD 21244-1850. Posted 03/30/99 (I-SN314220). (0089)

As you can see, an RFP offers a concise description of the project that is being "put out for bid." Most RFPs start out with the title of the project, the solicitation number (SOL), and the point of contact (POC). Then, these advertisements concisely describe the project for bid.

In the example RFP in Figure 2.1, for instance, the Health Care Financing Administration (HCFA) is looking for someone to submit proposals to "evaluate health outcomes and cost effectiveness of lifestyle programs with coronary artery disease." The remainder of the RFP describes in greater detail the kind of project proposals that the HCFA is seeking. Later in the RFP, the restrictions on time and the types of bidders eligible are also provided. You should notice that the client, the HCFA, is offering to mail another RFP that would, more than likely, provide further details.

Let us consider a quite different kind of RFP. Figure 2.2 shows the summary of an RFP for research in the Antarctic from the National Science Foundation. The actual RFP (NSF 00-72) is the length of a small book.

FIGURE 2.2

Summary of an RFP from National Science Foundation

Program Name: United States Antarctic Program
Program Description: The National Science Foundation invites scientists at U.S. institutions to submit proposals

- To perform research in Antarctica
- To perform related research and data analysis in the United States

Successful candidates will be provided funds and operational support needed to perform the research.

Scientific research, and operational support of that research, are the principal activities supported by the United States Government in Antarctica. The goals are to expand fundamental knowledge of the region, to foster research on global and regional problems of scientific importance, and to use the region as a platform from which to support research that can be done only in Antarctica or best from Antarctica.

In the U.S. Antarctic Program, three year-round research stations, additional research facilities and camps, airplanes, helicopters, surface vehicles, and ships support approximately 130 research projects each year throughout the continent and its surrounding oceans.

This announcement summarizes research opportunities, describes the support available, explains how to prepare a proposal, connects to an online system (the Electronic Support Planner) that can be used in describing needed operational support, and suggests sources of further information.

Program Officers: See the Office of Polar Programs, Antarctic Sciences Section, roster at http://staff.nsf.gov/subdiv.cfm?key=287.

Applicable Catalog of Federal Domestic Assistance (CFDA) No.: 47.078–Polar Programs

The ability to properly interpret RFPs is a valuable skill all its own. Companies will sometimes hire an RFP manager who coordinates the routing of RFPs within the organization. This manager's job is to look for proposal opportunities by monitoring the *Commerce Business Daily*, business periodicals, databases, and incoming mail. Then, the RFP manager often coordinates relations between the manager's company and the clients, ensuring that a client's RFP and any amendments reach the right people.

The RFP manager, in some special cases, may even provide feedback to the client on drafts of an RFP. In these cases, clients will release a draft of an RFP to solicit feedback from probable bidders. By providing comments on the draft, an RFP manager can help the client refine the advertisement, usually to the advantage of both client and bidder.

Determining Stasis

Whether you are responding to an RFP or an unsolicited proposal opportunity, it is important to first determine the *stasis,* or status, of the opportunity. In rhetoric, stasis is the meeting point at which two sides agree to have a discussion. In other words, before negotiation can take place, the two sides need to agree about what exactly is being negotiated. Indeed, often the primary reason why negotiations break down in politics, business, and even personal relations is that the two sides can never agree about what is actually being discussed (e.g., labor/management relations, gun control, peace treaties).

In proposal writing, determining stasis is your responsibility as the writer of the proposal (i.e., the bidder). The clients, after all, presumably know their situation and what they want. It is your responsibility to research their current situation, so you can show them you understand the problem or opportunity they are trying to address. But even if your clients don't understand their situation, it is still the bidder's responsibility to help them figure out the problem or opportunity to which the proposal is responding. Determining stasis will allow you to help the clients' sort out their own situation, so you can propose an effective plan.

The first step in determining the stasis of a proposal opportunity is to analyze the elements of the writing situation. Most people are familiar with the *who, what, where, when, why,* and *how* method that journalists use to develop a news story. Real life is never simple, but journalists know that all stories need to address these Five-W and How questions in order to be complete.[1] When sorting out the details of a story, they often start out by asking these six questions to help them cut through the complexities of a story. *Who* is involved? *What* happened? *Where* did it happen? *When* did it happen? *Why* did it happen? *How* did it happen? The answers to these questions form the basis of the story.

---

[1] A twentieth-century rhetorician, Kenneth Burke, used these elements to create the "Pentad," a tool that rhetoricians use to understand complex rhetorical situations. In his book, *Grammar of Motives,* he defines the elements of the Pentad the following way: Agent (who), Act (what), Scene (where and when), Agency (how), and Purpose (why). This book will use the who, what, where, when, why, and how vocabulary because it easier to remember.

Proposal writers also use this journalistic method to sort out the elements needed to understand the clients' current situation:

- Who is the client, and who else might be involved?
- What does the client need?
- Where is the work site? Where do we need to submit the proposal?
- When are the deadlines for the proposal and the completed project?
- Why is the client looking for someone to do this project?
- How should the project be completed?

Even simple answers to these questions will provide an initial understanding of the stasis of the situation for which the proposal is being written. As you move deeper into the proposal writing process, however, you will need to answer these questions in greater depth to fully understand what the client is seeking.

Interestingly, you will find that the *why* question is rarely answered up front in an RFP or by the client. For example, in the RFP in Figure 2.1, the HCFA never really tells us why it needs "an evaluation of outcomes and cost effectiveness." As proposal writers, we can initially only speculate about answers to the *why* question: Is an outcomes assessment a new legal requirement? Have they had any recent complaints that created the need for more objective scrutiny? Were they sued because they did not have an outcomes procedure in place? Of course, knowing *why* the RFP was written would greatly improve our proposal's chances of winning this contract. And yet, the RFP from the HCFA tells us almost nothing about why they are asking for bidders to handle this project. Later in this chapter, we will discuss how to address the why question.

You will notice that another question left unanswered by an RFP is the *how* question. That is, how should the project be completed? Answering the *how* question is your responsibility as the bidder for the project. In essence, the purpose of any proposal is to provide the clients with an answer to the how question by offering a plan, strategy, or methodology for solving the problem or taking advantage of an opportunity. For example, in response to the RFP from the HCFA in Figure 2.1, a successful proposal would answer the question by offering a plan for evaluating "health outcomes and cost effectiveness of lifestyle modification programs for people with coronary artery disease." Answering the how question (i.e., "How will the assessment be done?") is what a proposal is designed to do.

Proposal writers and RFP managers will often use a worksheet to help them initially sort out the elements of a proposal writing situation. The worksheet in Figure 2.3 illustrates how an RFP or other proposal writing opportunity can be broken down into categories that reflect the Five W and How questions.

Writers of unsolicited proposals can also use the Five-W and How method to help them understand the stasis of a proposal-writing situation. When writing an unsolicited proposal, the elements of the current situation are not stated directly, as they are in an RFP. Rather, unsolicited proposals usually begin with a good idea at a meeting or a conversation with a client. By working through the Five-W and

FIGURE 2.3
Proposal Opportunity Worksheet

PROPOSAL OPPORTUNITY WORKSHEET

Instructions: Draw who, what, where, when answers directly from client, RFP, or POC. If you don't know answers to these questions, write a question mark next to information you don't know.

Project Title:
Solicitation Number:
Date Advertised or Received:

Client:
Point of Contact (POC):
Deadline for Proposal Submission:
Address for Proposal Submission:

Summary of Proposal Opportunity
(In this area, specify any objectives mentioned by the client, RFP, or POC)

Comments and Recommendations
(In this area, speculate about why the client is requesting the work. Also, speculate about what kind of projects might meet the client's needs.)

Accept or Reject
(In this area, state whether a proposal should be written or not. Offer a rationale for your decision.)

Reviewer:	**Reviewer Initials:**	**Date Reviewed:**
Phone Number: e-mail address:		

How questions, you and your readers can come to an initial understanding of the problem or opportunity.

To sum up at this point, when interpreting an RFP, start out by identifying answers to the who, what, where, and when questions. Then, make some guesses that tentatively answer the why and how questions. When you are finished answering these questions, you will be half finished determining the stasis, or status, of the current situation.

A Description of the RFP Interpretation Process

Lisa Miller is a computer engineer who works for Insight Systems, a consulting firm that specializes in designing local area networks (LANs) and intranet systems. Recently, one of Insight Systems' sales representatives told her that Earl Grey Designs, a growing architecture firm in downtown Chicago, was looking for ways to expand without overextending themselves financially. The salesperson told Lisa that the company would soon be sending out an RFP that would seek plans for helping them manage their growth. He said their deadline for a proposal would be tight, but it might be a project that Insight Systems would want to pursue.

Lisa went to work researching Earl Grey, finding out as much as she could about their principal managers, their typical clients, and their business philosophies and objectives. A couple weeks later, the sales representative faxed her the RFP (see Figure 2.4).

Lisa noticed that the RFP left a good amount of room for interpretation. As you can see in Figure 2.4, the RFP could not possibly fill all gaps in Lisa Miller's knowledge of Earl Grey's situation. Specifically, it does not say exactly *why* the proposal is needed, though it did offer some hints that might help answer the why question. There were also many missing details about the current situation. Nevertheless, Lisa turned to her computer and began filling out a Proposal Opportunity Worksheet (see Figure 2.5).

As usual, using the RFP to identify answers to the Five-W and How questions only brought up more questions for Lisa to answer. So, after sending the Proposal Opportunity Review Form to her boss and co-workers, Lisa continued researching Earl Grey through the Internet, business magazines, and past editions of the business section of the *Chicago Tribune.* Later that week, she took the tour of Earl Grey's office and had a good talk with Grant Moser, the office manager and Point of Contact for the proposal.

While touring the Earl Grey office, Lisa could see immediately why Earl Grey sent out the RFP. The people in the office were already tightly packed into the current office space. Until recently, according to Mr. Moser, there was more than enough space, but the latest boom in construction around Chicago had doubled their business. Mr. Moser proudly told Lisa that the award-winning interior of the office was designed by Earl Grey's president, Susan James. The view of Lake Michigan was stunning. With a sour look, Mr. Moser confided to Lisa that most of the people who had scheduled tours were contractors and owners of office buildings in the Chicago suburbs.

FIGURE 2.4
Earl Grey Design's RFP

Earl Grey Designs

300 S. Michigan Ave., Suite 1201
Chicago, Illinois 60001
800-555-9823

March 29, 2001

RE: Request For Proposals for Managing Office Growth
Contact Person: Grant E. Moser, Office Manager

Earl Grey Designs, one of the top ten architecture firms in Chicago, invites pre-proposals from qualified consultants to develop plans for managing the physical growth of its architectural design operations. Due to growth in business, we find ourselves needing more room for our architects and their staff. From the pool of submitted pre-proposals, we will choose three finalists who will be invited to submit full proposals and deliver a presentation on the merits of their plan.

Earl Grey is open to innovative approaches to managing the growth of its office needs. A premium will be placed on proposals that cause the least disruption to our current operations. Our architects and staff are fully engaged in complex projects, so we cannot accept any proposal that suggests we shut down our operations, even temporarily.

Cost is an important issue but not the most important issue for the successful pre-proposal. At this stage, exact cost estimates are not expected; however, pre-proposals should include a general cost estimate. Earl Grey will negotiate for a final fee with the firm that submits the most feasible final proposal.

Pre-proposals should not exceed 10 standard pages, including any diagrams. They should be addressed to Grant E. Moser, Office Manager, and should arrive at Earl Grey Designs by April 30, 2001, by 4:00 p.m. If you would like to tour our current facilities or have any questions about this project, please contact Mr. Moser at 1-800-555-9823. Ask for extension 284.

While at Earl Grey, Lisa picked up as many of their promotional materials as she could, and she jotted down some measurements of their current office space. She asked Mr. Moser if there was a diagram of the office available. He gave her an old diagram that showed the office layout before Earl Grey's recent hiring growth.

When Lisa returned to her office, she did more research on Earl Grey, its principal owners, its mission statement, and their architects' current and past projects. Her research gave her the strong feeling that these people would not be happy in

FIGURE 2.5
Lisa Miller's Assessment of the Earl Grey RFP

PROPOSAL OPPORTUNITY WORKSHEET
Instructions: Draw who, what, where, when answers directly from client, RFP, or POC. If you don't know answers to these questions, write a question mark next to information you don't know.

Project Title: "Request For Proposals for Office Expansion"
Solicitation Number: None Given
Date Advertised or Received: March 29, 2001

Client: Earl Grey Designs (Architecture Firm)
Point of Contact (POC): Grant E. Moser (800-555-9823 ext. 284)
Deadline for Proposal Submission: Pre-Proposal Due by 4:00 on April 30, 2001
Address for Proposal Submission: 300 S. Michigan Ave., Suite 1201, Chicago, Illinois 60001

Summary of Proposal Opportunity
   The RFP requests a pre-proposal that helps the client "manage the physical growth of its architectural operations." The client has experienced recent growth in business, allowing them to hire more architects and staff. With this hiring, though, their office space is becoming a bit cramped.
   The RFP names two goals: (1) manage their need for more office space, and (2) cause the least disruption in their current operations.

Comments and Recommendations
   I think the client is experiencing some growing pains in this strong market. They want to keep growing their business, but they don't want to overextend themselves in case the market drops again. Also, looking at their Web site (www.earlgreydesigns.net), I notice they seem to take a great amount of pride in their current office, which they designed and which has won several interior design awards. Also, since business is hot, they don't want to disrupt their current projects. Frankly, I think they want to stay in their current office, but they cannot figure out how to do so.
   They probably aren't thinking about telecommuting right now, but my hunch is that we could sell them a plan that employs a LAN and an intranet, allowing some of their architects to work at home. Telecommuting might free up the office space they need. Also, architects, being "creative" people, might like to work at home where it's quiet.
   They are offering a tour of their facilities. I will take the tour and report back.

Accept or Reject
We should write a proposal for this project. We are taking a small chance by proposing something they might not expect. But, I think we can meet their goals.

Reviewer: Lisa Miller	**Reviewer Initials:**	**Date Reviewed:**
Phone Number: 5-4144 e-mail address: lmiller@insight_ system.com	*L M*	3/30/91

some bland, cubicle-filled office in the suburbs. After talking over the project with her boss, she decided to write the pre-proposal.

Most of Lisa's activities to this point have been devoted to answering the Five-W and How questions that will help her define the stasis of the current situation. Even though a typical RFP provides basic answers to most of the who, what, where, and when questions, most proposal writers will research much further to gain a better understanding of the factors and people involved. After all this research, Lisa was now just starting to answer the why question and the how question. Why is this project out for bid? What changed? How can we help Earl Grey solve this problem? In this chapter and future chapters, we will see how Lisa writes a pre-proposal to bid for the project at Earl Grey.

Defining the Problem or Opportunity

It is almost a cliché for consultants to say, "There are no problems, only opportunities." And, in the eternally optimistic world of business-speak, that's probably true—a problem *is* just an opportunity to improve. The word *problem,* though, lends a sense of urgency and importance to a project. Moreover, "problem-solving" or "working the problem" are positive, action-oriented ways to look at the proposal-writing process. Proposals are problem-solving tools. This statement is true whether you are pursuing a golden opportunity or proposing a way out of a tricky situation.

The writing of a successful proposal begins with a clear understanding of the underlying problem. For example, in the HCFA RFP in Figure 2.1, the surface problem is easy to identify: The HCFA needs someone to "evaluate the health outcomes and cost effectiveness of lifestyle modification programs for people with coronary artery disease." But is that really the problem? Or, is the need for an evaluation merely evidence of a deeper, underlying problem that the HCFA is trying to address?

In fact, more than likely, the need for this evaluation is a symptom of a more important, underlying problem. Perhaps the HCFA was mandated by the U.S. Congress to request this kind of evaluation. Or, perhaps a court ordered it to commission an independent survey due to a settlement. These are the underlying problems that must be addressed before the proposal can solve the surface problem mentioned in the RFP. In other words, we need to answer the why question to fully understand the problem that the client is trying to solve.

So, before starting to write, you should first use the clues offered by the client (in an RFP or in a meeting) to start determining *why* the problem exists. When you put all those clues together, you will be able to accurately define the stasis, or status, of the problem. To help you answer the why question, you might try out another stasis tool from rhetoric. Cicero (106–43 B.C.), a Roman rhetorician, suggested that identifying stasis requires a writer to initially answer three important questions:

1. Is there a problem?
2. What exactly is the problem?
3. What kind of problem is it?

When you can answer each of these questions confidently in detail, you will have a clearer notion about how to go about beginning the proposal-writing process.

Is There a Problem?

This first question might seem a bit odd until you realize that sometimes the best proposal is no proposal. At your office, for instance, business is going so well that your boss is growing anxious. So, at the first sign of a dip in sales, your boss suggests that you write a proposal to completely restructure the manufacturing operations. In this case, perhaps there really isn't a problem at all. Your best move might be to first propose a research study that determines whether the dip in sales is just a natural fluctuation in the market.

Another situation in which you might first ask, "Is there a problem?" is when you are seeking new clients. Often, in the rush to drum up new business, we are tempted to sell our clients products or services they really don't need. But, an old saying among consultants is, "You can only sell an empty box once." In other words, it is wise to only write proposals that solve real problems at a client's company. After all, the short-term gain is soon more than offset by the loss of future opportunities, especially when your clients realize you misled them. It is best to honestly answer no to the question, "Is there a problem?" than lose future sales.

What Exactly Is the Problem?

The second stasis question, "What exactly is the problem?" is usually the most important question to answer before writing a proposal. In most cases, when you answer this question, you will confirm the clients' gut feelings about their current situation. By defining the problem for the readers, you will develop a common ground on which you and the clients can begin negotiating the plan and even the costs.

In some cases, though, clients believe they have one problem, but the actual problem is something a bit deeper. In these situations, the surface problem is only a symptom of a more fundamental problem. For example, let us say a school district in an affluent community is having trouble attracting a faculty of top-notch teachers. The school board wants you to come up with a plan to entice strong teachers to the district. As you research the problem, however, you soon discover that some of the best teachers left the district because they could not afford to live in the community. When you interview these former teachers, they tell you that they wanted to stay, but housing is too expensive in the area. Meanwhile, they say, the commute from other areas was grueling and dangerous. You quickly see that the root problem is not attracting good teachers; it is retaining good teachers. Of course, your proposal would most likely include a plan to attract strong teachers, but you could also enhance your proposal by addressing the root problem of affordable housing for teachers.

As stated before, the secret to defining the problem to be solved is to ask yourself, "What changed?" When you look over the who, what, when, and where, pay special attention to any of these elements that have shifted recently. For example, in the affluent community that is having trouble attracting and retaining teachers, what changed in this community that created this problem? Have housing costs increased suddenly? Have property taxes gone up? Are the more experienced teachers retiring? By paying attention to changes, you can usually identify the specific problem that needs to be solved.

This second stasis question, "What exactly is the problem?" urges us to look for a root problem beneath the obvious. After all, the apparent problem might be merely a symptom of a deeper problem. Addressing these symptoms may provide a short-term fix, but the problems will return if the root problem is not addressed, too.

What Kind of Problem Is It?

The final question, "What kind of problem is it?" helps us identify what kind of proposal is needed in a particular situation. Proposals tend to fall into the four categories shown in Figure 2.6.

The type of proposal you need to write depends on two things: (1) the problem or opportunity you are trying to address, and (2) the deliverables you are expected to provide the clients when the project is completed. Deliverables are the

FIGURE 2.6
Four Types of Proposals

Type of Proposal	Problem	Purpose	Deliverables
Research Proposal	Needs insight or empirically produced facts	Proposes a research project; often requests funding	Report or publication that describes and analyzes results of study; might offer recommendations
Planning Proposal	Needs a plan that outlines a general strategy	Proposes to develop a strategic plan for addressing a problem/opportunity	Plan that describes a general strategy for solving the problem or taking advantage of the opportunity
Implementation Proposal	Needs to implement a strategic plan	Offers a detailed plan for implementing a project	Completion of the project and a completion report that demonstrates and measures results of project
Estimate Proposal (Sales)	Needs to provide a costs for a product or service	Provides a cost estimate for a product or service	A product or service

tangible objects or services that result from the project. In other words, deliverables are the things (e.g., reports, plans, products) that are handed over to the readers during the project and when it is finished.

Let us look more closely at the four types of proposals and their deliverables:

Research Proposals

Research proposals describe methods for gaining insight into a particular problem or opportunity. Scientists often use research proposals to request funding and approval to conduct an empirical study or develop a prototype. An electrical engineer, for example, might write a research proposal to figure out why an undersea robot shuts down when it dips 500 meters below surface. A biologist, meanwhile, might write a research proposal to the National Science Foundation in order to study the yearly migration of a sandhill crane population. The intent of a research proposal is to propose a study that will generate data or observations and fill a gap in our understanding. The deliverable for a research proposal is typically a report or article that explains the results of the research. In some cases, a prototype machine or service is also a deliverable.

Research proposals are also written for clients who need understanding of a situation, problem, or opportunity. For instance, perhaps a client has experienced the sudden loss of key employees to its competitors. A research proposal would propose a study to determine the causes (e.g., salaries, morale, benefits, stress) for this problem. This type of research proposal would describe the methodology that would be used to gather information (e.g., marketing studies, legal research, environmental impact testing, customer surveys, audits, or product quality studies). The "deliverable" for this kind of proposal would be a final report in which the findings are presented and explained. In some cases, research proposals might conclude with recommendations for taking action.

Planning Proposals

Planning proposals offer plans for improvement or recommendations for taking action. A planning proposal might be used to devise strategies to increase sales, describe new manufacturing techniques, or suggest changes to current business practices. For example, a planning proposal might be used to design a new bridge or suggest a better way to handle toxic waste. In most cases, the deliverable is the plan contained within the proposal itself. In other cases, the deliverable promised to the readers is an *implementation plan* that describes in detail (i.e., dates, times, personnel) how the project will be completed. Essentially, the recommendations in a planning proposal are the most important outcome. Your proposal's recommendations are what the clients are paying you to develop.

Implementation Proposals

Implementation proposals are written when the readers already have a plan that needs to be implemented. Contractors often write these kinds of proposals, showing how they would turn an architect's drawings (plan) into an actual structure. In this kind of proposal, the clients are looking for specific timelines, the names of involved personnel, a list of materials, and an itemization of costs. The deliverables for an implementation proposal are the promised final products or services and a "completion report" that documents the implementation process and describes any deviations from the original plan.

Estimate Proposals (Sales)

Estimate proposals, often referred to as *sales proposals,* offer a product or service for a specific cost. In these cases, the clients know what product or service they need. They simply want you to tell them how much you would charge for that service or product. Estimate proposals offer bids for standard services, like legal representation, janitorial services, maintenance work, or clerical services. When used for sales purposes, estimate proposals are often unsolicited. They describe your company's products and services, showing the customer why these products or services would be beneficial to them. The deliverable for these proposals is the product or service itself.

Of course, these proposal types overlap, and in many cases two different types of proposals might be merged. For instance, a planning proposal might include both a research phase in which an empirical study will be conducted and a planning phase that develops a strategic plan after the assessment is completed. It is often prudent, though, to urge the client to accept one type of proposal at a time. Let us say you discover that the clients lack a clear understanding of their current situation; yet they want your company to write a proposal to implement a solution. The client is essentially telling you, "We have no idea what is wrong, but we want you to fix it." In these cases, you are being asked to implement a plan when you are not even sure what the problem is—always a bad idea. Instead, you should urge the clients to accept one type of proposal (i.e., a research proposal or a planning proposal) for the time being. Then, promise them a follow-up implementation proposal when you have isolated the problem or developed a strategic plan.

Similarly, before expending the effort to write an implementation proposal, it is usually best to first write a planning proposal that offers a more general strategic plan. Once you and the clients agree on the strategic plan, an implementation proposal can be written. As you might have noticed already, proposals sometimes become stepping stones to future proposals. Research proposals often lead to planning proposals. Planning proposals lead to implementation proposals.

Applying Stasis Questions

As mentioned earlier, one of the main reasons proposals fail is because their writers misinterpret the stasis of the problem. The three stasis question discussed earlier in this chapter should help you determine the problem, or opportunity, that brought about the need for a proposal. These questions offer you a place to start writing a proposal by helping you to answer the why question.

Let us return to Lisa Miller's proposal to Earl Grey. After finding answers to the who, what, where, and when questions, she was ready to start tackling the why and how by working through the stasis questions. First, she asked herself,

"Is there a problem?" Her visit to Earl Grey only confirmed to her that the client had a problem that needed to be solved. At the Earl Grey office, people, desks, computers, and copiers seemed to be stacked on top of each other. The people had little room to operate comfortably. Yes, there certainly was a problem.

Second, she began answering the question, "What is the problem?" The RFP seemed to be suggesting that Earl Grey needed more office space. But she sensed a reluctance from Mr. Moser to leave their current Michigan Avenue office. So, to answer the why question, Lisa tried to think beyond the surface problem (lack of physical space) toward identifying a deeper, underlying problem. Specifically, she asked herself, "What changed to create this problem?" The office manager, Mr. Moser, said a recent surge in construction in Chicago forced them to hire more architects and staff. He called it the "usual boom and bust cycle" in the Chicago market, and he complained that two years from now, when the market goes down, they might need to let some of these extra people go. The problem, Lisa concluded, is indeed a lack of office space, but the problem might be only temporary. If the market went down, Earl Grey would not want to be financially overextended with a larger facility.

Finally, she began thinking about what kind of proposal she would need to write. It seemed as though the people at Earl Grey had a pretty good grasp of their problem. They wanted a plan for solving that problem. So, a planning proposal seemed like the best option for this project. Lisa's pre-proposal would sketch out a general plan for solving their problems. If her pre-proposal was accepted, then she would write up a more detailed planning proposal for creating new space in their current office. As she noticed in the RFP, the clients did not want an implementation proposal or even an estimate proposal. In other words, they were not looking for specific times and dates when the workers would show up to start redoing their offices. Instead, they were looking for a general strategy for addressing their growth problem.

By working through the stasis questions systematically, Lisa gained a deeper understanding of the client's problem and she figured out that the clients needed a planning proposal.

Talking to the Point of Contact

Once you have worked through the Five W and How questions and you have answered the three stasis questions, you are probably ready to contact the Point of Contact listed on the RFP. In most cases, you will find that POCs, especially those who handle government projects, are not forthcoming with additional details. POCs usually want to give the impression that they are impartial, fair, and not playing favorites among bidders.

Nevertheless, once you have worked out the stasis of the situation, you can ask the POC specific questions that will confirm or challenge your understanding of their problem or opportunity. At this point, the POC can usually confirm or deny your answers to the why question, sometimes offering further information that will help you understand the situation. You should also ask about the expected deliverables. Finally, confirm with the POC that your proposal will promise the tangible results that the readers are expecting.

FIGURE 2.7
Talking to the Point of Contact

Comment or Question	Intent of Comment or Question
"Here is our understanding of your current situation"	Allows you to confirm your answers to the who, what, where, and when questions. Here is also your opportunity to clarify any uncertainties about the details of the project.
"What created the need for this RFP?"	Essentially, you are trying to find out two things with this question. First, what *changed* at the client's company or organization to create this proposal opportunity? Second, *why* are they asking for proposals?
"Here is our understanding of why you are looking for someone to do this work."	Allows you to test out your best answer to the why question. Talk about how changes in the current situation brought about this opportunity for the client. Also, in most cases, phrase your answer to the why question as an "opportunity," not a problem.
"What are the specific deliverables you expect when the project is complete?"	This question has two purposes. First, the POC's answer may give you an idea about what the clients expect bidders to propose. Second, the answer should tell you what kinds of documentation the clients expect when the work is finished.
"Are there any other sources of information we might access to help us write a proposal that fits your needs?"	In some cases the POC has a packet of information that is available if you ask. Also, published reports or Web sites may be available that refer to their current situation.
"Do you have a price range into which the project must fit?"	This question is somewhat risky. Most POCs will not offer specific numbers. However, they may give you a range in which the clients are expecting the project to cost.

Of course, there is no script that you can use to talk with a POC. Figure 2.7, however, shows how statements and questions to the POC might be phrased to gain the most valuable feedback.

The ability to ask the POC specific questions is one of the great benefits to determining stasis up front. When talking to the POC, you will often receive only yes and no answers to your questions. So, if you have not developed a reasonable answer to the why question before calling, the POC will likely offer only unhelpful and agitated responses to your clumsy questions. However, if you are ready with informed, specific questions, the POC will tend to be more helpful, often giving you even more insight into the problem the company is trying to solve.

Last Word

The basic assumption behind stasis theory is that disputants must first "agree to disagree" on an issue. In other words, you and I may disagree strongly about something, but we must first agree on what we are arguing about. Otherwise, there is no basis for negotiation.

In a proposal, you need to initially agree with your clients about the elements of the current situation. You need to agree about the who, what, where, when, why, and—with some solid research—the how. You also need to agree that there is a problem, what the problem is, and what kind of proposal is needed to solve that problem. Only then will you be able to write an effective proposal. In this chapter, you learned how to read RFPs and you learned two important steps for determining the stasis of the proposal writing opportunity (i.e., the Five-W and How questions, and the three stasis questions). In the next chapter, we will build on this understanding of stasis by defining the rhetorical situation in which you are submitting the proposal.

CASE STUDY **What Is Elmdale Hill's Problem?**

At the Elmdale Hill Cafe, John Legler, Karen Sanchez, Thomas Lee, and Sally Johnson met to discuss the future of their businesses and the Elmdale Hill business district. Each of them could think of various reasons for the downturn in sales. They pointed to the new Wheatmill Mall. They also mentioned an increased perception of crime by customers, more homeless people, and more graffiti in the neighborhood. Other problems like higher prices, limited parking, and unpredictable weather seemed to be obstacles that made it even more difficult to compete directly with the mall.

"And it doesn't help when every little crime around here leads off the local evening news," said Thomas.

All four owners soon realized that their problem was very complex, and they agreed that there wasn't a silver bullet solution that would fix the problem. All of them also concluded that complaining wouldn't get them far. They needed to come up with a proposal for taking action. Only a written document would focus their efforts, give them a plan for action, and help them involve others in the community.

To begin developing a proposal, they began by answering the Five-W and How questions. Pulling out a piece of notebook paper, they wrote down answers to the who, what, where, and when questions, putting question marks next to information they were unsure about (see Figure 2.8). They decided to leave the spaces for the why question and the how question blank for the moment, because even obvious answers to these questions seemed hard to come up with. The why and how questions would need to be answered later when they had a better understanding of the problem.

FIGURE 2.8

Answers to the Five W and How questions

Questions	Answers
Who?	Ourselves, fellow merchants, our customers, the city government (?), news media (?), Wheatmill mall (?)
What?	Loss of sales, loss of customers, local and small businesses closing. Perception of crime problems, graffiti, more homeless people, parking
Where?	Present plan at meeting of Elmdale Hill merchants (?) Elmdale Hill Neighborhood Association (?) City Chamber of Commerce (?) Town Hall Meeting (?)
When?	As soon as possible, definitely before holiday shopping season starts in September
Why?	(?)
How?	(?)

With the who, what, where, and when questions tentatively answered, they turned to the why question. Using the three stasis questions, they began to isolate and identify the problem they face. They started by tackling the first stasis question, "Is there a problem?"

Karen answered, "Of course. Why would we be meeting if there wasn't a problem?"

Thomas said, "Yes, but our 'problem' could be just another seasonal dip in our sales or the beginning of a recession. Or, maybe our reduced sales are just a coincidence. Maybe other merchants aren't having the problems we are."

"But my records show this year has been my slowest in the ten years I've been in business. Summer has never been this slow before, even when we were at the bottom of a recession," Karen said.

"Yeah, it's been pretty bad," agreed John, "I don't think it's just a coincidence that most businesses in the Elmdale Hill district have seen their sales go down. The economy is still doing well, so we should be doing at least average business."

Sally said, "I know I'm getting clobbered by that mega-bookstore at the mall. They can often sell books for 25% less than I can."

"So, what do you think is the problem?" Thomas asked, moving on to the second stasis question.

"Wheatmill Mall is a big chunk of the problem," said John.

"Yes, but what is the real problem we are facing, assuming there's not much we can do about Wheatmill?" asked Thomas.

"Well, we're losing sales. That's a problem," said Sally.

"But why? What changed that is causing us to lose sales?"

John paused for a moment and said, "Well, fewer people are coming down to Elmdale Hill anymore. In the past, people would go shopping, then grab dinner at my restaurant, and go see a movie. They would spend time down here, visiting several different businesses."

Karen added, "Now, people see Wheatmill Mall as a place where they can do their one-stop shopping. They window-shop like they used to do here, and then they go get dinner at the mall's food court and perhaps catch a movie at the metroplex theater."

"Oh, but those awful food courts. The grease! How can they eat that stuff?" groaned John.

"And those tiny screens for movies," said Thomas.

"But that's our *real* problem," said Karen, "Some people are willing to sacrifice quality for convenience. The Elmdale Hill shops offer more quality than the mall, but less convenience. The customers who value quality have stayed with us, and the mall took those customers who prefer convenience. That's at least half our business right there."

As Karen pointed out, the problem might not be declining sales after all. The drop in business might be merely a symptom of a deeper problem. Specifically, fewer people were coming to the Elmdale Hill district because they found it less convenient than the mall. Many people prefer to go to only one place to handle their shopping, food, and entertainment needs. Perhaps these customers saw the Elmdale Hill district as a group of single shops, not realizing that they could spend the whole afternoon there doing a variety of different things.

After a little more discussion, the four store owners became increasingly convinced that the problem was "fewer customers due to a lack of convenience."

Feeling like they accomplished something by isolating the problem, John, Karen, Thomas, and Sally decided to tackle the third stasis question, "What kind of problem is it?"

John started out, "I don't know about you three, but I don't feel like I have a very good grasp of the problem. But, I also don't want to spend months running marketing studies to con-

firm that this 'lack of convenience' problem is true. We need to do something sooner than that."

"I think we should do *some* kind of research before creating a plan," said Sally. "Why don't we write a proposal that includes a 'research phase' and a 'planning phase?' In the research phase, we could survey the other merchants, interview reporters and police about crime and graffiti issues, and check out the local shelters to see why there are more street people in our area. We could then write up the results in a report that would be delivered to all the other merchants. In the planning part of the proposal, we could promise to use this research to refine any plans we might develop."

"But we can't just do it ourselves. We need to come up with a plan that involves the whole Elmdale Hill business community. Otherwise, we're just wasting our time," said Karen.

Sally agreed, "We need to get others involved first. That's why, in my opinion, it is probably too early to think about implementing anything on our own. We need to start out by doing some research and sketching out a strategic plan. Once we persuade some people to join us, we can start working out how we will put that plan into action."

They decided to write a hybrid *research* and *planning* proposal in which they would first describe their research methods for gaining insight into the problem. Then, the proposal would loosely sketch out a possible plan that would be refined when the research phase was completed.

By the end of the evening, they felt as though they were gaining a grasp on the proposal process. They didn't have a plan yet, but they felt as though they were moving in the right direction. They agreed to meet again the next day to work on the proposal a bit more.

Questions and Exercises

1. Find an RFP in the *Commerce Business Daily,* the *Federal Register,* a grant RFP database, or the newspaper classifieds. Write a memo to your instructor in which you use the Five-W and How questions to summarize the RFP. Then, discuss *why* you think the client is looking for someone to do the work

described in the RFP. Specifically, discuss what might have "changed" to create this proposal opportunity. And finally, discuss some possible projects that might be suitable for this RFP.

2. Analyze an RFP in your field or area of interest by using the Proposal Opportunity Worksheet shown in Figure 2.3 of this chapter. According to the Worksheet, what kinds of information would you still need to gather if you were to respond to this RFP? What questions would you need to ask the Point of Contact in order to clarify what kind of work is needed and why it is needed?

3. Research a problem or opportunity on your campus, in your workplace, or in your community, such as parking, healthcare, or safety. What has changed recently and brought these problems/opportunities about? What are the underlying problems that created these problems? Write a memorandum to your instructor in which you discuss how change has created these problems/opportunities. In your memo, speculate about some of the reasons why these problems/opportunities have not been addressed yet.

4. Apply the three stasis theory questions to a problem on your campus, in your workplace, or in your community. Is there really a problem that can be addressed? What exactly is the problem? What kind of proposal (research, planning, implementation, or estimate) would be needed to address this problem?

5. Call a Point of Contact listed on an RFP. Politely tell the POC that you are learning how to write proposals. Then, if allowed, interview that POC, asking what kinds of questions might be appropriate for a proposal writer to ask. Ask what kinds of answers the POC is allowed to give to proposal writers who call. Report your findings back to your class.

6. With a team, analyze the following RFP using the Five-W and How questions and the three stasis questions.

> RFP: Campus Safety Assessment. SOL 45-9326. DUE 100801. POC James Sanchez, Assoc. VP/Student Affairs (318) 555-4503. Bentworth University, a research university serving over fifteen thousand on-campus and commuter students and located near downtown Bentworth, is soliciting proposals for an assessment of safety on campus. The objective of such an assessment would be to determine the causes for a recent increase in reported crime on campus. We are especially interested in addressing forms of crime like assault, graffiti, and theft. Depending on the outcome of the report, special priority will be given to those consultants who can also help develop a plan for reducing the amount of crime on campus. Also, special consideration will be given to proposals that offer non-intrusive methods for collecting data and information. Interested parties should submit a 5–7 page pre-proposal that offers a general sense of how they would go about assessing crime on campus. The Student Affairs office will select 5 parties to submit full proposals. At that point, more information will be offered. Due

date for pre-proposals is October 10, 2001. Full proposals will be due on December 1, 2001.

Answer these questions: What might be the problem underlying the current situation? What might have changed to create this opportunity? What kind of proposal is the client looking for the bidders to write? What information do you still need to write the proposal? What are some questions you would need to ask the Point of Contact?

Purpose, Readers, Context

Overview

This chapter will show you how to begin inventing the content of a proposal by defining the rhetorical situation in which the proposal will be used. The chapter will meet the following learning objectives:

1. Define what is meant by *rhetorical situation.*
2. Discuss subject, purpose, readers, context, and objectives of proposals.
3. Show how to analyze readers.
4. Show how to analyze contexts.
5. Discuss the use of the rhetorical situation to focus writing groups.

The Proposal-Writing Process

As discussed in Chapter 1, the proposal-writing process includes four stages: invention, drafting, revision, and editing. Though these stages imply a progression from invention to editing, the process is not strictly linear. Rather, writers cycle forward and back among the four stages as they compose a proposal. Revising can lead to more drafting. Editing often highlights places in the proposal where more invention is needed.

Writers sometimes make the mistake of diving into the drafting phase without first taking time to fully invent their ideas and plan out the proposal. They try to write the proposal from introduction to conclusion without first taking the time to fully consider the readers' characteristics or the contexts in which the proposal might be used—often with unfortunate results. By diving right in, they think they are saving time. But really, they end up wasting time, because soon they write themselves into corners or dead ends. Or, worse yet, they sit at their desk staring at the blank screen or piece of paper, hoping words will magically leap onto the page. We have all been there.

Writing proposals is an especially tough challenge. When you sit down to write a proposal, there is so much to say. And yet, that blank screen or piece of blank paper just stares at you. It dares you to start putting words together. Your mind goes blank. The problem is not that you do not have anything to say. Instead, you have too much to say, and you are not sure how to start writing it all down.

How should you begin developing a proposal? One helpful strategy is to start by defining the rhetorical situation in which your proposal will be used. The *rhetorical situation* includes the proposal's *subject, purpose, readers, context*, and *objectives*—the angles you will need to address as you are writing the proposal. A simple way to think about the rhetorical situation is to visualize the readers of the proposal looking over the document. What unique reader characteristics will influence how they interpret your proposal? What elements in their context will shape how they weigh your ideas? If you can identify these factors before you start writing, your path toward developing a proposal will be far clearer.

Something to keep in mind is that your readers are completely responsible for creating meaning from your words. As they read your writing, you cannot sit behind them clarifying your words and ideas. Therefore, it is critically important that you tailor your proposal to the readers and the contexts in which they will be reading. In this chapter, you will learn how to make common-sense assumptions about the psychology of your readers and the contexts in which they will use your proposal. You will learn how to interpret the rhetorical situation to identify the various psychological, social, and political factors involved in the reading of proposals.

The Rhetorical Situation

Before putting words on paper, professional writers often try to visualize the situations in which their texts will be used. For example, a writer developing a user manual will try to imagine their readers using the text. Are they reading the instructions on the floor? in the kitchen? on a workbench? What tools do they have available? Why did they decide to look at the user manual—to install something? to troubleshoot a problem? What is the readers' attitude? Are they angry, excited, frustrated? These types of questions help writers put themselves in the minds of their readers. By imagining themselves in the readers' place, writers can develop the most appropriate content, organization, style, and design for the documents they are creating.

Rhetoricians have developed various analytical tools to help writers visualize rhetorical situations. One of the most flexible of these analytical tools is the following list that prompts the writer to consider five different elements of the rhetorical situation:

- **Subject**   What is my proposal about? What is it not about?
- **Purpose**   What is my proposal supposed to achieve?
- **Readers**   Who will read my proposal?
- **Context**   Where will my proposal be read, and how does that context shape the reading?
- **Objectives**   What are some other goals, besides the purpose, that my proposal should achieve?

When preparing to write a proposal, or any document, answering these questions up front will immediately clarify the rhetorical situation in which the proposal will be used. Moreover, these questions will help you develop a deeper understanding of the content, organization, style, and visual design that the proposal will require. Let us consider each area of the rhetorical situation in greater depth.

Subject

Essentially, the *subject* is what your proposal is about. In Chapter 2, you learned how to determine the stasis of a problem or opportunity. Answers to the three stasis questions (i.e., Is there a problem? What exactly is the problem? and, What type of problem is it?) will already provide you with a large amount of insight into the subject of your proposal.

Now that you have a good idea of the problem you are trying to solve, you should start thinking about the boundaries of that problem. Specifically, ask yourself two questions—

- What do my readers "need to know" to make a decision about my proposal?
- What information, no matter how interesting to me, is *not* needed to make a decision about my proposal?

These questions are important because readers tend to interpret a proposal from a "need-to-know" perspective. In other words, they only want to spend time processing information that will help them make an informed decision. Writers, on the other hand, often approach a text from a "want-to-tell" point of view. That is, after spending weeks, perhaps months, collecting information on the subject, writers very much want to tell the readers everything they collected, no matter how insignificant.

The problem, as anyone who has struggled to read a bloated document will agree, is that readers quickly grow frustrated with all the tidbits of want-to-tell information. The seemingly endless details can distract the readers from the more important need-to-know issues in the proposal. As a result, a thirty-page proposal that includes want-to-tell information is almost always less effective than a leaner fifteen-page proposal that is limited to need-to-know information, because the leaner proposal highlights the crucial points for the readers. The bloated proposal, meanwhile, blurs the crucial points by hiding them among noncrucial details.

To help you sort out the need-to-know from the want-to-tell information, you should pay close attention to the boundaries of you proposal's subject. First, ask yourself what is *inside* the subject (i.e., what do the readers need to know?). Then, ask yourself what is *outside* the subject (i.e., what don't the readers need to know?). In some cases, this second question concerning what is outside the subject can be most useful for defining the boundaries of the subject. By consciously deciding what topics will *not* be discussed in the proposal, you can better define what will go into the proposal.

Purpose

The purpose of the proposal is what you want the proposal to achieve. As you think about your purpose, you should try to determine exactly what you want your readers to believe or do when they are finished looking over your proposal.

One of the most common problems with proposals is that the writers are not absolutely clear about their purpose. Of course, they have a good grasp on what they are trying to achieve. But, when they are asked to state their purpose, they ramble for a couple minutes with a laundry list of items. "Well, it should do this, this, and this . . . and, oh yes, it should do that, too." This kind of shotgun approach to the purpose almost guarantees that the proposal will sound unfocused and vague to the readers. After all, if the writer cannot articulate the purpose of the proposal succinctly, the reader certainly will not be able to articulate the purpose, either.

The secret to writing a good purpose statement is to limit yourself to expressing the purpose in one sentence. In one sentence, try to complete the phrase, "The purpose of this proposal is to . . ." If you cannot squeeze your purpose into one sentence, then your proposal might not be focused enough for the readers.

Fortunately, once you have hammered down a one-sentence statement of your proposal's purpose, you will have created a foundation for guiding the entire proposal-writing process. As you write the proposal, you can look back at your statement of purpose to see if your proposal is indeed achieving what you set out to do. Meanwhile, you can use that purpose statement to help you carve away all the distracting, noncrucial information that tends to creep into the writing of larger documents. A good purpose statement acts like a knife to help you cut away the fat in your proposal.

In the introduction to your proposal, this statement of purpose is often used as a guiding claim that the rest of the proposal will support. For instance, if you state in your introduction, "The purpose of this proposal is to provide a strategic plan for renovating the downtown of Albuquerque, turning the city center into a center of shopping, entertainment, and learning," then you have clearly told your readers what your proposal is designed to achieve. They can then keep this purpose in mind as they read through the details you offer in the body of the proposal. In most cases, your statement of purpose need not be stated so directly in the introduction. Merely dropping "The purpose of this proposal . . ." phrase leaves you with a direct statement like "This proposal will provide a plan for renovating. . ." Your intentions for the proposal will still be clear.

Readers

Experienced proposal writers will often tell you that developing a complete understanding of the readers is the most important part of the proposal writing process. In fact, some professional proposal writers will actually collect whole dossiers of information on their readers, trying to find out what motivates them to say yes to a proposal. The methods offered here are a bit less thorough, but you should find that they provide you with a great amount of insight into the psychology of your readers.

When analyzing your readers, you should first recognize that there are different levels of readers who will pick up your proposal:

Primary Readers

The primary reader is the person or persons to whom the proposal is addressed. In most cases, the primary readers are the people who can actually say yes to your proposal. They are the *decision makers* in the proposal process, because they are most responsible for assessing the merits of your ideas. If you are unsure who your primary readers are, ask yourself who actually has the power to accept your proposal. Who can say yes?

Secondary Readers

There are also numerous secondary readers who will influence the acceptance or rejection of your proposal. Think of secondary readers as the people to whom your primary readers might turn for advice. They could be supervisors, experts, accountants, or lawyers who check over the methods, facts, and figures of the proposal. Compared to the primary readers, these secondary readers often have different motives for reading the proposal. As experts, they are usually looking for more specialized information than the primary readers. For example, the senior engineer at a company might not have final say about whether a proposal is accepted; nevertheless, her opinion may greatly influence the primary readers' decisions about the technical feasibility of your ideas. As you write the proposal, you should keep that senior engineer in mind.

Tertiary Readers

Tertiary readers are the people who you did not expect to read your proposal but would have a stake in what you are proposing. For example, tertiary readers could include reporters, hostile lawyers, program assessors, historians, politicians, the public, or your competition. At first, it might seem odd to keep the interests of these distant readers in mind, but these tertiary readers often prove to be people who can unexpectedly sabotage (or support) your plans. You should always identify these potential readers to make sure that you are not writing something that would make you or your organization vulnerable to their challenges.

Gatekeepers

Gatekeepers are the readers who have the most direct influence over you and your proposal. They could include your supervisor, the CEO of your company, an accountant, or your company's legal counsel. Gatekeepers are the readers who need to endorse your proposal before it is sent to the primary readers. Again, it might seem strange to keep the needs of these readers in mind as you invent your ideas. But if your proposal is not acceptable to your boss or the legal department, then the primary readers will never have the chance to say yes. You need to make sure you understand what these gatekeepers want to see in the proposal before you start writing it. Otherwise, the proposal may end up in an endless loop of revisions as various gatekeepers ask for further changes.

If you haven't noticed already, these four classes of readers represent many individuals who will influence the development of the proposal. How can you identify all

FIGURE 3.1
Writer-Centered Worksheet

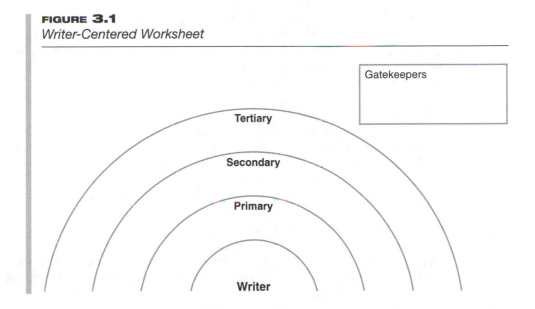

these different people and their interests? One way is to use a *writer-centered work-sheet* to help you identify and sort out all these different readers (see Figure 3.1).[1]

Here is how the worksheet is used. Imagine yourself in the middle half-circle labeled *Writer*. Then, in the area labeled *Primary*, write down the primary readers, preferably by name, who will be directly responsible for making a decision on your proposal. You should have only one or two primary readers, because only a few people will have the power to say yes or no to your proposal. In the *Secondary* area, write down all the readers who might serve as advisors to the primary readers. Think about the people to whom the primary readers might turn for information or advice. In most cases, you will find that there are many more secondary readers than primary readers. In the *Tertiary* area, try to imagine anyone else, no matter how remote, who might have a stake in your proposal. Write down the people who might use your proposal, even if you never intended for them to possess a copy. And finally, write down some gatekeepers in the *Gatekeepers* box on the top right of the worksheet. As you think about gatekeepers, try to write down people who need to approve your proposal before it is sent to the primary readers.

The writer-centered worksheet helps you visualize your potential readers by spatially viewing their relationship to you. Your primary readers are usually the most important part of your audience, so they occupy the circle closest to you. The secondary and tertiary readers occupy places a bit further away. The gatekeepers are a bit off to the side because they are not really the intended readers of the proposal, but they will supervise your work.

---

[1] Note: The audience worksheets in Figure 3.1 and 3.2 are similar to those provided by J.C. Mathes and Dwight Stevenson in their book *Designing Technical Reports* (pp. 15–23). The worksheets used here, however, are designed differently to focus on the audience issues important to proposals.

Now it is time to address the psychology of the people you identified in the writer-centered worksheet. It is time to get inside their minds to figure out why they might say yes or no to your proposal. To begin, readers react positively or negatively to the content of proposals for a variety of reasons. Specifically, they tend to react on four different levels:

Motives

Readers are motivated to take action when they think a plan will improve their personal, professional, or organizational lives. For example, perhaps a particular reader is motivated by a higher profit margin. A successful proposal would address that motivation by stressing the enhanced profit margin created by the proposed project. Another reader might be motivated by a "do the right thing" approach, so a successful proposal written to this reader might show how the proposal is socially beneficial. In our culture, the word *motives* has a slightly negative undertone, as though people with motives have hidden reasons for behaving a particular way. Here, we are using the word to suggest that people always have motives for taking action. When you identify someone's motives, you will know what moves them to act.

Values

Readers often react positively or negatively because an idea or plan touches their personal, professional, or organizational values. Usually, it is not hard to find out the readers' values. Often, companies publish documents like mission statements, policy statements, and ethics policies that spell out the values that the company publicly holds. An individual reader's professional or personal values can often be found in biographical statements, speeches they have made, or their past actions. The Internet is a great place to figure out your readers' values, because people are often more revealing in their corporate and personal Web sites than they would be in person.

Attitudes

Readers typically start out with a positive or negative attitude toward a given proposal. In some cases, they are looking forward to moving into new markets or fixing a long-standing problem in the organization. In other cases, however, readers will approach a proposal with a negative attitude, because the proposal resulted from a personal or organizational failure. For example, sometimes the in-house experts at a client company have a negative attitude toward your proposal because they think their managers' decision to solicit proposals implies a lack of faith in the experts' ability to solve the problem themselves. Of course, readers' attitudes are always hard to judge, but you should pay close attention to what the readers say and how they say it. Sometimes the readers' body language or tone can tell you a great amount about their attitude toward you, the project, and your proposal.

Emotions

Readers also react to proposals emotionally in ways that go beyond the simple logic or costs of your proposal. For instance, if you are proposing to renovate a landmark building, the readers may have strong positive or negative emotions. They may feel joy, frustration, pride, or even anger. You should always take these emotions into account as you write the proposal. Positive emotions can be used to energize your proposal, while negative emotions should be addressed by stressing the benefits of taking action.

Again, a worksheet can help us sort out all the complex motives, values, attitudes, and emotions of the various readers. By listing out the different readers in a *reader analysis worksheet* (see Figure 3.2), you can start to anticipate the psychological factors that will affect the reactions of the four different types of readers previously discussed.

Using the reader analysis worksheet is a simple process. First, in the left-hand column, list out the readers you identified in the writer-centered chart. Then, working from left to right, fill in what you know about each reader's motives, values, attitudes, and emotions. If you need to leave a space blank because you do not know something about the readers, just put a question mark in that space. Blank spaces or question marks signal places where you need to do some research on your readers. Of course, you cannot know everything about your readers, but eventually you should be able to put notes of some kind inside each of the spaces in this table.

Some writers may mistakenly believe that all this reader analysis is not necessary for writing a proposal. And perhaps, for smaller proposals, it might be too much. But as proposals grow larger and more complex, the stakes start to grow higher and the competition more intense. The more important the proposal, the more critical it is that you develop a high awareness of how and why your readers react in specific ways. Try using the writer-centered worksheet and reader analysis worksheet, and you will almost certainly feel more able to shape your proposal specifically to the needs of the readers. In most cases, your deeper understanding of the readers will increase your chances of winning the contract or funding.

Context

Analysis of the context is strongly related to your analysis of the readers, because context involves the physical, economic, ethical, and political environments in which the readers will evaluate your proposal. If, for example, you know that the decision on a contract will be made by a large committee that will receive several other fifty-page proposals, you might want to find a way to use executive summaries, lists, and graphs to highlight your main points. After all, you can safely predict that committee members will first scan all the proposals and choose only a few to study in greater depth. By recognizing the readers' physical context, you can highlight your main points, thereby increasing the odds that your proposal will make it into the "keep" pile and away from the "reject" pile.

But there are also more complex contextual factors to consider when writing a proposal. In addition to physical constraints, contextual factors include the economic, ethical, and political issues that shape the reading of a proposal. Let us look at these contexts separately:

FIGURE 3.2
Reader Analysis Worksheet

Readers	Motives	Values	Attitudes	Emotions
Primary Readers				
Secondary Readers				
Tertiary Readers				
Gatekeepers				

Physical Context

As mentioned earlier in this chapter, professional writers will often try to visualize the physical context in which a document might be used. Do the readers expect a large document or a smaller document with appendices? Will they be reading many proposals at the same time? How will the proposals be discussed? Will the proposal be read in a large meeting or at someone's desk? These elements of the physical context will influence how you organize and design your proposal.

Economic Context

Of course, the bottom line *is* the bottom line for any proposal. When bidding for a contract, you should always take into account the client's economic status. In some cases, an expensive plan might solve all the client's problems, but economically they are only able to afford something more modest. On a larger scale, the economic context might involve studying forecasts for the client's industry or developing an understanding of the health of the current market for the client's products or services. Overall, you should always pay close attention to the money issues in a proposal. You can be certain that your readers will.

Ethical Context

Clients often shy away from proposals that sound ethically questionable. In an increasingly litigious society, the ethics of any project are important in any proposal. Therefore, you need to be mindful of plans that might leave the readers facing ethical pitfalls, leaving them open to lawsuits or damage to their public relations. Moreover, short-term gains at the expense of the environment or society might sound tempting, but these ethical transgressions have a way of returning later to hurt the client and yourself. As a result, proposals should always evaluate the risks of litigation and public condemnation. As you analyze the context, you should try to identify any potential ethical problems, even the most obscure.

Political Context

In proposals, political issues come into play on two levels. First, as corporate citizens, most company executives are well aware of the national, local, and industrial political issues that might affect their business. Proposal writers should be well aware of the politics in a particular industry and how they play out in the local, state, and federal sectors. The second level of politics involves the office politics that influence the review of proposals. It is important to recognize that proposals are usually treading on someone's turf or offering ideas that other people in the company believe they could have provided. In some cases, the good-old-boy or good-old-gal network might give one proposal an edge over others. These office political issues are unavoidable, but you should be aware of them so you can better plan your proposal-writing strategy.

Figure 3.3 shows a *context analysis worksheet* that can be used to help you sort out all these complex contextual issues. It is divided into three different levels, primary readers, industry/community, and writers, to represent the various levels on

FIGURE **3.3**
Context Analysis Worksheet

	Physical	Economic	Ethical	Political
Primary Readers				
Industry/ Community				
Writers				

which these contextual issues tend to influence the readers. The *primary reader* level is for your notes about the different contexts that face the primary readers of the proposal. As you think about this level, imagine the outside influences that will impact how your readers make their decision about your ideas. The *industry/community* level is for observations about current trends in the readers' industry or community. This part of the chart might also include the concerns of the secondary or tertiary readers described in the reader analysis worksheet. And finally, the *writer* level concerns you or your organization's context. It is important not to forget that many of the same contextual factors that are influencing your readers and their industry/community are also the factors that influence you and your organization. You may need to modify your proposal to fit your own contextual-based interests.

As in the reader analysis worksheet, put question marks in spaces where you do not know enough about the readers' context. These question marks signal places where you may need to do more research on your readers.

Objectives

Objectives are the goals, besides the purpose, that you would like the proposal to achieve. When you were writing your proposal's purpose statement, you probably noticed that there were many other goals, besides the purpose, that you wanted the proposal to achieve. For example, you might want an external proposal to build a sense of trust between your company and the client. Or, perhaps you want your proposal to spark a discussion on how your company can use the Internet to improve sales and service.

Essentially, objectives are your other reasons, besides the purpose, for writing the proposal. Before composing a draft of the proposal, writers often list out the objectives the proposal should achieve. Then, as they write the draft, they try to keep these objectives in mind.

Why should you write down some other objectives besides the purpose? Because even if your proposal is rejected, you may have other reasons for sending it to the readers. Sometimes bidders will answer an RFP merely to introduce themselves to a potential client or funding organization. These bidders might know that their chances of winning the contract are slim. Nevertheless, they submit the proposal, because they want to put their name in front of the client, describing the services and products that the bidder would be able to offer. At a minimum, even a rejected proposal is a good opportunity to introduce a potential client to your company or organization.

International Readers and Contexts

International trade and globalization, which have been accelerated by the growth of the Internet, are bringing new challenges to writers of proposals. In some cases, the proposal genre familiar to North American readers is quite different from equivalent types of documents in other countries. In some cultures, the use of proposals is actually something quite new. For example, in one interesting case, the author of this book found himself teaching Ukrainian scientists and engineers how to write proposals for high-technology firms in the United States. These Ukranian scientists and engineers said they did not know how to write proposals, because the Soviet Union tended to allocate funds from the top down. Consequently, proposals were not needed, because the government simply sent funds that the scientists and engineers were expected to use as they saw fit. In the Soviet system, they really did not need to "propose" projects in ways that would be familiar to North Americans.

Cultural differences can influence almost every aspect of a proposal, from content to organization to style to design. For example, in North American and Western European countries, the credibility of a proposal's content is usually based on observable evidence (i.e., facts and data). Quite differently in Asian countries, the credibility of a proposal's content is far more reliant on interpersonal relationships, the bidder's standing in the community, and past experiences with the bidder. In Mexico and some other Central and South American countries, details about the bidders' personal lives are often as important as the proposals' plan itself. Some Mexican readers might even expect details about your managers' family lives in the qualifications section of the proposal.

Likewise, the organization of a proposal often needs to change to suit an international audience. Organizational structures that Americans perceive to be "logical" or "common sense" may be seen as confusing and even rude in some cultures. For instance, in Arabic cultures, documents often start out with statements of appreciation and attempts to build common bonds among writers and readers. Asians, meanwhile, often prefer to start out with contextual information about nonbusiness issues. To some Asians, American documents seem abrupt, because Americans tend to bluntly highlight goals and objectives up front.

Style, as you probably know, is problematic for most Americans who are writing proposals to international readers. North Americans tend to use an informal writing style, sometimes even using first names and contractions in otherwise formal documents. In Mexico and most Central and South American countries, use of this informal style in a proposal would suggest a lack of respect for the project and the readers. Similarly, the American reliance on "plain speech" can often rub against the sensibilities of Arab readers, who prefer a more ornate style in formal documents.

Design expectations can also change with the culture. Some icons that show hand gestures, like the OK sign, a pointing finger, or a peace sign with the back of the hand facing outward, can be highly offensive to some cultures. Other seemingly benign icons or graphics can also have negative meanings. For example, in some Asian cultures a white flower or white dress can symbolize death. Another design problem is that Western conventions for creating graphs and charts can make data almost meaningless for some international readers. Even simple page design issues like the use of white space can change with the culture. European readers, for example, find that American texts use too many graphics, leaving too much white space. Americans often find European texts crowded and dense due to a lack of white space.

How should you write proposals to international readers? Fortunately, in our increasingly global economy, readers are becoming more familiar with cultural differences. So, mistakes that once "offended" readers are now simply unpleasant. Nevertheless, a good rule of thumb is to listen carefully to your readers' expectations. Careful listening is a valued quality in all cultures, and you will learn a great amount by simply paying attention what your readers tell you they expect the proposal to include and how it should look. Then, do some solid research into your readers' cultural expectations for proposals. International readers will usually be gratified that you took the time to learn their conventions, as long as it does not look like you are trying to fit them into a stereotype (e.g., the cliché of mentioning cherry blossoms in a letter to a Japanese reader). You might also find some model texts from the readers' culture, using them to help guide your decisions about content, organization, style, and design.

Overall, when you are writing proposals to international readers, listen to what your readers tell you, do some research into your readers' expectations for proposals, and be ready to learn from your mistakes.

The Rhetorical Situation at Earl Grey

In the last chapter, we saw how Lisa Miller used stasis techniques to identify the who, what, where, and when of the RFP sent out by Earl Grey. We also saw how she used the three stasis questions to isolate Earl Grey's problem. Lisa was now ready to start developing a deeper understanding of the rhetorical situation.

Subject

From her notes on the RFP, Lisa knew that her subject was the lack of office space at Earl Grey Designs. This subject, Lisa decided, called for a planning proposal in which she would suggest that Earl Grey use a local area network (LAN) and an intranet site to free up some office space. Specifically, she was going to propose that some of Earl Grey's employees be asked to telecommute from home at least a few days a week, using the LAN and intranet site.

Along these lines, she wrote, "The subject of this proposal is the use of a LAN and intranet site to free up office space at Earl Grey by allowing some employees to telecommute." This sentence itself already hinted what the readers would need to know in order to make a decision. First, the proposal would need to define what LANs and intranet sites are, while showing how these communication tools could be used to conduct the firm's business. Second, she would need to show the readers how telecommuting works and why it would be beneficial to their company. And most important, she would need to show the readers exactly how much office space would be freed up by her plan.

Purpose

The purpose of the proposal was tough to write, but Lisa ended up jotting down, "The purpose of this proposal is to persuade Earl Grey Design that telecommuting will free up space in their office, allowing the company to avoid the disruption and cost of moving to a new location." Of course, this purpose statement was rough and it would need to be modified for the proposal itself; nevertheless, it seemed to sum up what Lisa wanted the proposal to do. This sentence was fine as a working statement to guide her planning and writing of the proposal. It would help keep her on track as she invented the proposal itself.

Readers

She then analyzed the readers, using a writer-centered worksheet and a reader analysis worksheet. Her research on the Internet and her discussion with Grant Moser, the office manager, confirmed that the primary readers for the proposal would be the two principal architects in the firm, Susan James and Thomas Weber. From Earl Grey's Web site, Lisa discovered that Susan James was a progressive, modernist architect who preferred simplicity when she designed buildings. Lisa noticed that Ms. James' designs and a couple of speeches published on the firm's Web site showed a strong preference for innovation and creativity above all else. Thomas Weber was a bit more conservative, though still a modernist in approach. He seemed more responsible for the day-to-day functions of the firm, though he was also the principal architect on the ordinary projects handled by the firm. From her conversations with Mr. Moser, Lisa came to believe that both the primary readers wanted to stay in their current Michigan Avenue office. They were also concerned about the disruption in business created by a move to a new building.

The secondary readers, Lisa noted on her writer-centered worksheet, were the financial officers, staff, public relations agents, and clients associated with the firm. She knew the financial officers would probably not want to spend a great amount of money on moving or renovation, because these expenses might overextend the firm's resources. Staff and PR agents, she guessed, would also resist a move to the suburbs. Most members of the staff lived downtown, so moving to the suburbs would mean more commuting. Meanwhile, Lisa guessed that Earl Grey's PR agents would regret their client giving up such a posh address in Chicago. The firm's clients, too, would probably react negatively to a move to the suburbs. After all, one of the advantages of hiring Earl Grey was the accessibility of their offices and—to be honest—the appeal of having a "Michigan Avenue" architecture firm drawing up the plans.

Tertiary readers included the press, local politicians, and the competition. The press and local politicians, Lisa felt, would react positively to her idea for telecommuting, because it kept an important architectural firm downtown. Lisa's competition for the project, of course, would not like her proposal. They were motivated by larger, more expensive solutions that would put their people to work and more money in their pockets. Certainly the competition would work hard to undermine her project if they received a copy of the proposal. They would probably point out that telecommuting is new and untested as a work environment.

Gatekeeper readers included Lisa's boss and the chief engineer at Insight Systems. Lisa's boss, Hanna Gibbons, would be enthusiastic about the project.

Lisa knew Hanna valued these higher profile cases, because they seemed to attract business with other affluent customers. In the proposal itself, Lisa's boss would want the biographies of key employees at Insight Systems to play a prominent role. Her boss believed high-profile clients put added emphasis on relationships, so extensive biographies would be important. The chief engineer, Frank Roberts, was far more interested in the technical details of a proposal. He would, as always, insist that the technology be clearly explained in the greatest detail. In fact, his insistence on "full disclosure," as he termed it, had almost sabotaged Lisa's last proposal because the clients could not comprehend some of the technical parts of the plan. Lisa would need to figure out another way to satisfy Frank this time.

Context

The proposal's context was complicated also, so Lisa pulled out a context analysis worksheet to help her sort out the outside influences on the readers. The primary readers would certainly feel a great amount of political pressure inside and outside the firm to stay in downtown Chicago. After all, both employees and clients would be trying to influence them to keep their current office. Economic concerns were also important, because it was not clear whether the current growth in Earl Grey's business could be sustained in the long term. Lisa also considered the physical context in which her proposal would be read. The primary readers were certainly very busy people, so she needed to make her proposal highly scannable and visual. She would also need to keep sections and paragraphs short and simple, so the primary readers could look over the proposal even when they were being interrupted.

Lisa also did some research into the industry/community issues that might influence the reading of the proposal. Recent stories in the business sections of the Chicago papers talked about the "explosive" rebirth of downtown Chicago. It seemed like this rebirth was leveling off, though, and there was good reason to believe the fast pace of downtown renovation and construction would be slowing down. Of course, local politicians were taking a great amount of credit for bringing people and businesses back to Chicago. The local alderman would probably call Earl Grey as soon as he heard rumors that the firm might leave his jurisdiction.

Objectives

Finally, Lisa listed out some objectives, besides the purpose, that she wanted the proposal to achieve. She wanted the proposal to show a high level of professionalism. She also wanted the proposal to build a bridge for her company into the highly competitive downtown Chicago market. And, she believed that a successful project for a reputable architect firm might lead to further business referrals. Lisa was certain that telecommuting was going to be the way of the future, and the Earl Grey account offered a high-profile way to start moving business environments in that direction.

As you can see, by working methodically through the rhetorical situation, Lisa discovered a great amount about her purpose, her readers, and the contextual factors that influence her readers. Already, some important themes, like the internal and external politics of moving, were becoming clearer to Lisa. She was also discovering ways she might try to match the proposal to the personalities and values of her primary readers. Of course, Lisa could have just jumped into the writing of the proposal, but she more than likely would have missed many of these subtle influences on the readers. She knew the little time she invested toward defining the rhetorical situation would pay off later with a much more informed proposal.

Focusing a Writing Team with the Rhetorical Situation

To this point in the chapter, we have discussed using the five areas of the rhetorical situation (subject, purpose, readers, context, and objectives) as an invention tool. These areas might sound a bit abstract, and with the deadline looming for your proposal, you are probably tempted to just jump ahead to the drafting stage. In most cases, though, skipping the analysis of the rhetorical situation only leads to a much shallower, less creative proposal. Skipping ahead also wastes your time, because your supervisor, your co-workers, and unforeseen circumstances will send you off on tangents and wild goose chases. Moreover, if you have not clearly defined your purpose, readers, and context, you are almost certain to misread many of the clients' suggestions about what they are looking for in the proposal.

Perhaps the most effective use of the five areas of the rhetorical situation is to help you organize team projects. All too often, when writing with a team, you and your co-workers will discuss a project and agree verbally about what needs to be done. But then, each person walks away from the meeting with a slightly different idea of what the project involves. We have all found ourselves in these kinds of situations. As time passes and the project moves forward, each members' ideas only grow further apart. Soon, your co-workers and you are trying to patch together a Frankenstein proposal that was written to multiple audiences for multiple reasons.

If you sit down with your co-workers before writing the proposal and simply agree up front on the subject, purpose, readers, contexts, and objectives, you are well on your way to writing an effective proposal. To avoid problems with writing a proposal with a team, try working through the five-part analysis of the rhetorical situation with them:

- **Subject.** Use the stasis questions to figure out (a) if there is a problem, (b) what the exact problem is, and (c) what type of proposal will solve that problem. Then, discuss what information the readers need to know to make a decision on your ideas. Also, try to identify information the readers do not need to know.
- **Purpose.** State the purpose of the proposal in one sentence. Period. That is, complete the following phrase, "The purpose of this proposal is to . . ." If

you need two or more sentences to state your purpose, your ideas might be too unfocused.

- **Readers.** Identify the various readers (primary, secondary, tertiary, gatekeepers) and their individual characteristics (motives, values, attitudes, and emotions). To identify the readers and their characteristics, fill out the writer-centered worksheet (Figure 3.1) and the reader analysis worksheet (Figure 3.2).
- **Context.** Identify the various contextual issues (physical, economic, ethical, and political) that influence the writing and reading of the proposal. Fill out the contextual analysis worksheet to sort these issues into levels that influence the primary readers, the industry/community, and you and your organization (Figure 3.3).
- **Objectives.** List out any other corporate or organizational objectives, besides the purpose, that you would like the proposal to achieve.

More than likely, you will find that this analysis will start your proposal-writing process off on the right foot.

Last Word

This chapter and the previous chapter were designed to help you start thinking about the problem/opportunity your proposal is pursuing. You learned how to clearly define the problem and anticipate the rhetorical situation in which your proposal will be used. Now it is time to start learning how to write the proposal itself. In the next chapter we are going to discuss the writing of the Situation section of the proposal.

CASE STUDY   **Defining the Rhetorical Situation**

In their previous meeting at the Elmdale Hill Cafe, John, Karen, Thomas, and Sally agreed that the recent sales decline in the Elmdale Hill business district was due to the "real or perceived lack of convenience" for customers. They agreed that some of their regular customers were beginning to shop at places that they thought were more convenient, specifically the Wheatmill Mall.

To help them begin writing the proposal, the four business owners decided to begin identifying the rhetorical situation for their proposal. John said, "All right, let's start out by figuring out what we're up against. Who are we sending this proposal to, and what do we want it to do?"

"Can the mayor or the City Council help us?" asked Sally.

"Maybe," said John "but I don't think they can really solve our problem for us. The Wheatmill Mall has a whole load of influence in this city. Anyway, City Hall can't really bring us more sales."

"If you want the truth," Thomas said, "if we want to survive, the businesses in Elmdale Hill business district are going to need to compete better. In my opinion, the business owners in Elmdale Hill are ultimately our primary readers for this proposal. It all starts with them."

The others seemed to agree that the Elmdale Hill merchants were the primary audience, so

John wrote down "Elmdale Hill Business Owners." He then said, "Good. Now what do we want this proposal to do?"

After a moment, Karen said, "We need to convince the shop owners that we can all work together toward improving the convenience of the Elmdale Hill district."

Thomas added, "We also need to work together to improve the perception of the convenience of our shopping district."

With this tentative idea of their purpose in mind, they began filling out the rhetorical situation in the following way:

Subject: Improving sales in the Elmdale Hill District

Purpose: The purpose of our proposal is to develop a plan for improving the convenience and the customers' perception of convenience in the Elmdale Hill district.

Readers: Store owners in Elmdale district (primary readers)

Context: Offices of store owners. A Town Hall meeting?

Objectives: Unify business owners. Resist urban sprawl? Preserve historic business districts?

With these elements tentatively defined, they then studied each of them individually:

Subject

Defining the subject of the proposal only took them a few moments. The subject, after all, was essentially the flipside of the problem that they identified when they last met. If the "problem" was a loss of sales due to a real or perceived lack of convenience in the Elmdale Hill business district, then the subject was simply how to improve that situation. The challenge, however, was for John, Karen, Thomas, and Sally to determine what was "inside" the subject and what was "outside." In other words, they needed to distinguish between "need-to-know" and "want-to-tell" information, so they could narrow the subject to its basics.

For example, they found themselves ruling out their personal gripes about the mall's unhealthy fast food, cheap clothing, tiny-screen theaters, and generic bookstores. After all, their primary readers (the other Elmdale Hill business owners) probably would not need to know about these issues to make a decision on the proposal. Rather, the subject of the proposal needed to be confined to issues that impacted the readers directly, not the frustrations of the writers. So, they decided to limit the proposal specifically to issues that related to improving the customers' convenience or perception of convenience in the Elmdale Hill shopping district.

Purpose

They then defined the purpose of the proposal. What did they want the proposal to do? Confining themselves to one sentence, they shaved their purpose down into a clear, crisp statement. They wrote, "The purpose of our proposal is to develop a plan for improving the convenience and the customers' perception of convenience in the Elmdale Hill district." This statement of the purpose, though still generic, offered them two immediate tools for writing the proposal. First, it specified their overall goal for writing the proposal. Second, it gave them a knife to cut away the noncrucial details so they could focus on the need-to-know information.

Readers

They then turned to the writer-centered worksheet to identify their other potential readers (see Figure 3.4).

The primary readers, as John, Karen, Thomas, and Sally decided earlier, needed to be the Elmdale Hill business owners themselves. These readers, after all, were the people who could actually "do" something to change the current situation. They would be the decision makers. Secondary readers were the people who might be able to also exert influence on the project. The mayor and the City Council seemed like good candidates for this role. Also, the city's Police and Chamber of Commerce might be valuable allies, because they could offer guidance during the development of the plan. Of course, secondary readers would not change the situation themselves, but they might serve as advisors to the primary readers.

FIGURE 3.4

Elmdale Hill Proposal's Writer-Centered Worksheet

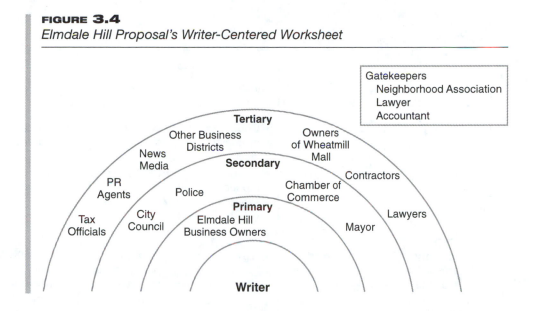

The tertiary readers, at first, seemed a bit more problematic. Who else might be interested in obtaining a copy of the proposal? Karen immediately pointed out that the local media might be interested in a copy. "We might decide not to send them the proposal, but my guess is that they will eventually obtain a copy. We need to keep them in mind as we're writing." John then pointed out that the owners of the Wheatmill Mall and their lawyers were probably going to find a way to track down a copy of the proposal. Sally mentioned that they also better keep their competitors in mind, being careful not to make statements that could be used against Elmdale Hill merchants in court.

Finally, they wrote down a few gatekeepers. Karen pointed out that the officers of the Elmdale Hill Neighborhood Association would probably want to be consulted before the proposal was sent out. These people might even have some further insights into how business owners and home-owners could work together to improve the Elmdale Hill area. Thomas suggested that they should have a lawyer and an accountant look over the proposal before sending it out, so they would feel confident that they were not leaving themselves legally liable or financially vulnerable.

Having identified their various readers, they filled out a reader analysis worksheet, as shown in Figure 3.5.

Context

With their readers identified and described, John, Karen, Sally, and Thomas decided to look more closely at the context in which the proposal would need to operate. It wasn't long before they realized the complexities of the issues that would be influencing their proposal and their plan for change.

The context analysis worksheet seemed to especially highlight the economic and political issues that would influence how the other merchants would read the proposal (Figure 3.6). On the one hand, they knew the other merchants would not react favorably toward a proposal that cost them a significant amount of money. On the other hand, the other merchants would also weigh the costs against any potential profits the proposed plan might generate. Meanwhile, it became clear that the proposal would need to negotiate the politics of City Hall and its cozy relationship with developers and large merchants.

FIGURE 3.5
Elmdale Hill Reader Worksheet

Readers	Motives	Values	Attitudes	Emotions
Primary Readers (Business Owners)	• Stay in Business • Make Profits • "Be your own boss"	• Good customer service • Love of products or services • Independence	• Want to find solution to problem • Dislike the mall • A bit doubtful	• Fearful of losing their business • Pride in owning their own business
Secondary Readers (Mayor and City Council, Chamber of Commerce)	• Increased tax revenue • Increased development • Diverse business environment	• Stay in office • Good public reputation • Lawful behavior	• Want to protect small business • Want to balance small business and large business interests	• Sympathy for small businesses (perhaps) • Fear of being voted out of office
Tertiary Readers (Press)	• Raise awareness • Likes an interesting story	• Leans toward underdog • Values diversity	• Presently apathetic • Could become an ally in preserving Elmdale Hill district	• Could take up a story as a "cause." • Rooting for the underdog
Tertiary Readers (Competitors/ Wheatmill Mall)	• Stamp out their competition • Profits • Protective of image	• Profits • Efficiency • Good public relations	• Hostile or dismissive of small businesses • Sees small businesses as old-fashioned	• Respond angrily to attacks from competitors • Annoyance
Gatekeepers (Neighborhood Association, Lawyer, Accountant)	• Preserve Elmdale Hill district • Decrease crime • Legal issues • Money issues	• Want a nice place to live and work • Safety	• Want to preserve a diverse district • Encourage financial health of district	• Concerned about crime • Pride in neighborhood

FIGURE 3.6
Elmdale Hill Proposal's Context Analysis Worksheet

	Physical	Economic	Ethical	Political
Primary Readers	• Initially, received in the mail, read in their office • Later, proposal might be used in large meeting of business owners	• Loss of sales means money is limited for large-scale changes • Low-cost changes will be met more favorably	• Feel as though large businesses are lowering prices to run out smaller businesses	• Lack clout with politicians due to limited money • A willingness to fight the odds against bigger corporations
Industry/ Community	• Issue of sprawl vs. renovation of neighborhoods and businesses • Raise proposal awareness on a Web site?	• Industry being driven by large, high-profit businesses • Development brings in tax dollars	• Movement of most businesses toward chains and warehouses • Move toward Internet	• Sympathy for small businesses among nonpoliticians and press • City Hall has cozy relationship with developers and large merchants
Writers	• Can meet personally with other business owners • Can lobby in person with politicians and press	• Limited means for printing and publishing proposal • Need to run business	• Importance of local ownership of businesses • Small business money stays local	• Can appeal to readers through interpersonal connections • Connections with Neighborhood Association • Friendships

Objectives

Finally, John, Karen, Thomas, and Sally considered the objectives, besides the purpose, that they would like their proposal to achieve. Karen thought the proposal would be a first small step toward preserving historic business districts in the city. John wanted the proposal to unify the business owners in the Elmdale Hill district. He said, "We've just been working in isolation too long. It would be nice if we began to see each other as allies rather than the people who just happen to work on our block." And Thomas saw the proposal as an opportunity to strike a blow against urban sprawl. "We need to stop the sprawl somehow. Why not start here?"

Describing the rhetorical situation for their proposal ended up taking them an hour and a half. When they finished addressing the five different areas, they had developed a much richer sense of the content, purpose, and social/political factors surrounding their proposal. The foundation for writing the proposal had been set.

They were ready to start inventing the Situation section of the proposal.

Questions and Exercises

1. Using a proposal from your workplace or a proposal you found on the Internet, write a two-page analysis in which you discuss how the writers handled the proposal's purpose, readers, and context. Can you find any places in the proposal that seem tailored to the specific readers or context? Do you think the proposal achieves its purpose? Are there places in the proposal where the writers stray from their purpose? How might the proposal be improved to fit its rhetorical situation?

2. With a team, choose a problem on campus, at your workplace, or your community that might warrant a proposal. Analyze the rhetorical situation in which that proposal would need to operate. Use a writer-centered worksheet and a reader analysis worksheet to identify the readers and their characteristics. Then, fill out a context analysis worksheet to work through the physical, economic, political, and ethical factors that might influence the readers. Write a memorandum to your instructor in which you summarize the important issues that relate to the proposal's readers and context.

3. In the Elmdale Hill case study, what are some reader-related issues that will probably need special attention when John, Karen, Thomas, and Sally write the proposal? Look closely at how the writers filled out the reader and context worksheets. What are some issues that jump out at you? What are some issues that the writers will need to keep in mind as they write this complex proposal? Are there any issues you might add to these worksheets? What are some of the political and ethical issues that the writers might be neglecting?

4. Writing with a team can be challenging. How might you use the methods and worksheets in this chapter to help you manage a writing team for a proposal? What might you do differently if you were writing a proposal with a team that you might not do if you were writing alone?

5. Study the RFP in Question 6 at the end of Chapter 2. What are the contextual issues (physical, economic, political, and ethical) that might be influencing this rhetorical situation? What political issues would you need to keep in mind as you write a pre-proposal for this RFP? What ethical issues might also be involved?

4

Describing the Current Situation

Overview

This chapter discusses the writing of the Situation section in a proposal. The chapter will meet the following objectives:

1. Discuss the importance of describing the current situation accurately for the readers.
2. Show how to argue logically with reasoning and examples.
3. Illustrate how mapping can be used to invent the content of a Situation section.
4. Define the basic parts of a proposal section.
5. Discuss the drafting of a typical Situation section.
6. Describe how to write the Situation section in a scientific research proposal.

Why Describe the Current Situation?

Having defined the problem and analyzed the rhetorical situation, you are now ready to start writing the proposal itself. In Chapter 1, you learned that proposals tend to follow a pattern, or genre. This genre includes the following areas:

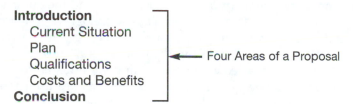

Introduction
   Current Situation
   Plan
   Qualifications   ← Four Areas of a Proposal
   Costs and Benefits
Conclusion

The proposal genre is not a formula to be slavishly followed. Rather, it is a pattern that can be manipulated to fit the needs of any proposal. In fact, clients may ask you to conform to proposal-organization schemes that vary widely from the one shown here. They might ask you to put qualifications or costs up front in the proposal. Or, they might expect you to merge the discussion of your qualifications with the plan. Nevertheless, you will find that these four areas are handled one way or another in almost all proposals.

In this chapter, we are going to discuss how to write the Situation section of a proposal. The purpose of a Situation section is to explain your understanding of the existing problem/opportunity, its causes, and its effects. This section shows the readers that you completely comprehend their current situation, thus increasing the likelihood that you can offer a reasonable plan for addressing their needs. Granted, in many cases, the readers already have a good understanding of their current situation. In these cases, your aim in the Situation section is to confirm to the readers that *you* understand their current situation. Your clients will only trust your plan after you have thoroughly demonstrated that you have a firm grasp of their needs.

Arguing Logically

One way to interpret the current situation is to identify the logical framework that holds it together. Aristotle was perhaps the first rhetorician to suggest that there are three paths that can be followed when inventing an argument. In his *Rhetoric*, he points out that a writer can devise arguments based on the following:

- **logos**—the use of deductive reasoning and inductive examples to support claims
- **ethos**—the reputation or credibility of the writers and the persona they portray to the readers
- **pathos**—the attitude, feelings, or tone projected by the text.

The Greek words *logos, ethos,* and *pathos* do not translate directly into English. Nevertheless, these words can be roughly equated to "logic," "character," and "emotion."

All three paths are addressed in any given argument; but one path of argument will tend to be dominant over the other two. For example, advertisers rely heavily on emotional arguments (*pathos*), because appeals to the audience's feelings typically require less time than arguments based on logic (*logos*) or character (*ethos*). Of course, advertisers also use logical arguments (e.g., "If you are looking for the safest car built, you should test drive the new Antera") and character arguments (e.g., "IBM has been a leader in the computer industry for over four decades"). In advertising, however, emotional arguments are used most often, while logical or character arguments play a supportive role.

Proposals tend to be built on logical arguments (*logos*), because these arguments provide the soundest method for persuading readers to adopt a position or change their minds. Logical arguments, however, often lack the intensity of arguments based on character and emotion. The advantage of logical arguments—i.e., the reason they are best for developing proposals—is that they are more firmly rooted in empirical evidence. After all, readers can dismiss a proposal's attempts to influence their emotions (*pathos*), or they can question a proposal's claims about the bidder's character (*ethos*). But logical arguments in a proposal are harder to dismiss, because they tend to be rooted in facts that can be validated independently by the readers. As a result, proposals that rely on logical arguments tend to make the most stable, credible cases for their acceptance.

In Chapters 6 and 9, we will discuss arguments based on character and emotion, so let us now look closer at how to argue logically. There are two basic methods for arguing logically: *reasoning* and *examples*. A proposal based on logic employs both these methods to create a well-balanced argument.

Reasoning

Reasoning tends to rely on variations of *if–then, either–or,* and *cause–effect* statements. When reasoning with someone, you are essentially arguing, "If you believe *X*, then you should accept *Y* also." Or, you are saying, "Either you accept *X* or you accept *Y*." Or, perhaps you are pointing out that "*X* causes *Y* to happen." For example, in a proposal you might claim, "If you agree that it is important to increase your manufacturing capacity, then you will need to modernize your current facility." Or, "Increased speed limits on State Highway 6 will almost certainly lead to more fatal accidents." Reasoning is essentially the use of deductive logic to construct an argument that leads the readers from their current opinion to a new opinion.

Examples

Examples are used to highlight predictable patterns for the readers. When arguing through examples, you are essentially showing that similar events in the past or present allow us to predict events in the future. For instance, historical examples can be used to prove a pattern: "In the years 1954, 1970, and 1999, low unemployment was accompanied by significant drops in crime. In 1928, 1962, and 1988, on the other hand, the crime rate increased dramatically, along with sharp rises in unemployment. These facts show that keeping unemployment low is the best way to fight crime." You might also use examples to point out the parallels in different situations. For example, a death penalty advocate might say, "When a rabid dog attacks a child, we don't try to reform the dog and then release it back into society. We put it to sleep. Should our response be anything less for a man who attacks a child?"

In a proposal, reasoning and examples are often used to support each other. In the State Highway 6 example, the best way to back up the claim that "higher speed limits leads to more fatal accidents" would be to cite some real examples where increased speed limits caused more deaths. An effective logical argument works back and forth between reasoning and examples, using both to develop a solid, supported case.

As you may have also noticed, logical arguments require observable or empirical support (e.g., facts, data, and evidence) to be successful. After all, if you want to argue that raising speed limits will increase the highway death toll, you would need to back up your claims with some solid evidence taken from historical examples, expert testimony, or scientific tests. Logical arguments provide the strongest foundation for your position, but they are only as strong as the empirical evidence that backs them up.

Inventing the Situation Section

Now, let us use these logical techniques to invent the Situation section for a proposal. Put concisely, your aim in the Situation section is to explain to the readers the *causes* and *effects* of a problem or opportunity. Essentially, in this part of the proposal you will use logical reasoning and examples to break down the current situation into its smaller parts. Then, when you describe the client's situation in your proposal, you can reconstruct these parts into a whole description of their problem or opportunity.

As you write the Situation section, you should keep three guidelines in mind:

Guideline 1: Problems are the effects of causes.

Guideline 2: Ignored problems tend to grow worse.

Guideline 3: Blame change, not people.

Guideline 1: Problems Are the Effects of Causes

This first guideline urges you to seek out the logical elements of change that are at work behind the current situation. Problems and opportunities do not just happen—they are caused because something in the current situation *changed* to create them. As the writer of the proposal, one of your first tasks should be to figure out what caused the problem or opportunity to exist.

One way to identify the causes of a problem or opportunity is through a technique called *logical mapping,* or just *mapping* for short. Mapping helps you sort out the problem on a piece of paper, so you can visualize the logical relationships between the problem and its causes.

To map out the logic of the current situation, write down the problem in the center of a blank sheet of paper. Put a circle around the problem. Then, ask yourself what are two to five major causes of that problem. Write them separately around the problem. Circle them and use lines to connect them to the original problem (see Figure 4.1).

Then, map further to identify the minor causes that created the two to five major causes. In other words, treat each major cause as a separate problem and continue mapping further out. In Figure 4.1, for instance, there are four major causes (the ones closest to the problem). By mapping further, we can identify the minor causes that created these major causes.

As you map out the causes of the problem or opportunity, keep asking yourself, "What changed?" As discussed in Chapter 1, proposals are tools for managing change. By paying attention to the evolving elements of the current situation, you will begin to visualize how the problem or opportunity came about.

To illustrate, let us go back to Lisa Miller's proposal for Earl Grey. When she mapped out Earl Grey's office space problem, she began by writing "lack of office space" in the center of a sheet of paper (Figure 4.2). Then, she identified some of the major causes of that problem:

FIGURE 4.1
A Problem–Causes Map

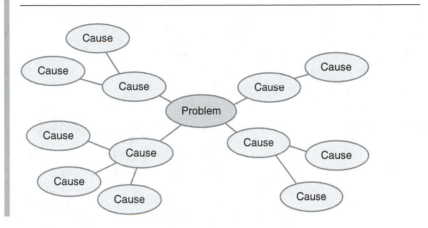

FIGURE 4.2
A Map of Earl Grey's Problem

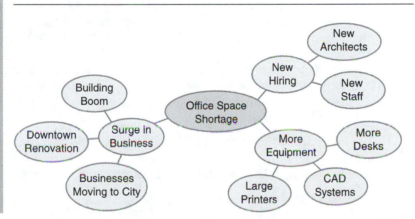

1. Earl Grey had hired several new architects and staff members over the last year, thereby increasing the amount of people, desks, computers, and equipment taking up space in the office.
2. Earl Grey had experienced a surge in business, forcing the firm to handle several projects at once. This surge seemed evident in the many plans for various projects laid out in Earl Grey's office.
3. She noticed the large amount of computer and printing equipment in the Earl Grey office. When Earl Grey was founded, architects relied on simple drafting tables. Now, computer-aided design (CAD) systems and large format printers were taking up a great amount of space.

Her causes for the problem seem to be (1) new hiring, (2) surge in business, and (3) an increase in office equipment.

Once Lisa identified the major causes of the problem, she treated each of the causes separately as a new "problem" and mapped out further to explore the minor causes.

When mapping, you could keep charting the causes indefinitely, teasing out the most obscure reasons for the problem. But, eventually, you will find that you have invented plenty of detail to describe the problem to the readers. At that point, mapping further would not be helpful. That's when you have enough material for the Situation section.

Guideline 2: Ignored Problems Tend to Grow Worse

When faced with a description of their problem and its causes, your readers will be tempted to just ignore the problem or wish it away. The interesting thing about change, though, is that current problems tend to grow worse over time, not better. Consequently, if these problems are not addressed, they often evolve into much larger problems. Because ignored problems tend to grow worse, you should also explore the effects of not addressing the problem or opportunity.

Logical mapping can be used to help you analyze the effects of a problem or missed opportunity. On a new sheet of paper, again put the problem in the center of the page (see Figure 4.3). Then, start mapping out the effects of the problem. This time, though, instead of asking what caused this problem, ask yourself, "What are the effects of not addressing this problem?"

As you map out the potential effects of the problem, try to tease the further effects that might come about if the problem or opportunity were not addressed.

Lisa Miller, for example, began mapping the effects of ignoring Earl Grey's office space problem (Figure 4.4):

1. The limited working space would make Earl Grey's operations far less efficient. If employees were required to climb over equipment and other people to do their jobs, a great amount of time would be wasted.

FIGURE 4.3
A Problem–Effects Map

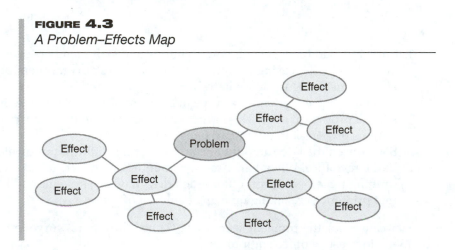

FIGURE 4.4

Mapping Out the Effects of Earl Grey's Problem

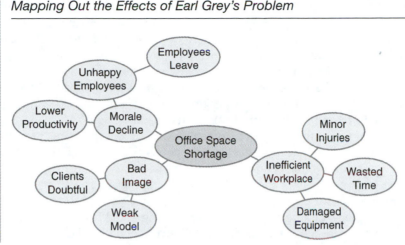

2. Employee morale was almost certain to drop, if it hadn't already. Good employees tend to leave when they feel uncomfortable at work. In the tight labor market for architects and staff, it would be hard to replace good architects and staff.

3. Earl Grey's crowded office implied to clients that the company does not practice what it preaches. In their own promotional materials, Earl Grey advertised functional, comfortable workspaces; yet its own office did not meet these goals. When visiting Earl Grey's office, potential clients might become skeptical whether Earl Grey could create the functional workspaces they promised.

Once she identified the major effects of the problem, Lisa kept mapping out even further to explore some of the minor effects.

When mapping out the effects, there is no need to become apocalyptic about the situation. You should avoid giving the readers the impression that the whole situation is hopeless and not worth saving. After all, no one wants to put more money into a sinking ship. Nevertheless, you can come up with some effects that will add a sense of urgency to your proposal and prove that the problem should not be ignored.

Guideline 3: Blame Change, Not People

This final guideline reminds us that problems and opportunities come about because reality is always changing around us. As you map out the causes and effects of the problem, it might be tempting to point the finger of blame at someone. But blaming people in a proposal, even your competitors, is almost always a bad idea.

After all, in most cases the readers of a proposal (or people closely associated with them) could be partly deserving of blame, so assigning fault will not gain you any positive points from the readers. For instance, imagine the sour taste in the readers' mouths if a proposal stated, "If your chief engineer, Steve Wendell, had chosen to pay for regular servicing of the GH-7000 router, then your company would not be looking to purchase a new machine right now." Even if this statement is true, Steve Wendell is not going to be eager to accept this proposal, and neither will his supervisors. Accepting the proposal would be an admission that Steve and his supervisors made a serious mistake.

Even when the people to blame are your competitors, you should avoid pointing the finger at them. Let us say your company was hired to fix a problem that your competitor created. Blaming your competition might score you some short-term points with the readers, but this approach is also risky. For one thing, someone at your client's company was responsible for hiring your competitor in the first place, and he or she is already taking some heat for that choice. Second, your competition has almost certainly been trashed by the client already. Placing more blame on your competitor might remind the clients to be more cautious, right when they are reading *your* proposal. By blaming your competitor, you are only reminding the clients to keep their guard up—something you want to avoid if you are urging them to say yes to your ideas.

In almost all cases, your Situation section will be stronger if you *blame change, not people*. Change is ultimately the one aspect of our lives that we can do little about. Roads eventually start to crumble, machines break down, markets shift, companies alter strategies. Change is the culprit behind all these things.

Moreover, change will not be offended if you put the blame on it. By blaming change, you will avoid messy political tensions that will only hurt your proposal. So, in the case of Steve Wendell and the GH-7000 router, you could just blame change by writing "Over time, the GH-7000 router begins to lose its precision and eventually needs to be replaced. Meanwhile, new advancements in the field require upgraded machines to stay competitive." If you want to mention the importance of paying for regular maintenance, make sure that issue is mentioned with your plan later in the proposal, without reference to Mr. Wendell.

Researching Logical Relationships

Essentially, the purpose of mapping is to highlight the logical relationships that underlie the problem or opportunity you will address in the proposal. It helps you identify the if–then, either–or, cause–effect arguments that you can use to reason with your readers. A causes map illustrates the statement, "These causes are having this effect," and the effects map points out, "If we don't do something about this problem, then here is what will happen." That's logical reasoning.

Mapping also tends to bring out examples that can be used to fill out the argument in a Situation section. As you keep mapping further, you will more than likely discover that you or members of your writing team can remember examples of real situations similar to the one you will describe in the Situation section. These examples might come from your personal experience, your company's history, or even cultural history. Perhaps you might draw examples from outside sources like newspapers, magazines, the Internet, or journals to back up your claims about the causes and effects of the current problem.

In most cases, mapping alone will not allow you to write a good Situation section. Once you have mapped out the causes and effects, it is time to start collecting print sources, data, and studies that will substantiate your understanding of the current situation. For example, Lisa Miller's mapping of Earl Grey's current situation might sound reasonable. But if she is going to prove that her understanding is accurate, she needs to back up her ideas with some solid facts and data. In her causes map, for instance, she claims that one reason for the lack of office space is a "surge in business." To back up this claim, she could draw growth figures from Earl Grey's annual report or a recent article about Earl Grey in the business section of the *Chicago Sun-Times.* In her effects map, meanwhile, Lisa pointed out that a lack of office space would lead to a "decline in morale" among Earl Grey's employees. She might back up this kind of claim by referring to published research that shows how cramped office spaces lead to lower productivity and unhappy employees.

Solid research is the backbone of any Situation section. Mapping may help you highlight logical relationships behind the problem or opportunity, but your follow-up research will provide the support on which those logical arguments stand.

Mapping in Teams

Writing teams probably gain the most from cognitive mapping, especially on large projects. As you probably know, it is hard for groups of people to write a document together, sentence by sentence. However, team members can easily participate in the mapping process. When you are working with a team, find a whiteboard, chalkboard, or some large sheets of paper. With a marker in hand, you can encourage the team to brainstorm about the causes and effects of the problem. As they explore the logical relationships in the problem, write down their comments and fill the board or paper with their ideas.

The mapping process is a uniquely visual way of bringing out the team's ideas. You will find yourself and team members coming up with ideas you never would have considered if you had been trying to write the document sentence by sentence. Meanwhile, mapping also allows your team members to visualize the overall problem or opportunity that is being addressed in the proposal. It provides them a global understanding of the changes in the current situation that the proposal is trying to manage.

Once your team is finished mapping out the problem, you can then assign each person on the team a cause or effect to research. Send them to the Internet, the library, company files, or government offices to dig up more data and facts to support the logical relationships your team discovered in the mapping process.

Writing the Situation Section

When writing the Situation section of a proposal, you will transform your maps and your research into readable sentences and paragraphs. The Situation section, like most large sections of a proposal, will tend to include three parts: an opening, a body, and a closing (see Figure 4.5). In other words, each section of the proposal is like a miniature essay with three parts: an introduction, body, and conclusion.

Each part of a section plays a different role. Let us consider each of these three parts separately in more depth.

Opening

The opening paragraph or paragraphs set a context for the body by telling the readers a few important things up front. Directly or indirectly, it will tell the readers the following:

- The subject of the section
- The purpose of the section
- The main point of the section

For example, Lisa Miller might identify the *subject* of her Situation section with a heading, like "The Office Space Shortage at Earl Grey." Then, in the opening paragraph, she might identify the *purpose* of the section by writing, "Before describing our plan, we want to first identify some of the factors that created Earl

FIGURE 4.5
The Basic Organization of a Proposal Section

Typical Section

Opening—identifies the subject, purpose, and main point of the section

Body—provides reasoning and examples to back up the main point of the section

Closing—reinforces the main point of the section and begins transition to next section

Grey's office space shortage." And finally, she might state her *main point,* "We believe this shortage is a result of Earl Grey's success and growing influence in the Chicago market. The downside to this growth has been less free space in Earl Grey's office."

Most sections require only a one-paragraph opening. The purpose of the opening paragraph or paragraphs is to simply set a framework for the body of the section. Therefore, try to keep the opening of each section as concise as possible.

Body Paragraphs

The body of the section is where you will provide the majority of the details you mapped out in your cause and effect maps. Three approaches to writing the Situation section are most effective: the causal approach, the effects approach, and the narrative approach.

Causal Approach

This approach structures the body of the Situation section around the causes of the problem. When using this approach, each major cause will typically receive one or more paragraphs in the body of the section. For example, the body of Lisa's Situation section might include three paragraphs that reflect the three branches in her map of the problem's causes. The first paragraph in the body might discuss the impact of Earl Grey's surge in business. The second paragraph might talk about the new hiring at Earl Grey. And the third body paragraph might discuss the office space demands of more equipment. Essentially, the causal approach structures the body of the section around the different major causes.

Effects Approach

This approach structures the body around the effects of not taking action. Usually, this approach is most effective when you and the readers of the proposal are already fully aware of the causes of the problem. There is little reason to dwell on these causes or prove they exist, because everyone already agrees they exist. In this case, the causes might be concisely mentioned in the opening paragraph or they might be discussed generally in the first body paragraph of the section. Then the remainder of the section can be devoted to the effects.

When using the effects approach to write the body of the Situation section, each major effect receives one or more paragraphs in which consequences of inaction are discussed. For example, if Lisa Miller were to use an effects approach in her Situation section, she would devote at least a paragraph to each of the major effects in her effects map. Specifically, her Situation section would discuss topics like the "decline in employee morale," "inefficient workspace," and "bad impression on clients."

Overall, the effects approach is most successful with readers who know why a problem exists but are reluctant to take action. By devoting most of the Situation section to a discussion of the effects of the problem, you urge them to face reality.

Narrative Approach

This approach tells the readers a story about how "change" created the current situation. Each paragraph moves the readers sequentially along a timeline, showing how changes in and around the organization have created the need to take action. For example, let us say you are trying to convince a local company that they should hire your accounting firm to handle their taxes. When the clients started the business, their company was small, so they could handle their accounting in-house. Ten years later, however, they are now a multimil-lion-dollar corporation, and their in-house accounting methods are no longer adequate. With the narrative approach, you would start out at the beginning and then lead them toward the present, showing them how their growth over the years has led to their need for the more sophisticated accounting services that your company provides.

The best approach for organizing the body of the Situation section depends on the kind of situation you are trying to describe and the readers to whom you are describing it. The causal approach is most effective if you are educating your readers about the issues that brought about their current problem or opportunity. The effects approach works best if the readers already know the causes of the problem, and you are worried that they might not recognize the importance of doing something. The narrative approach is most effective when you want to show the readers how the problem or opportunity evolved over time. The causal and effects approaches to organizing the situation section work best at describing the situation as it stands now. The narrative approach allows you to describe the historical events that led up to the present.

Closing

The closing of a section can be written a few different ways. The most effective closings are those that summarize the main point of the section while helping make a transition to the next section in the proposal. Above all, the closing should be concise.

The closing for a Situation section is a good place to stress the importance of the problem or opportunity. If you used the causal or narrative approach to orga-nize the body of the Situation section, you might then use the closing to discuss some of the effects of not taking action. The closing thus becomes an opportunity to stress the importance of the problem, giving the readers extra incentive to pay attention to your plan, which usually appears next in the proposal. If you are using the effects approach to organize the body, you might summarize the major effects of inaction or generally discuss what the readers might "need" to solve the problem. By discussing what is needed, you will begin making the transition to your discussion of the plan.

In some cases, however, proposal writers do not include a closing in their Situation section, preferring instead to go straight into their plan. Shorter propos-als can certainly do without closings, because closings tend to repeat what was just said in the body of the section. Larger proposals, on the other hand, usually require a closing to round off the section and reinforce main points.

Lisa Miller's Situation Section

According to Earl Grey's RFP guidelines, Lisa Miller needed to write a pre-proposal that would not exceed ten pages total, including any graphics or diagrams. The limited available space meant all the sections in the proposal would need to be concise. Lisa also wanted to leave extra space for the Plan section, because she believed her plan was going to be the most important part of the proposal. So, she decided the Situation section should be as concise as possible. In this section, she would need to show the readers at Earl Grey that she understood their situation, but she did not want to spend too much time telling them what they already knew. Lisa decided to limit the Situation section of her proposal to about one or two pages.

Looking over her maps of the causes and effects of the problem, Lisa decided to use the narrative approach to describe the current situation, because she felt the readers already had a rather strong grasp on the causes and effects (Figure 4.6).[1] The narrative approach would allow her to highlight Earl Grey's growth and success, while stressing that the office space problem exists because of this success. This approach would also help her bring the readers into the story, warming them up for the Plan section that would follow.

In her Situation section, Lisa had a few goals:

1. She wanted to turn the office space "problem" into a positive by pointing out that the current office space shortage is the result of Earl Grey's success. By reframing the problem in positive terms, she hoped to show that the problem was created by change and that it was not anyone's fault.
2. She wanted to reinforce the award-winning nature of the current office. Her competitors for the contract would almost certainly propose that Earl Grey move out of the current office, something she knew the firm's management was reluctant to do. So, she reminded them of the award-winning history of their current office, using examples to stress the historical importance of the office to their firm.
3. She reinforced that the current growth in business might just be a short-term "surge" related to the good economy in Chicago. From her discussions with Grant Moser, the POC, she knew the readers were concerned about overextending the firm's expenses. She wanted to reinforce that concern by hinting that the growth in business is due to recent trends that may or may not continue.

---

[1] This example and following examples in this book are not intended to be viewed as final drafts. They are unpolished, much like a typical rough draft. If you would like to see a finished draft of this section, please turn to the example proposals in Chapter 12.

FIGURE 4.6
The Situation Section for the Earl Grey Proposal

The Office Space Shortage at Earl Grey

Before describing our plan, we would like to first highlight some of the factors that created the office space shortage at Earl Grey Design. Actually, we believe this shortage is a sign of Earl Grey's success and growing influence in the Chicago market. The downside to this growth has been the loss of free space in Earl Grey's downtown office.

In 1982, Earl Grey moved into its current office on Michigan Avenue. At the time, the firm employed five architects and fifteen staff members. The office seemed roomy, because Susan James designed it with functionality and growth in mind. The five original architects each had a couple of drafting tables and a large desk. Meanwhile, desks for staff members were placed strategically throughout the office to maximize the efficiency of the workspace. The design of Earl Grey's office won accolades and awards as a masterpiece of modernist design. In a 1983 interview with *Architectural Review,* James explained that the workspace was designed to be both "aesthetic and pragmatic, a balance of form and function." She also wanted it to be a model office that would show clients the advantages of the modernist design.

Almost two decades later, the office is still a modernist masterpiece, but Earl Grey's growth has made the space feel a bit limited. This surge in business began in 1992 when the economy began to rebound from a recession. Soon, downtown businesses began renovating their neoclassical-style offices, adopting the modernist style. By the late 1990s, companies were returning to downtown Chicago from the suburbs. Earl Grey soon found itself one of the firms leading a movement that the *Chicago Tribune* dubbed the "Downtown Renaissance." Earl Grey's revenues doubled from 1992 to 1995 and then doubled again from 1995 to 2000.

To meet this increased demand, Earl Grey added ten architects and twenty new staff members during the 1990s. As a result, an office that once seemed roomy was becoming increasingly snug. More architects and staff meant more drafting tables, more desks, and more equipment. Meanwhile, new kinds of equipment not used two decades ago, like CAD systems and large-format copiers, also began using up precious floorspace, further restricting the limited room available.

Left unaddressed, this lack of office space may create some further problems in the near future. According to a Spenser Institute study, a restrictive office tends to undermine employee morale, leading to lower productivity and overall employee discomfort. The workspace will also become increasingly inefficient, wasting employees' time and causing them minor injuries, while also causing damage to equipment. A cramped office also presents a bad image to clients, especially since Earl Grey prides itself on designing functional workspaces that enhance business activities. Clients may come to believe that Earl Grey does not practice what it preaches.

The problems faced by Earl Grey are simply the downside of the firm's success and growing influence in the Chicago market. Now, the challenge faced by Earl Grey is to free up office space without disrupting current projects or jeopardizing future growth. We believe we can help you meet this challenge.

4. Lisa decided to mention the effects of inaction, but she handled them with a soft touch. She assumed the readers would already be well aware of these effects. Merely mentioning them would be sufficient to motivate the readers to take action.

Overall, Lisa conceded that her Situation section was telling the readers things they already knew. Nothing in her Situation section would come as a surprise to Earl Grey's management. Nevertheless, Lisa was showing them that *she* understood their problem, its causes, and its effects. She also wanted to remind them why they wanted to stay in their current office. By taking this approach, she believed her readers would be most receptive to her proposed plan.

A Note on Situation Sections in Research Proposals

Proposals for primary research, like scientific or historical research, require us to think a bit differently about the current situation. In research proposals, the Situation section is usually referred to as the Background, Research Problem, or Literature Review. These kinds of sections are designed to meet three specific goals:

- They show how the proposed research enhances or differs with prior research on the subject.
- They show why the research is important.
- They establish the credibility (*ethos*) of the study and authors by showing familiarity with the scientific community's conversation on the research subject.

To meet these three goals, the Situation section of a research proposal needs to summarize previous research on the subject, while identifying a gap in the previous research or raising a question about previous research. (Swales 1984).

At first glance, it might seem as though Situation sections in research proposals are quite different from those in other kinds of proposals. But once you look closer, the similarities become apparent. Like other proposals, research proposals suggest ways to solve problems. The problems being solved, however, are gaps in our current knowledge of a subject or a problem with the prior research that needs to be amended.

In research proposals, the causes and effects of the problem are still important. A research proposal should still identify the changes in the field that created the current problem. For instance, perhaps another study highlighted a gap in the knowledge base. Or, perhaps a new discovery threw the results of prior studies into doubt. The proposal should also identify the effects of not doing research on the subject. Perhaps a new cure might be missed. Perhaps we may lose the opportunity to learn more about an important subject.

The largest difference between Situation sections in research proposals and other kinds of proposals is the use of a literature review to describe the current situation. That is, the "situation" described will be made up of a review of other research papers, articles, and studies on the subject. In their Situation section, the writers of the proposal weave together other studies, showing where a gap exists or a question can be raised.

Last Word

The Situation section is often the most neglected part of a proposal, because many writers mistakenly assume that the readers already understand the current situation. That is not always true.

Readers need a well-written, well-reasoned Situation section for two reasons. First, the readers (your clients) often do not fully understand the problem or opportunity that they are facing. If they did, why would they be looking to you for help? By identifying the causes of the current problem and its potential effects, you are often providing them insight that they lack. If they agree with your assessment of their situation, they will be more likely to agree to your plan.

Second, even if your clients understand the problem, its causes, and its effects, they still want to see that *you* fully understand the situation. Nothing frustrates clients more than the one-size-fits-all, cookie-cutter plans that are forwarded by some large consulting firms. Each individual client is unique, and so are its problems. A well-written Situation section shows the readers that you are addressing *their* problem, not fitting their problem to a predetermined solution.

In many cases, a well-written description of the current situation is the difference between success and failure when bidding for a project or seeking funding for research.

CASE STUDY Describing the Situation in Elmdale Hill

After defining the rhetorical situation for their proposal, John, Karen, Thomas, and Sally believed they had a rather clear understanding of their purpose, their readers, and the contexts in which their proposal might be used. They had examined their readers' motives, values, attitudes, and emotions, and they explored the physical, political, ethical, and economic contexts that shaped the writing and reading of the proposal. With all their notes in front of them, they decided to start writing the Situation section of the proposal.

First, they used a cause–effect map to explore the causes of the current problem. Placing the problem "lack of convenience" in the middle of a sheet of paper, they began mapping out the causes for that problem.

"One cause that comes to mind is parking-related problems," said Karen. "The parking meters limit people to one hour, and it costs a dollar per hour. In my experience, I find it's hard to shop for only an hour, and I know you can't see a movie or have dinner in an hour."

"Also," added John, "the meter readers seem especially aggressive in Elmdale Hill. It's almost like they're waiting for people to be late."

Sally added, "One other cause of the parking problem is that the parking lot on the corner of Central and Second was replaced by that new

FIGURE 4.7
Problem–Cause Map for Elmdale Hill

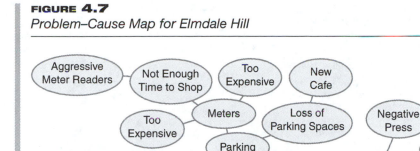

Starbucks. That took away much of the free, longer-term parking that was available."

"Lack of good public transportation in this area is also a cause," said Thomas. "Even if people wanted to leave their cars at home, the buses in this area only come around every hour. The buses also look like they are fifty years old. It's no wonder people just hop in their cars and drive to the mall."

On the sheet of paper in front of them, they mapped out issues surrounding the parking issue (see Figure 4.7). "Lack of parking" soon branched out into its minor causes, including "parking meters" and "lack of free parking." Branching from each of these causes were other causes. Under "parking meters," for example, they wrote down, "expensive," "only one-hour time limits," and "overly aggressive meter readers." The public transportation issue became its own major cause that they explored a bit further.

John looked up from his map. "All right, there are two causes already. Any more?"

Karen said, "Well, it seems like the mall is doing a much better job promoting itself. Every day I see advertisements on television that promote the mall as a whole, not just individual stores."

Thomas responded, "Yeah, but advertising is expensive. I certainly can't afford television advertising."

"It's the same for those folks at the mall," said Karen, "They just pool their resources, selling the whole mall experience rather than a single store."

"Meanwhile," said Sally, "Elmdale Hill gets bad press because we can't counter negative stories with our own advertising. We also don't present a consistent image to the public. People see us as individual shops, not a unified collection of shops like the mall."

After a few minutes, they had developed another branch of the situation called "negative public relations." Under this branch, they wrote "minimal advertising for Elmdale Hill," "bad press in local newspapers," and "lack of consistent image for Elmdale Hill shopping district."

Finally, they began exploring a third major cause—"actual or perceived problems with safety." In this branch, they wrote down "graffiti," "too many panhandlers," "too few police walking the streets" and "bad publicity from newspapers." When they finished this branch, their map had grown into a detailed description of the problem.

FIGURE 4.8

Problem-Effects Map for Elmdale Hill

With the causes of the problem mapped out, they decided to look at the potential effects of the problem. Again, putting the problem, "lack of convenience," in the center of a sheet of paper, they began mapping to find the effects of not taking action.

"Certainly, we're going to lose even more sales if we don't do something soon," said Karen.

"If that's true, our situation is just going to keep getting worse because we will be advertising even less than we do now. We will also need to cut back on improvements to our businesses," said Sally.

"As more shops close, customers will have even fewer reasons to come down to the Elmdale Hill district," Thomas stated.

"Unfortunately, when shops close, they are usually replaced by more marginal businesses like pawn shops and porn shops. That means our core customers are being replaced by customers that don't frequent specialty stores like book stores, your movie theater, my restaurant, or your clothing store," said John.

"It's a very different clientele. Frankly, I'd rather move to a different part of the city than work next to a bunch of pawn shops," said Karen.

Within a few minutes, they had developed a full problem-effects map (See Figure 4.8).

The two maps they developed put the problem, its causes, and its effects out on paper where they could study them more closely. They agreed that each of them would research the causes and effects in more depth at the library or on the Internet.

A few days later, after some research, they began to compose the Situation section of their proposal. They decided to focus on the causes of the problem in the Situation section because they wanted to avoid giving the impression that the problem was beyond fixing.

After sketching out a small outline, they wrote the following rough draft of the Situation section by describing the problem and its causes. They ended the Situation section with a concise description of the effects of ignoring the problem (Figure 4.9).

Looking over what they had written, Sally said, "Seems a bit rough right now. And, I'm not sure we handled the homeless issue correctly."

Looking over the draft, Thomas replied, "That's all right. We can clean it up when we finish writing the rest of the proposal. The basic information is all here."

"Let's move on to solving the problem," said John.

FIGURE 4.9

A Situation Section for the Elmdale Hill Proposal

The Reasons For Elmdale Hill's Recent Loss In Profits

Over the last few years, most of the merchants in the Elmdale Hill Business District have experienced a significant decline in sales. After conducting an informal survey of Elmdale Hill, we found that over X percent of the merchants in this area took in fewer sales this year than last year. Indeed, several business owners told us that this year is their worst one on record.

Of course, the reasons for the recent revenue losses in Elmdale Hill are complex. Many merchants we talked to mentioned the recent construction of the Wheatmill Mall. But, we believe the problem is not the mall itself, but the way we compete against it. Specifically, our problem is that our customers perceive a lack of shopping convenience in Elmdale Hill. So, they take their business to a place that they believe is more convenient (i.e., the Mall). We believe there are four main reasons why customers believe Elmdale Hill is not convenient.

First, the lack of parking has become a severe problem in the Elmdale Hill area. Until recently, the parking lot at Central and Second provided free long-term parking for our customers, but the new Starbucks built on that empty lot took away most of the convenient parking in the area. Now, when customers drive down here to shop, they discover that parking spaces are almost impossible to find. And even when they are lucky enough to find a parking space, they are forced to shorten their shopping time, because all the meters have one-hour limits. Under these conditions, window-shopping is out of the question. Seeing a movie, meanwhile, or dining at a restaurant is just about impossible. If customers decide to stay longer, the aggressive meter readers in this area slap them with a 25-dollar parking ticket.

Second, public transportation is minimal in this area. Customers could avoid the parking problems by taking the bus. Unfortunately, buses only come through once an hour, often forcing customers to wait outside for a long time in freezing or sweltering conditions. Also, the buses do not run at night, restricting shopping hours to 8 to 6 business hours.

Third, Elmdale Hill suffers from a lack of positive publicity. Whereas the businesses at the Wheatmill Mall either pool their advertising dollars or rely on national chains to buy advertising, the Elmdale Hill businesses tend to advertise individually on a very limited basis, usually in newspapers or on the radio. This minimal, sporadic advertising means that

(continued)

FIGURE 4.9

Continued

we are not tapping the television viewers who make up the majority of our paying customers. Moreover, our use of individual advertising does not give Elmdale Hill a unified image; therefore, customers view us as a group of single shops rather than a place where they can come to fill all their shopping needs.

A more serious publicity-related problem is the increasingly negative portrayal of Elmdale Hill in the local media. Because we are not actively projecting a positive public image of ourselves, the media only reports the negatives. As a result, the few criminal acts committed in this neighborhood seem to receive significant coverage without any counter-response. Meanwhile, the positive aspects of Elmdale Hill are rarely known outside the district, because we lack a unified voice and we have no source for keeping the media informed about the people and events that make Elmdale Hill a fun place to live, work, and shop.

Finally, another reason for our loss in sales is our customers' perception that safety has decreased in the Elmdale Hill area. Of course, we can blame some of this problem on the media. But, we must concede that we have experienced an increase in activities that are usually associated with crime. For example, the amount of graffiti on our walls has jumped significantly over the last couple years. Graffiti gives customers the impression that Elmdale Hill is a "bad" or at least questionable neighborhood where they might not be safe. Another safety-related problem is the increase in panhandlers on our streets. The merchants of Elmdale Hill and their customers have always been friendly and generous to panhandlers, probably attracting more homeless people to our area. Even though we know that these panhandlers are mostly harmless and generally nice people, our customers may see their increased numbers and occasional rude behavior as further evidence that Elmdale Hill is not a nice neighborhood anymore. Whether safety has really decreased in our area or not, many of our customers have come to believe that they are not safe here, especially after dark.

Unfortunately, if we choose to ignore these problems, they will only become worse over time. Soon, customers will just stop shopping at Elmdale Hill. As existing businesses continue to be replaced by pawn shops, porn stores, and check-cashing operations, the reputation of the Elmdale Hill Business District will degrade in the media and the minds of the public. Furthermore, the current "perception" of crime might be replaced by real increases in crime as businesses in Elmdale Hill start to cater to a more marginal, transient customer. Essentially, the small problems we are experiencing now will eventually become large problems if we do not take proactive steps in the near future.

Questions and Exercises

1. Find a problem on your campus, in your workplace, or in your community that you believe needs to be addressed, like commuting, health, or safety. Using the mapping techniques discussed in this chapter, map out the causes of that problem. Then, map out the effects of not taking action.

2. For the problem you mapped out in Exercise 1, outline three Situation sections that follow the three approaches discussed in this chapter (causal, effects, narrative). Which approach would be most effective for the readers of this Situation section? How does your choice of approach influence how the readers will respond to your subject and purpose?

3. Following your work in Exercises 1 and 2, write a two-page Situation section in which you describe the problem, its causes, and its effects.

4. Locate a proposal on the Internet that includes a substantial Situation section. What are some ways in which the writers use logical reasoning or examples to support their arguments? Identify specific examples where the writers use reasoning (if-then, cause-effect, either-or). Identify different kinds of examples used in the document. Can you find places where the writers need to use better reasoning to support their points? Where might some examples help illustrate their claims.

5. Using the proposal from Exercise 4, recreate the problem–cause and problem–effects maps that may have been used to write these sections. In other words, place the problem in the middle of a sheet of paper. Then, map out the causes you see in the Situation section of the proposal. Map out the effects that the proposal identifies.

6. Look at your food choices available on your campus or at your workplace. Write a one-page Situation section in which you describe the current status of the food (healthy or not) where you learn and work. What is the problem with the current food choices? What are some of the causes and effects of that problem? Remember to blame change, not people in your description of the current situation.

7. The Situation sections for the Elmdale Hill proposal is still rather rough. How would you change the section to make it stronger or more persuasive? Are the writers missing anything you would add? Write a memo/e-mail to John, Karen, Thomas, and Sally in which you suggest improvements to their Situation section.

5 | Developing a Plan

Overview

This chapter discusses the development and writing of a plan in a proposal. The chapter will meet the following objectives:

1. Discuss the purpose and importance of the Plan section.
2. Illustrate how to set primary and secondary goals.
3. Show how to answer the "how question" by mapping a solution.
4. Show how to invent and organize the plan.
5. Discuss the importance of answering the "why questions" in the plan.
6. Illustrate the writing of the Plan section.
7. Comment on the writing of a scientific methodology.

The Importance of the Plan Section

A thorough description of the plan is the heart of any successful proposal. A proposal's Plan section—sometimes called the *Approach, Methodology, Research Program, Solution,* among other titles—typically describes a detailed step-by-step process you will follow to solve the problem or take advantage of the opportunity. When describing your plan, you are going to tell the readers *how* the problem should be solved and *why* the problem should be solved the way you prescribe. You will also identify the *deliverables,* the tangible results of your proposed plan. Overall, an effective Plan section explains how change will be managed to your or your clients' advantage.

When writing the Plan section, the hardest task facing you is the invention of something completely new. In other words, the project you are proposing does not currently exist, so you need to peer into the future and use your imagination to see your plan in action. In some cases, writing the Plan section might mean simply adapting a previous plan to the new situation. In other cases, writing this section will require the invention of a whole new product, organization, or approach from the ground up. That is why writing the Plan section can be exciting and challenging—and also frustrating. In this chapter, you will learn how to avoid some of that frustration by setting goals, answering the how and why questions, and writing a well-organized plan that will attract your readers.

Setting Goals

Goal setting is always a good way to determine the objectives you want your plan to achieve. If the goals of the plan are not clear, the proposal will seem unfocused and nonspecific. But if you set some goals up front, the chances increase that you will develop a successful plan for reaching those goals.

Setting goals for a proposal's plan can take a few minutes, but it is well worth the effort. To start out, check whether the clients have already set goals for you. Often, clients will have defined their objectives in the RFP. Or, in conversations with you, they might have said something like, "Here are the three things we need accomplished," and then listed out what the project should achieve. If your readers have already specified some of their own goals, it would be wise to adopt them as the goals of your plan. After all, by telling you their goals, the readers have more or less handed you the criteria on which they will be evaluating the proposals they receive. These goals are the benchmarks they will use to judge the merits of various proposed projects.

If the readers have not specified some goals, you should take a few minutes to list the objectives that *any successful plan for this project should be able to meet.* Ask yourself what are the two to five goals that your plan will need to achieve, given the situation you described in the Situation section. In other words, if you were to boil the current situation down to its very essence, what goals would you need to achieve to solve the problem or take advantage of the opportunity? List these goals.

In most cases, one of the goals you or your readers have identified stands above the rest in importance. We will call this goal the *primary goal,* because it is the core issue that the readers want addressed. The primary goal is typically the antithesis of the problem, or it is a restatement of the opportunity. For example, if the problem is, "Gecko Industries lacks name recognition in the general public," the primary goal would be, "Our primary objective is to raise the profile of Gecko Industries in the eyes of the public." If you are pursuing an opportunity, you might say something like, "Our principal aim is to help Mesa Equipment capture 20 percent of the climbing harness market." Essentially, the primary goal is the bottom-line objective that your plan is designed to achieve.

Other goals for your plan will be referred to as *secondary goals.* Secondary goals usually concern *how* you are going to carry out the plan rather than the overall result. In other words, secondary goals focus on the *process* you will use to achieve the primary goal. For instance, your clients may require that the successful plan meet specific requirements, like achieving specified quality control levels, maintaining high environmental standards, adjusting to a preexisting operating schedule, or complying with government standards (e.g., ISO-9000 regulations). These kinds of secondary goals concern *how* you will carry out the plan. Make no mistake, secondary goals are still very important to the readers. In your plan, you will need to prove to the readers that you can meet their primary goal, while also satisfying these important secondary goals.

When possible, it is always a good idea to go over your list of primary and secondary goals with the readers before writing your plan. In many cases, an agreed-upon list of goals can serve as a place where you and your readers reach a common understanding. Your goals can be used to slice through the complexities of the current situation, giving you and the readers a focal point on which to develop a solution to their problem. If the readers agree with you on the goals, you are much more likely to develop a plan that satisfies their needs.

Setting goals is also a good way to focus the efforts of your own team of colleagues or employees. By specifying directly what your team is trying to achieve, you can focus the team's efforts toward meeting specific results. This goal-setting process will help keep your team on track; meanwhile, the list of primary and secondary goals will help you determine whether your proposal's plan is satisfying the client's and your requirements.

Setting Goals for the Earl Grey Project

Formally and informally, the people at Earl Grey had already furnished Lisa Miller with a list of goals that her plan would need to meet. The original RFP provided a clear idea of the plan's primary goal when it stated that the plan should "manage the physical growth of [Earl Grey's] architectural design operations." This primary goal, Lisa noted, was the antithesis of the problem, lack of office space, that she discussed in the Situation section.

A couple secondary goals also stood out in the RFP. For one thing, the RFP mentioned that the plan should "cause the least disruption to our current operations." The RFP also mentioned cost. Though costs were not stressed in the RFP, Lisa had the impression that a less expensive solution would strongly appeal to the readers at Earl Grey.

Looking over her notes from her meeting with Grant Moser, Lisa further identified a few other secondary goals. First, she sensed that the clients wanted to find a way to retain Earl Grey's award-winning Michigan Avenue office, even though they had reluctantly conceded that their office space shortage might require them to relocate. Another unstated secondary goal Lisa picked up from Mr. Moser was the client's wish to avoid overextending the firm's revenues. Mr. Moser seemed to suggest that the Chicago architectural market would not always be this strong, so the firm did not want to chain itself to an expensive office that would be a burden when the market weakened. A final secondary goal, Lisa noted, was to maintain high employee morale at Earl Grey. In her Situation section, she had pointed out that employee morale would suffer if Earl Grey did not address the office space problem. On the other hand, the employees also seemed resistant to relocation to the suburbs. Maintaining morale would be an important goal, Lisa felt, even though the RFP and Mr. Moser had not mentioned it directly.

On a worksheet, Lisa wrote down her primary and secondary goals (Figure 5.1). Where possible, she tried to rephrase these goals in positive terms that implied action and progress.

As you will notice, Lisa's goals are all somewhat abstract. They are not solutions to the problem. Rather, they are milestones that any successful plan would

FIGURE 5.1
Goals Worksheet

Objectives for the Proposal's Plan
Our primary objective is to manage the physical growth of Earl Grey's architectural design operation. While meeting this primary objective, we should also strive to meet the following secondary objectives:

- Minimize disruption to Earl Grey's current operations.
- Minimize costs, so the firm will preserve financial flexibility.
- Retain Earl Grey's current office on Michigan Avenue.
- Foster a dynamic workplace that will be appealing to Earl Grey's architects and staff.

---

be able to meet. This simple act of identifying goals creates some boundaries for a potential solution while providing a method for determining which plans are suitable and which are not. By setting goals, Lisa provided her team with a measuring stick to determine whether her plan would work. Moreover, she hoped, these goals would be the criteria on which the readers at Earl Grey would evaluate the viability of her proposal's plan.

Answering the How Question

With the goals set, we are faced with a question that has followed us since we started the proposal writing process: *How* are we going to solve the problem or take advantage of the opportunity? *How* are we going to achieve these primary and secondary goals? One way to answer the how question is to begin mapping out a solution on a sheet of paper. In the last chapter, you learned how to map out the current situation for the readers. We can use this same mapping technique to invent a plan for solving the problem.

To begin, it is important to recognize that goals are met when people take specific steps to reach those goals. A plan is like a roadmap of steps that will take us from the current situation to a better situation in the future. So, when mapping out the solution to a problem, you want to identify all the steps, some larger and some smaller, that will allow you to meet the goals you have set for yourself.

Move 1: Identify a Possible Solution to the Problem

To begin the mapping process, you first need to identify a solution that might meet the primary and secondary goals you have identified. In other words, you need to invent a solution that would address the problem or opportunity you described in the Situation section. Fortunately, while writing the Situation section, you more than likely started to identify one or two possible solutions that might work. You have a hunch that at least one of these solutions will allow you to reach the goals you just articulated, but you are not sure about the individual steps that will help you achieve those goals.

On the first try, you do not need to identify the right solution. You might even list out a few possible solutions. Then, you can map them out separately, seeing which one best meets your primary and secondary goals.

Move 2: Map Out a Possible Solution

As we discussed in the last chapter, mapping allows you and a team of others to highlight the logic behind your ideas. In this case, we can use mapping as a logical method to construct the steps in a plan.

Place your most promising solution in the center of a piece of paper and circle it. Or, put the solution on a whiteboard or chalkboard. Then, ask yourself and your team, "What are the two to five major steps needed to make this solution a reality?" Write down those major steps around the solution, circle them, and connect them to the solution (Figure 5.2). Then, treat each major step separately. Ask yourself or your team what minor steps are needed to make each major step a reality.

As you map further out, each level of the plan should be supported by levels of smaller steps. For example, let us say one of your major steps is "collect information." Some smaller steps connected to this major step might be "survey client's customers," "interview clients," and "study client's marketing plan." Each of these smaller steps might have further substeps attached to them. The step "survey client's customers" might branch out with even smaller steps like "create survey," "secure a mailing list," "user-test survey." Of course, you and your team could probably keep mapping out as far as you like, identifying even the minutest steps that might be required. However, there comes a point in the mapping process where you begin generating too much detail. When you begin identifying steps that probably will not be mentioned in the proposal, it is time to stop.

FIGURE 5.2
Mapping the Solution

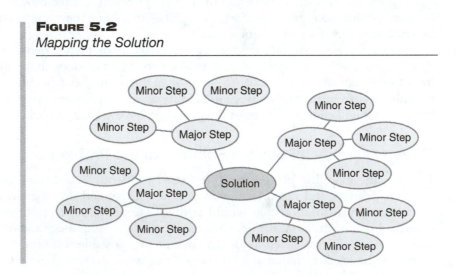

When you map out your plan, you will often find yourself and your team coming up with steps that might never have occurred to you otherwise. This added creativity is the advantage of the mapping process. Because you are working visually and spatially, not linearly, your mind can more freely associate different thoughts. Also, you will likely find yourself crossing out whole areas on your worksheet, because certain steps are nonstarters. In some cases, you will find that one of your steps really isn't a major step after all. Rather, it belongs under one of the other major steps.

A rule of thumb, again, is to try to limit your plan to five or fewer major steps. A plan that includes too many major steps will become unmanageable for the readers, because it will force them to wade through a seemingly neverending list of tasks. If your map of the solution includes more than five major steps when you are finished mapping, consider whether some of the less-significant major steps could be consolidated with one of the other major steps. If consolidation will not work, then you should sort the major steps into two or three larger *phases* that bundle larger steps together.

The Importance of an Evaluation Step

One step that should appear in almost all proposals is an *outcomes assessment* or *evaluation phase* in which the results of the project are measured after completion. The purpose of an evaluation step (i.e., customer satisfaction surveys, product testing, or impartial evaluators) is to reassure the clients that your work met the goals listed in the proposal. The strongest outcomes assessment tools yield quantifiable (i.e., numerical) ways of measuring whether the project was a success. In most cases, the evaluation step is the last step in the plan.

Move 3: Review Your Primary and Secondary Goals

When you are finished mapping, look back at the goals you identified earlier. Does your mapped solution meet those goals? Are there any goals, especially secondary goals, that are not being met? When reviewing your goals, you may find yourself adding some new major and minor steps to your map. In some cases, you may cross out major or minor steps because they go beyond the needs specified by the goals. You may even find that your map does not meet your goals at all. In these cases, try mapping out another solution to see if another plan will meet your goals.

In the end, mapping will allow you to answer the how question. Your map of the solution illustrates roughly how you are going to achieve the primary and secondary goals you identified, thus solving the problem or taking advantage of the opportunity.

Mapping a Plan for the Earl Grey Proposal

Lisa Miller knew there were several possible solutions to Earl Grey's office space problem. However, her company, Insight Systems, could only offer one particular type of solution, a local area network (LAN) and intranet that would allow Earl Grey's employees to telecommute from home.

To help her rough out a solution, Lisa called a planning meeting that included a few other engineers at her company. She gave each of them a copy of her proposal's Situation section, which they read and discussed. Then, on a whiteboard, she wrote "Telecommuting" and circled it. With a marker in hand, she asked the engineers to help her identify the major steps needed to develop a telecommuting system at a company like Earl Grey.

As the group brainstormed, Lisa jotted down some of the major steps needed to achieve that solution. Around the solution, she wrote, "Build Computer Network," "Study telecommuting needs," "Train Earl Grey employees," and "Conduct outcomes assessment." She was already beginning to visualize the plan through the map developed with her team (Figure 5.3).

Once they had roughed out the major steps, Lisa and the other engineers began mapping further to identify the minor steps required to achieve each major step. For instance, under "Train employees," they wrote smaller steps like "Offer workshops," "Develop training materials," and "Create a help desk for new telecommuters." Their map began to fill the sheet of paper.

After mapping the plan with her team of engineers, Lisa looked back at the primary and secondary goals she listed out before (Figure 5.1). For the most part, she felt their mapped plan was meeting those goals. Even in its rough form, their plan seemed to show how Earl Grey could manage its office growth while minimizing disruption, minimizing costs, and fostering a dynamic workplace. Best of all, their plan would allow Earl Grey to keep its Michigan Avenue office—an

FIGURE 5.3
A Map of the Telecommuting Solution

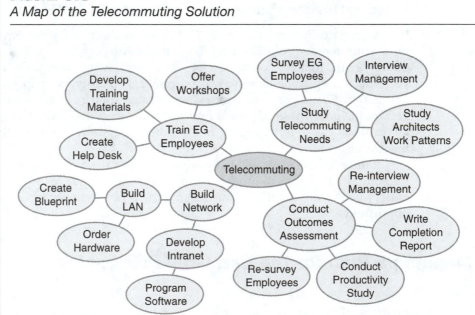

unstated goal that she thought would be appealing to the readers. Lisa was ready to begin organizing and drafting her Plan section.

Organizing the Plan Section

After mapping out the logic of your plan, you need to organize the major and minor steps into a pattern that the readers will understand. To start, it is important to recognize that a proposal's Plan section is simply a description. When describing something, whether an object or process, your first task is to *partition* that something into its larger parts.

For example, if someone asked you to describe your house or apartment, you would probably start out by saying something like, "My house has a kitchen, three bedrooms, two bathrooms, a living room, and a garage." With this statement, you just partitioned the house into its larger parts. Now you are ready to address each of the parts separately. You might continue by describing the kitchen separately: "The kitchen is about 500 square feet. It has a large tile countertop, a gas oven, a dishwasher, and a refrigerator. There is an oak table in the middle of the kitchen floor where we like to eat our meals."

Describing a process is similar to describing an object. A description of a process—sometimes called a *methodology*—first requires the task to be partitioned into its major steps. For instance, "Baking a cherry pie requires four major steps: (1) make the cherry pie filling, (2) prepare the crust, (3) pour the filling into the crust, and (4) bake the pie." Once you have partitioned the process into its larger steps, you can then describe the minor steps under each of these major steps. Instructions for making the pie filling would require some smaller steps like (a) combine cherries, sugar, and cornstarch, (b) heat mixture until thickened and bubbly, (c) cook for one more minute, and (d) remove from heat and allow to cool.

Your proposal's Plan section is simply a description of a process. When you mapped out the plan, you partitioned the plan into its major and minor steps. Now, on another worksheet, list out these major steps in the order they will be followed. Then, fill in the minor steps under each of the major steps. For example, Lisa Miller might outline her plan as shown in Figure 5.4. In this outline she organizes the major steps into the order they will be taken.

Of course, like any outline, Lisa's description of the plan was still rather crude and skeletal. Nevertheless, the transfer of the visual map into an outline form shows the basic structure of the plan. Now Lisa could begin putting some muscle on that skeleton.

Answering the Why Questions

When clients read a proposal, their overriding question is always *why*? *Why* should we do it this way? *Why* is this step necessary? *Why* not try doing it a different way? As the proposal writer, your job is to answer these why questions as you

FIGURE 5.4

Outline of Office Space Solution for Earl Grey

Our Plan: Telecommuting

In order to provide suitable working space for Earl Grey's employees, we propose a program that allows some employees to telecommute from home. Implementation of this program would require a procedure that includes the following four steps: studying telecommuting options, building a telecommuting local area network (LAN), training employees in telecommuting strategies, and assessing the telecommuting program.

Step One: **Study telecommuting options.**
- Survey employees to determine work patterns.
- Interview management to determine most suitable telecommuting system.
- Research architects' work patterns.

Step Two: **Build telecommuting network.**
- Develop blueprint for hardware.
- Build hardware structure for LAN system.
- Code intranet software.

Step Three: **Train employees in telecommuting strategies.**
- Offer telecommuting workshops.
- Create a help desk for telecommuting employees.
- Develop training materials.

Step Four: **Conduct outcomes assessment.**
- Survey employees and management.
- Study employee productivity.
- Write completion report offering recommendations for improvements to telecommuting system.

---

explain the various steps in your plan. Answers to the why questions are the muscles that hold the plan together.

One way of developing answers to the readers' why questions is to chart them out in a why table like the one in Figure 5.5.

In this table, simply write down one of your major steps on the top line and offer a short answer to the why question. Then, write down the minor steps that support this major step and provide answers to the why questions next to each

FIGURE 5.5
A Why Table

Major Step:	Why?
Minor Steps 1. 2. 3. 4.	Why? 1. 2. 3. 4.
Deliverables?	

smaller step. Finally, looking over the contents of the table, ask yourself whether there are any deliverables that will result from these steps.

Deliverables are the tangible results of each major step. They are what you will "deliver" to the readers as your project progresses and when it is completed. In some cases deliverables are finished products of some kind (e.g., a machine, a building, a software package, or some noticeable physical change). In other cases, a deliverable might be some form of communication to the readers (e.g., a completion report, a progress report, or even just a regular summary at a meeting). Whenever possible, though, you should try to come up with some kind of deliverable for each major step, even if you are just offering a phone call to update your readers on your progress. After all, your readers should be able to observe the tangible results of your work as you finish each step. They should feel as though they are receiving something they could see or touch in return for their investment in your project. By identifying those deliverables, you will show the readers that they are receiving something tangible for investing their financial and personal faith in you and your company.

When you are finished with the why tables, you should have created the basis for a well reasoned argument. When you turn these why tables into paragraphs in your Plan section, you will be answering both of the readers' main questions (i.e., how and why). You will also have specified the tangible results of your work. To illustrate, Figure 5.6 shows how Lisa Miller might fill out one of these why tables.

The advantage of a why table is that it helps you invent answers to the how and the why questions that the readers will be asking of your plan. Essentially, each of the why tables tells the readers *how* you are going to achieve a particular part of the plan, *why* you are taking particular steps, and *what* deliverables will result. Of course, you still need to track down sources, statistics, or facts that support your answers to the why questions. But when you have finished filling out the why tables, you are mostly ready to start writing your plan into its final form.

FIGURE 5.6
A Why Table for Earl Grey

Major Step: Study telecommuting options	**Why?** To identify specific workplace needs of employees and management
Minor Steps	**Why?**
1. Survey employees	To determine which employees might be eligible for telecommuting and why
2. Interview management	To understand management's strategies to adapt telecommuting system to management's needs
3. Research architects' work patterns	To determine what telecommuting system would best suit the needs of the principal employees of the firm

Deliverables? A report that summarizes the results of our research and describes the best telecommuting system for Earl Grey's needs

Writing the Plan Section

In Chapter 4, you learned that a proposal section typically has three parts: an opening, a body, and a closing. All three of these parts are usually found in a good Plan section. An *opening* is needed to tell the readers the purpose and main point of your Plan section. The *body* of the Plan section will describe the steps in your plan. And the *closing* will round off the plan section by summarizing some of the deliverables you are promising the readers.

The Opening of the Plan Section

Like the opening of any larger section in a document, the opening of the Plan section is designed to set a framework for the details that follow in the body of the section. But the opening of the Plan section is especially important, because here is where your readers need to make the critical transition from your description of the *situation* to your description of the *plan*.

This transition is difficult, because the Situation section sometimes sets a negative tone. After all, in many cases your Situation section just told the readers that they have a problem and that some rather unpleasant consequences will occur if they avoid taking action. Even in a Situation section that describes a golden opportunity, you will probably close your discussion by mentioning some of the negative effects of not taking advantage of the opportunity. The Plan section, on the other hand, needs to be as optimistic as possible. From this point forward in the proposal, you will leave the problem and its consequences behind, concentrating instead on the advantages and benefits of solving the problem a particular way.

Essentially, your opening paragraph in the Plan section needs to shift the readers from a negative viewpoint to an optimistic one. To negotiate this tricky transition, the opening of the plan section should make most, if not all, of the following important moves:

- **Transition**—signals to the readers that you are starting your discussion of the plan.
- **Statement of the Purpose of the Section**—tells the readers that the purpose of this section is to provide a detailed step-by-step plan.
- **Statement of the Plan's Goals**—lists out the goals that any successful plan would be able to meet.
- **Naming of the Overall Solution**—in a sentence or phrase, identifies your overall strategy for solving the problem.
- **Forecast of the Plan**—briefly lists the major steps of your plan.

Of course, these moves need not be made in this order, and some of them might not be made at all. However, if the opening paragraph, or paragraphs, of your Plan section accounts for these moves, you will have established a clear framework for the detailed plan that follows.

To illustrate, let us return to Lisa Miller's proposal for Earl Grey. As she drafts the opening of her Plan section, she tries to address each of the opening moves separately. For her transition, she writes, "Let us now turn to our strategy for managing Earl Grey's limited office space." It's a crude transition, but it will work for now. She then writes, "The purpose of this section is to provide a plan for providing suitable working space for Earl Grey." Then, she states her main point: "We propose that Earl Grey implement a telecommuting program that allows employees to work at home, thus freeing up space in the current office." And finally, she forecasts her plan: "We will follow a four-part process that studies Earl Grey's telecommuting options, develops a computer network to facilitate telecommuting, trains employees to be effective telecommuters, and assesses the outcomes of the telecommuting program." At the moment, these phrases are mere fragments, but they provide a basis for writing the opening of the Plan section. Putting all these fragments together, she writes the text shown in Figure 5.7.

FIGURE 5.7

An Example Opening of a Plan Section

Our Plan: Maintaining Flexibility Through Telecommuting

Management of Earl Grey's limited office space requires a plan that allows the company to grow while maintaining financial flexibility in the quickly evolving Chicago market. Therefore, we believe a successful solution must meet the following objectives:

- Minimize disruption to Earl Grey's current operations.
- Minimize costs, preserving Earl Grey's financial flexibility.
- Retain Earl Grey's current office on Michigan Avenue.
- Foster a dynamic workplace that will be appealing to Earl Grey's architects and staff.

To meet these objectives, we propose to collaborate with Earl Grey toward developing a telecommunication network that allows selected employees to work at home a few days a week. The primary advantage of telecommuting is that it frees up office space for employees who need to be in the office for the day; yet, it avoids overextending Earl Grey's financial resources during a period of significant growth.

Our plan will be implemented in four major phases. First, we will study Earl Grey's telecommuting options. Second, we will develop a computer network that will allow selected employees to telecommute from a home office. Third, we will train Earl Grey's employees to be effective telecommuters. And finally, we will assess the outcomes of the telecommuting program. With this program in place, Earl Grey will enjoy a more flexible workplace with even more room to grow.

In Lisa's opening to the Plan section, all of the *opening moves* are accounted for. The heading "Our Plan: Maintaining Flexibility Through Telecommuting" signals the transition into the discussion of the plan. In the first paragraph of the Plan section, she tackles these issues:

- She identifies the subject of the section (the plan).
- She states the purpose of the section (to offer a plan for managing Earl Grey's limited office space).
- She expresses the section's main point (telecommuting is the solution).
- She forecasts the structure of the plan (four steps).

In addition to these moves, the opening also states the goals that any successful plan should be able to meet, establishing a set of criteria that the readers can use to measure the success of the plan that will follow.

The Body of the Plan Section

The body of the Plan section is where you are going to describe your plan and tell the readers why you believe the problem should be solved a particular way. The structure of the body will be built around the major steps you identified earlier. For example, if you have four steps in your plan, the body of your plan section will likely have four major parts. Each part will describe one of the steps in detail.

Writing each of these parts should not be difficult at this point. Start out by looking over the why table that describes the first step in your plan. State the major action up front and then support that major action with a discussion of the minor steps that will be needed to achieve it. As you describe these major and minor steps for the readers, flesh out the discussion by answering those why questions that the readers will be asking at this point. Finally, at the end of the discussion of each step, you might discuss some of the deliverables that will be the end results of this part of the plan.

To illustrate, Figure 5.8 shows how one of Lisa's why tables (shown in Figure 5.6) can be developed into part of her plan.

This description of the plan's first step is rather concise. Lisa could expand it considerably by describing in greater detail how her company will conduct and analyze the surveys, interviews, and empirical studies. Or, she might spend more time answering the clients' why questions in greater depth.

In the end, though, the length of any part of the plan—and the plan altogether— depends on the amount of information your readers will require to say yes to your ideas. If your readers are unfamiliar with you, your techniques, or your field of expertise, you may need to spend more time explaining your methods and the reasoning behind your plan. If your readers are familiar with you and your methods, the description of the plan can be more concise and to the point. In Lisa's case, she decided to keep the discussion of each step concise because the RFP imposed a ten-page limit on the pre-proposal. She still needed to save room to discuss three more steps. She also needed to include the other sections of the proposal.

The text in Figure 5.8 also demonstrates how answers to the readers' why questions can be interwoven with the steps in the plan. As you compose your plan, you should imagine your readers asking you "why?" as you describe each aspect of the plan. If you can answer these questions while you describe the steps, you will help the readers understand the rationale for your plan. Meanwhile, you will immediately address any potential objections the readers might have toward your methods.

Finally, Lisa also mentioned a deliverable (a report) that will be provided to Earl Grey when this step is completed. Not all steps need to include deliverables, but if possible, you should try to come up with ways to deliver something tangible to the readers at the end of each major phase. Not only will these kinds of deliverables keep the clients informed, the clients will feel they are receiving something concrete for their money. Clients want updates and information. They want to feel like they are part of the plan, not just the recipient. By identifying deliverables clearly, you bring the readers into the process as active participants.

FIGURE 5.8
Example Description of a Step

Phase One: Analyze Earl Grey's Telecommuting Needs

Before moving forward, we believe it is important to analyze the specific workplace needs of Earl Grey's employees and management. This analysis would allow us to work closely with Earl Grey's management to develop a telecommuting program that fits the unique demands that a dynamic architecture firm like yours would put on such a system.

In this phase, our goal would be to collect as much information and data as possible, so the transition to telecommunication would be smooth and hassle-free.

- First, we would conduct thorough surveys of your employees to determine which people might be willing and able to telecommute. These surveys will tell us about their work habits and the way in which a telecommuting system might be adapted to their needs.
- Second, we would interview Earl Grey's management. These interviews will help us tailor the telecommuting system to your corporate culture and your managers' specific needs.
- Third, we will conduct empirical studies to identify and understand the office dynamics at Earl Grey. These empirical studies will help us replicate those office dynamics in a virtual environment.

We estimate this phase will require thirty days. At the end of that time period, we will submit a report to you in which we analyze and discuss the findings of our surveys, interviews, and empirical studies. In this report, we will also describe the various telecommuting options available and recommend the option we believe best suit the needs of Earl Grey.

The Closing of the Plan Section

The closing of the Plan section, like any closing of a major section, should not offer any new information to the readers. In the closing, you should summarize the section's major points and stress the importance of your plan. You might also summarize some of the major deliverables you promised your clients in the body of the plan. Your aim in the closing is to concisely round off the discussion, giving the readers an overall view of your plan and the tangible results that will come about if they say yes to the proposal. Some proposal writers use the Plan section's closing to show that their plan satisfies the goals mentioned in the opening of the section.

The closing of the Plan section is not the proposal's conclusion, so here is not the place to pour on the persuasion. The closing merely puts an endpoint on your description of the plan and prepares the readers to make a transition into a discussion of your company's qualifications.

A Comment on Research Methodologies

If you are writing a research proposal, the invention process described in this chapter might not seem exactly suitable to your needs. But when you recognize that a Methodology section is really just a description of a plan, you will see that this process actually works quite well.

A Methodology section in a research proposal describes how and why a subject will be studied a particular way. It needs to do more than simply describe the procedure of your study; it should also tell the readers *why* your approach is the most appropriate for this subject (Penrose and Katz 1998, p. 45). After all, the reviewers of your proposal will scrutinize your methods closely to determine whether they will yield useful results. If you are using a methodology adapted from other studies, it should be carefully described and cited. When inventing a new methodology, you need to justify your decision to carry out the study through a novel procedure.

In a research proposal, the methods section often begins with a list of objectives that the study will meet. In most research proposals, this list of objectives is specific about the kinds of quantifiable results that would mark whether the research project was a success. Indeed, much like a business proposal, the objectives of a scientific methodology establish the aims of the study and the guidelines for success.

A Methodology section will then define exactly the subject that will be studied and the conditions under which it will be observed. If the subjects are animals, insects, places, or people, the Methodology section should identify the class to which the subjects belong and the characteristics that distinguish the subjects from their class. The Methodology section should also precisely describe the environments and circumstances (e.g., time, temperature) in which the subjects will be studied.

After defining the subject, a Methodology section usually offers a step-by-step description of the process that will be used to study the subject. The description should be exact and complete, mentioning any materials, tools, formulas, and calculations that will be used during the study. Essentially, the description should be exact enough that other researchers could replicate the study and calculations to test its results.

Methodology sections often close with a discussion of the analysis tools that will be used to study the data generated by the experiment or observation. Any statistical procedures or software packages that will be used to process the data should be mentioned here. Some researchers even mention the types of computers that will be used to analyze the results of the study. That way, other researchers can exactly replicate the analysis of the results if they want.

In most cases, Methodology sections in research proposals are written in passive voice, because who did which step is often not important. For example, the passive sentence "The herons will be observed for 30 days from April 10 to May 10" would work just fine, because it is probably not necessary to say "Mandy Jervis will observe the herons from April 10 to May 10." Nevertheless, methodologies are increasingly being written in active voice, especially from a 'first person' perspective (e.g., "We will measure the PCB level of the lake every two days at 8:00 A.M."). Active voice reinserts the researchers into the study, reminding the readers that the researchers were part of the experiment and may have influenced the results.

Researchers should always remember that the Methodology section is the most scrutinized part of any funding proposal, because it establishes the validity of any results that will be generated by the research. If the proposal's reviewers have any doubts about the methodology of a study, they will more than likely choose not to fund the project. After all, a questionable methodology will invariably lead to questionable results. Consequently, it is crucial that the Methodology section answer all of the reviewers' how and why questions in exact detail.

Last Word

The Plan section is the heart of your proposal. It explains *how* the problem should be solved and *why* it should be solved a particular way. Most proposal writers see the Plan section as the most challenging part of the proposal writing process. From here, they usually find, the writing is a bit easier. In the next chapter, we will discuss the writing of the Qualifications section. There is definitely a sense of relief that comes when the plan is finished; however, a good plan is only as strong as the people who will put it into action.

CASE STUDY **A Plan for Creating Unity**

Describing the situation was hard work for John, Karen, Thomas, and Sally. As they described the problem, its causes, and effects, they grew increasingly anxious to come up with a plan that would solve those problems. So, when they finally turned to developing the plan, they felt reinvigorated. "Now we're finally going to *do* something," Thomas said as they began brainstorming about solutions.

John said, "Well, let's begin by identifying some of our goals. What would we like our plan to achieve? What goals would any successful plan need to meet?"

"I'll state the obvious to get us going," stated Karen, "We need to increase sales in the Elmdale Hill business district."

"Good," said John as he wrote, "Increase sales," on his sheet of paper.

After a moment, Thomas said, "We also need to heighten the public's awareness of the shopping opportunities in Elmdale Hill."

"Yes. I agree," said John, as he kept scribbling, "We also need to rebuild the reputation and image of the Elmdale Hill business district in the media."

Karen added, "One goal I would like us to meet is to make our shops more accessible to our customers. If our problem is a lack of convenience, then it seems like one of our goals should be to directly address some of the causes, like the parking problem and the public transportation problem."

"OK, this list of goals looks pretty good so far," said John, as he finished adding "make shops more accessible to customers" to his list. "Do you folks have any ideas about what kind of plan might help us reach these goals?"

After a moment, Thomas answered, "Well, I've been giving this some thought since we wrote the Situation section. Earlier we mentioned that the one thing the Wheatmill Mall has that we don't have is a common identity. People see 'the mall' as one place where they can handle all their shopping, dining, and entertainment needs. Quite differently, they see Elmdale Hill as a group of independent shops that have little to do with each other. A possible solution to our problem is to find a way to unify Elmdale Hill into some kind of cooperative community. That way, customers would say something like 'I'm going down to Elmdale Hill to do some shopping, eat, and catch a movie.' They would see all our various shops as part of one larger entity, much like they see the mall."

Sally said, "Great idea. Should we propose some kind of organization that gives us a common identity, like a merchant's association? That way, we could provide a common voice to the media in our public relations and advertising campaigns. Banded together, we would also have more influence with City Hall to change parking policies and public transportation to fit our needs."

They all agreed that forming a merchants association sounded like the basis of a good plan. At the top of his sheet of paper, John wrote, "Our Primary Goal: To form an Elmdale Hill Merchants Association that will (1) unify our shopping district, (2) allow members to pool resources, and (3) help us take political action." He said, "I like this idea. Let's map out a plan to see if it might work."

Mapping out the plan was easier than most of them expected. Putting "Form Merchants Association" in the middle of a sheet of paper, they began asking themselves what major steps would be required to make their solution a reality. Some of the larger steps included "Gather Information," "Design the Association Government," and "Hold Public Forum." Under each of these larger steps, they began mapping out the minor steps that would cause these major steps to happen. Figure 5.9 shows the map they created of their solution.

They were surprised at how quickly their plan grew in depth and detail. Their map illustrated their answers to the how questions behind their plan.

So, they turned to the why questions by filling out why charts for each of the major steps in their plan. Next to each of the smaller steps in their plan, they tried to write down a good reason why that step was needed. They also thought

FIGURE 5.9
Mapping Elmdale Hill's Solution

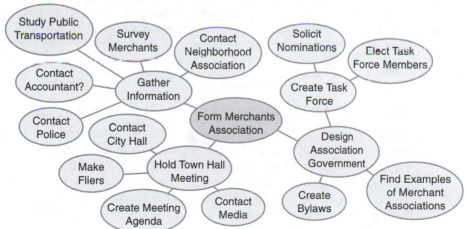

FIGURE 5.10

A Why Table for Elmdale Hill

Major Step: Hold Public Information Forum	**Why?** Explain advantages of merchant association. Rally support.
Minor Steps	**Why?**
1. Create forum agenda	To make sure we address important issues and leave room for discussion
2. Make fliers	To get the word out to business owners and local people about the forum
3. Contact City Hall	To invite the participation of mayor and police, and make them aware of our concern
4. Contact media	To show the media that we have a problem and are taking action. Also, to net some free, positive publicity
Deliverables? A newsletter that reinforces the points made at the meeting. It would include quotes and additional information.	

about some of the deliverables that might be appropriate with some of the larger steps. Figure 5.10 shows their why table for the major step called "Hold Public Forum."

With their why tables filled out, they decided to begin drafting the section itself. Figure 5.11 (see pages 96–97) shows their rough draft.

Karen looked over the plan after they had finished the first draft. "All this sounds so official and real. Yet, we just pulled this stuff out of thin air."

John smiled, "That's exactly what proposals do. They create. You have to admit, though, that this idea sounds pretty feasible now that it's written down. We're definitely done with the hard part."

Questions and Exercises

1. Find a proposal on the Internet, and analyze its Plan section. Do the writers of the proposal provide a step-by-step process for achieving some stated (or unstated) goals? Do they answer the how questions and the why questions in each part of their plan? Do they identify some deliverables at the end of each step or the end of the plan? Write a memo to your instructor in which you evaluate the effectiveness of this Plan section. Offer recommendations for improvement.

2. Using the proposal you found for Exercise 1, reconstruct the map they may have used to invent this section. Put the solution in the middle of a sheet of paper. Then, map out the major and minor steps that make up their plan. Looking over this map, does their solution seem logical and reasonable? Are there any gaps in content or organization you would like to see filled? Would you write the section differently?

3. Look closely at an RFP in your area of interest. With a team, identify the primary and secondary goals that the readers would like submitted proposals to achieve. Can you think of any unstated secondary goals that are not mentioned in the RFP but might be important to the readers? After you have identified the primary and secondary goals, write a memo to your instructor in which you identify your goals. Tell your instructor why these goals are the ones "any reasonable plan would be able to achieve."

4. Working with a team, find a problem on your campus, at your workplace, or in your community that needs a solution. Identify some goals that a successful solution would need to meet. Then, map out a plan to solve the problem. Look carefully over your map to determine whether your plan would be able to meet all the goals you identified.

5. Follow up on Exercise 2 by writing a two- to three-page Plan section in which you answer the how questions, the why questions, and identify some deliverables.

6. The Elmdale Hill proposal's Plan section still has some gaps in it. What are some major and minor steps that might still be missing? Do you think all the current steps in their map and Plan section are necessary? What would you do differently? Write a memo to John, Karen, Thomas, and Sally in which you identify the strengths in their Plan section and make suggestions for improving it.

7. You have been asked to develop a mentoring program at your college or workplace. The current problem is that new students or employees often feel overwhelmed by the immediate onslaught of work. As a result, they often drop out or quit within a couple of months. Your task is to set some goals, map out a solution, and write up a two-page description of your mentoring plan. Your plan should answer the how and why questions while providing some tangible deliverables.

FIGURE 5.11
A Draft of the Plan

Organizing Ourselves into a Merchants Association

Fellow business owners, we can stand aside watching our sales steadily decline, or we can begin working together to find ways to strengthen our businesses and our community. In this section, we would like to offer a plan for building unity among our individual businesses, so we can better compete with the large chain stores and the Wheatmill Mall. Specifically, we believe the merchants of Elmdale Hill should form a "Merchants Association" that would pool our resources and help us take action as a unified community when we address the city government, the police, the media, and the general public.

The Elmdale Hill Merchants Association would achieve a few important objectives. First, it would heighten the public's awareness of shopping opportunities in Elmdale Hill. Second, it would restore and promote a positive image of the Elmdale Hill shopping district. Third, the Association would devise ways to make our businesses more accessible to the public. And, most importantly, the Merchants Association would help Elmdale Hill businesses increase sales by recapturing previous customers and bringing in new customers.

To create this Merchants Association, we propose this three-part plan:

Gather Information

An important first step would be to gather demographic information from the merchants in the Elmdale Hill district. Using a blind survey, we will ask merchants about their needs, their concerns, and their level of interest in forming a merchants association.

The survey would meet a few different purposes. First, it would provide us with some baseline data that we could use toward deciding what kind of merchants association would be appropriate for Elmdale Hill's needs. Second, the survey would introduce business owners to the idea of a merchants association, raising their awareness that we are trying to create a tighter business community. And finally, it would prove that we are not alone in our recent drop in sales. Once we have collected the data, we will be able to show that the loss in sales is an important trend that needs to be addressed.

While the survey is being circulated, we will also contact national organizations that support the formation of merchant associations. Our aim will be to gather information on our options for organizing a merchants association. We can then devise several organizational alternatives that might suit the Elmdale Hill shopping district. When the surveys return, we can match the data to various alternatives so we can offer a recommendation about the best way to proceed in our development of an association.

When we complete our information gathering, we will send each merchant a small report that analyzes our findings and makes recommendations about the best way to move ahead with the formation of the association.

Hold a Public Information Forum

After sending out the report, we will schedule a public information forum to explain the advantages of a merchants association to Elmdale Hill. Invitational flyers will be sent out to all the merchants

FIGURE 5.11
Continued

and residents who work and live in the area. We will ask interested people to submit discussion points for the agenda. That way, everyone will have time to have his or her voice heard.

We would also like to invite City Hall (mayor and police chief) and the news media to the forum. The people at City Hall need to know that we are concerned about our loss of sales, lack of adequate public transportation, and the perception of crime in our area. By inviting the news media, we can notify them that we are working to improve the Elmdale Hill area. Their coverage would also provide us with some immediate positive press.

Design the Association's Government

At the public forum, we will describe the alternatives for merchant association governments and solicit comments from the attendees. At the end of the meeting, we will ask for nominations to a "steering committee" that will study these alternatives and make recommendations.

The committee will be charged with four tasks:

- First, the steering committee will develop a mission statement that describes the objectives and role of the merchant association in the community. This mission statement will be distributed throughout the Elmdale Hill shopping district, and commentaries on the mission statement will be encouraged. A month after the mission statement has been distributed, the committee will revise it to address the comments offered by fellow merchants.

- Second, the committee will design an organizational structure that is suited to the needs of the Elmdale Hill district. When they are completed with their deliberations, the committee will produce a short report to be distributed to Elmdale Hill merchants. Then, they will call another town meeting in which comments on the report can be made. Our hope is that this careful deliberation will encourage merchants to buy into the idea of a merchants association and feel as though their voices were heard. Since membership in the association will be voluntary, it is important that likely members feel as though they were given a fair opportunity to participate.

- Third, the committee will determine appropriate dues for membership in the association. The cost of the dues will depend on the mission statement and organizational structure that was determined.

- Finally, the committee will write an association constitution that will describe the procedures and guidelines by which the association will act. This constitution will finalize the mission statement, organizational structure, and policies on dues. It will also describe how officers in the merchants association will be elected. When the constitution is complete, it will be distributed to every business owner in the Elmdale Hill shopping district for a vote. Owners who are in favor of a merchants association will be asked to vote for or against the constitution. A majority of affirmative votes will lead to adoption of the constitution. If a majority votes against the constitution, it will be revised and resubmitted for a further vote. Merchants who do not favor a merchants association will be asked to abstain from the voting.

This process should take a few months. We think it is important that we pull together as a community. The Elmdale Hill Merchants Association will allow us to compete better against the chain stores and mall that have recently moved into our area.

6 | Describing Qualifications

Overview

This chapter discusses the writing of the Qualifications section in a proposal. The chapter will meet the following objectives:

1. Explain why Qualifications sections should be written as arguments.
2. Define the four types of Qualifications sections.
3. Show how "what makes you different makes you attractive."
4. Discuss the contents of a Qualifications section.
5. Show how to organize and compose a Qualifications section.
6. Illustrate how mapping can be used to create a persona.

The Importance of Trust

The Qualifications section occupies a sensitive place in the structure of a proposal. After all, your plan just energized the readers by showing them how their problem will be solved or how they are going to take advantage of an opportunity. Now, you want the Qualifications section to preserve that momentum as you make the transition from your description of the plan to a discussion of the costs and benefits of that plan. A well-written Qualifications section can maintain or even build the readers' interest by showing them your strengths and capabilities. On the other hand, a poorly written Qualifications section is sure to take some of the shine off your proposal at this crucial point.

The purpose of the Qualifications section is to certify to the readers that your team or company has the personnel, experience, expertise, and facilities to carry out the plan proposed in the Plan section. Going a step further, the Qualifications section should also prove to the readers that you are *uniquely* qualified to take on the job. You need to show them which special qualities set your team or company above the competition.

When writing the Qualifications section, you should remember that proposals do more than offer plans and costs. They create relationships between people. By saying yes to your proposal, the readers are essentially putting faith in you. They are agreeing to trust you. Indeed, the best plan is not worth a dime if the readers do not trust you or your company. The Qualifications section is the place in the proposal where you can best build your readers' sense of faith in you and your abilities.

Readers of proposals put great emphasis on the contents of the Qualifications section. Indeed, for many readers, the qualifications of the bidders are as important as their plan. As the writer, you should take advantage of their interest at this crucial moment in the proposal by persuading them you are the right people for the job. In this chapter, you will learn to go beyond standardized descriptions of qualifications. You will learn how to shape the Qualification section into a dynamic component of the proposal that keeps the positive momentum going.

Types of Qualifications Sections

As we discussed in Chapter 4, Aristotle suggested that arguments tend to follow three paths: logic, character, and emotion. In any given argument, one of these paths will tend to be dominant over the other two; however, elements of all three can be found in any text. The Qualifications section is a place where character arguments tend to take the lead. In proposals, character is built on the common motives, values, and attitudes that you, your team, or your company has in common with the readers.

As you begin to invent the Qualifications section, you should first identify the type of relationship that exists between your proposal's readers and your team or company. For example, internal proposals tend to stress the credentials of the people who will work on the project, because presumably the readers, as managers in the company, are already aware of the facilities and equipment available. On the other hand, external proposals, especially when the readers are not familiar with the bidder, require a much more thorough discussion of the bidder's personnel, facilities, and experience. In these kinds of proposals, you need to build your company's credentials by showing the readers your company's capabilities and values.

Depending on your relationship to the readers, there are four types of Qualifications sections you might write in a proposal:

Company to Company

Company to company sections describe your company's people and operations to the readers, demonstrating why your company is uniquely qualified to handle their needs. These Qualifications sections introduce the client to your company, showing them who will be working on their project and what kinds of resources will be devoted.

Team to Management

Team to management sections are written for internal proposals designed to make changes or propose new projects at your own company. In these cases, the Qualifications section would show management why your team is capable of carrying out the plan. In some cases, you might find yourself using a team-to-management Qualifications section to nominate a group of individuals for a team, drawing various experts at your company to your project.

Recommendation

Recommendation sections propose a specific outside contractor, consultant, or company to carry out the plan. In an internal proposal, this kind of Qualifications section recommends a specific company that the management should hire to carry out the project. Often, consultants also use these kinds of Qualifications sections to refer a company's management to the best outside company for putting the consultant's plan into action.

No Qualifications Section

Not all proposals need a stand-alone Qualifications section. In some cases, especially with short proposals, you can work the discussion of qualifications into other sections of the proposal. For instance, some proposal writers like to handle qualifications in their description of the plan, because any answers to the why questions in the Plan section rely heavily on who is handling the project and what facilities and equipment are needed. Therefore, a separate discussion of qualifications would unnecessarily repeat what was said earlier in the proposal.

These different types of Qualifications sections have different purposes. Nevertheless, they all are designed to show the readers *who* should do the project, *why* they are uniquely qualified for the project, and *what* kinds of resources will be used. More importantly, though, they highlight the relationship between the readers and the people who are proposing the project.

What Makes You Different Makes You Attractive

Some time in their life, most people have been asked to write a personal application letter for a job. In this kind of letter, your aim is to describe your qualifications, experience, education, skills, and any other qualities that make you right for the job. Meanwhile, your resume, which is usually submitted with the application letter, lists out details of your working life, like dates of employment and your specific responsibilities at each job.

One of the best ways to envision the writing of a Qualifications section is to think of this section as an application letter for a job. In an application letter, you want to show a potential employer that your experience, training, abilities, and special skills make you the best person for the job. You want to show them that you have common sense, a commitment to excellence, and a good attitude. In an application letter, it is not enough to simply show that you are qualified for the job, or even that you are the *most* qualified person for the job. After all, other candidates applying for the job are qualified too, perhaps even more than you. Rather, your application letter needs to illustrate why your *differences* from the other candidates make you especially attractive as a new employee. Stressing your unique strengths, you can craft your application letter into an argument that says, "Hire me, because I am uniquely qualified for your position."

Similarly, in a Qualifications section, it is not enough to merely list your company's personnel, experiences, facilities, and so on. Rather, you need to prove to the readers that your company or team is uniquely qualified for the project. You need to prove to them that your company's differences from the competition make you especially qualified to handle the work. Of course, something you should always remember is that all companies have their strengths and weaknesses—there is no perfect company or team for any project. By paying attention to what makes your company different, you can often persuade the readers that your company or team has the common sense, commitment to excellence, and attitude to best meet their needs.

Never let your differences be seen as weaknesses. For example, proposal writers at small companies will sometimes complain, "Our competitors are the big sharks in this field. It's hard to compete with their huge facilities and armies of consultants." Ironically, proposal writers at the large companies (feeling more like whales than sharks) complain that they are competing against all those aggressive smaller companies that are more flexible and can avoid the massive overhead costs of a large corporation.

The lesson to be learned is that *what makes you different makes you attractive.* If you work for the smaller company in the industry, you should look for ways to show that your company's size allows it to be flexible and innovative—unlike your larger competitors, who will try to sell all their clients the "same old prepackaged solution." And if you work for the larger company, you should stress your company's experience, facilities, and the ability to find the right people within your organization to handle this unique project. A successful Qualifications section capitalizes on your company's unique qualities, showing the readers why you stand out among your competitors.

How do you find out what makes you different? One good way is to list out your top competitors on a sheet of paper, assuming they are probably bidding for the same project (see Figure 6.1). Then, write down each of your competitors' strengths and weaknesses. Consider issues like size, experience, personnel, facilities, and previous history with the client. When you are finished, write down your company's strengths and weaknesses. Be honest with yourself at this point—you are trying to develop a candid assessment of where your company fits among its competitors. For yourself, not your clients, you want to be clear about your company's weaknesses, because you might need to address or avoid them when you write the Qualifications section.

When you are finished sorting out your and your competitors' strengths and weaknesses, note the places where your company is different from the others. On your worksheet, circle any of your company's strengths that your competitors lack. Then, turn any of your competitors' weaknesses into your strengths, and write them down in your company's strengths column. For example, perhaps your competitors lack an R&D department, which is a unique strength of your company. You might point out in your Qualifications section that your company's ability to commit researchers full time to the project gives your company an innovative advantage. Merely mentioning this fact in your Qualification section will draw attention to the absence of R&D departments at your competitors.

FIGURE 6.1
Strengths and Weaknesses Worksheet

My Company	Competitor 1	Competitor 2	Competitor 3	Competitor 4
Strengths	*Strengths*	*Strengths*	*Strengths*	*Strengths*
Weaknesses	*Weaknesses*	*Weaknesses*	*Weaknesses*	*Weaknesses*

Finally, look for ways in which you can turn your company's weaknesses into strengths. For instance, if your company is new to the client's area—though you have a long history of success in other areas—you could use this "weakness" to your advantage by pointing out that you are going to bring fresh ideas and new strategies to the client. Or, perhaps a "weakness" is that your company lacks the top-dollar research scientists employed by your competitors. In this case, you might point out that your company hires experts on a per-project basis, keeping overhead low and ensuring that the most knowledgeable people are involved in each project.

In the Qualifications section, you should concentrate only on your strengths and avoid directly mentioning your or your competitors' weaknesses. If your company has a weakness that cannot be turned into a strength, then it probably should be avoided in the Qualifications section altogether. It is better to discuss your weaknesses with clients in person, if you must, after they have received the proposal. You should also not directly mention your competitors' weaknesses, either. A hatchet statement like, "Our main competitor, Gopher Technologies, lacks the kind of experience you are looking for in this project," leaves a bad taste in everyone's mouth. You are better off throwing a barb at your competitors by turning their weakness into your strength. For example, "Unlike other companies in this area, our agency has five decades of experience in this field that we can draw upon for your important project." This kind of positive statement will stress a strength in your company while deftly planting a seed of doubt about your competitors in the readers' minds.

When you are finished weighing your strengths and weaknesses, identify the *main strength* that sets your team or company apart from the competition. That is, highlight the strength that makes you the most qualified team or company for the project. You will use this strength as the basis for your Qualifications section. The other strengths you have identified can be woven into the rest of the section where appropriate. We will use this main strength in a moment.

Inventing the Content of the Qualifications Section

If you were looking to hire someone new at your company, what would you like applicants to tell you in their application letters? Certainly, you would want them to tell you about their previous experience in the industry. You would want to know if they have the education and training to do the job. Also, you would want to know if they possessed the skills and abilities required for the position. And finally, you would want to see if any applicants had the right attitude for the position.

Readers of a proposal's Qualifications section are looking for much the same kinds of information, just on a larger scale. They want to know whether your company has a history of success in the industry with similar projects. They want to know whether your management and labor have the education and training to handle the complexities of the project. And, they will look closely to see if your company has the necessary facilities and equipment to carry out the project. The aim of the Qualifications section is to describe these qualities to the readers.

To address the readers' needs, a typical Qualifications section tends to break down into three areas:

Description of Personnel—biographies of management, demographics of labor force, special training of employees, security clearances.

Description of Company—corporate history, mission statement, business or research philosophy, facilities, equipment, patents or proprietary procedures, security and privacy procedures, quality-control procedures.

Industry Experience—past successful projects, experience of personnel in the industry, successful similar cases to proposed project.

Description of Personnel

The most critical part of the Qualifications section, perhaps the whole proposal, is the description of the personnel who will be involved in the project. Clients want to do more than check whether you and your employees can do the job. They want to see if there is a foundation for building a positive working relationship. Therefore, your descriptions of personnel should not simply list out their credentials; you should also offer a strong sense of the human qualities these people will bring to the project.

Descriptions of the personnel are typically divided into three areas:

Management includes project leaders, supervisors, and key employees who will occupy specific leadership roles on the project.

Labor includes members of the work force who will manufacture the product or provide the service.

Support Staff includes assistants, bookkeepers, secretaries, repair technicians, and other employees who will support management and labor.

Your description of the management team should offer concise biographies of the managers who will devote significant time to the project. Start out by describing the project leader's qualifications and qualities. Then, describe each of the remaining managers, supervisors, and key employees according to their importance in the project. Each manager's biography should run about one or two paragraphs. It should mention the manager's experience, education, capabilities and tell the readers why each specific executive is an important member of the management team.

Your biographies of the management should offer enough detail to familiarize the clients with your managers; however, avoid overwhelming the readers with each manager's life history. In most cases, the managers' resumes will be included in an appendix, so you want to provide just enough biographical information to demonstrate that your management team is experienced, educated, and able to succeed. Also, in each manager's biography, you might want to mention a personal attribute that offers some insight into the manager's personality. For example, use phrases like, "Jane's consensus-building management style . . ." or even, "A careful listener, Dr. Perkins has always prided herself on responding personally to her customer's needs." Never go too far with personal attributes. One small comment per biography is usually enough to give the readers a sense of the personality of each manager on the team.

The description of your company's labor and staff should provide demographic information on your company's employees. Tell the readers how many laborers and staff members are employed by your company. Also, identify their various roles in the organization. You might further identify their general level of education and any special training they have received.

You should not discuss each individual on your staff; rather, you want to give the clients an overall feel for the kinds of employees that your company tends to hire. For instance, let's say your company's manufacturing plant is in Ames, Iowa, a small university town just north of Des Moines. When describing the company's labor force and staff, you might mention the various levels at which employees work and their different responsibilities in the company. You might also highlight your employees' high level of education and their strong work ethic. Meanwhile, you might specify that the local university and community college helps you train and retrain your employees for new projects. Essentially, your description of your company's labor and staff support uses demographic information to give the readers a general feel for the kinds of people who work at your company.

Overall, the description of your management, labor, and support staff should demonstrate that the members of your team or the employees at your company are qualified to take on the client's project. It should also give the clients a sense of the people with whom they will be working on the project.

The Dreaded Organizational Chart

One eternal question faced by proposal writers is whether to include the requisite organizational chart, or *org-chart* for short, that identifies the management hierarchy for the project (Figure 6.2). Organizational charts take up a great amount of space in a proposal, so they should be used with care and only when needed.

Organizational charts are needed when the project is complex and there are numerous levels of managers involved. In these complex Qualifications sections, the organizational chart should be designed to help the clients figure out who answers to whom in the bidder's management structure. That way, the clients can quickly identify (1) who they should talk to when they have a comment, question, or problem, and (2) who at the bidder's company will be interfacing with specific people at the client's company.

Organizational charts should not be used in smaller projects where the management structure is apparent in the biographical descriptions of the managers. After all, the readers have limited time and patience. If an organizational chart is simply being used to show the obvious connections between managers at your company, then it is wasting the readers' time while unnecessarily adding to the length of your proposal. That limited time and patience would be better used in the rest of the proposal.

Description of the Company

Of course, as the writer of the proposal, you are familiar with your company, but your readers are likely unfamiliar with much of your company's history, mission,

FIGURE 6.2
An Organizational Chart that Is Not Helpful

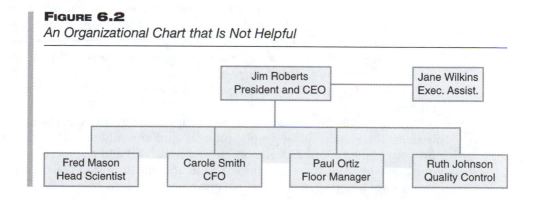

or operations. Even when two companies have longstanding business relationships, a thorough description of your company in the Qualifications section is often needed because relationships change over time. In other words, the two companies that began doing business together a couple decades ago no longer have the same managers and employees. Often, the companies' missions have changed, and their facilities are somewhat different.

In your description of the company, you want to offer the readers an overview of your operations. The following elements are often included in a description of the company:

Corporate History describes when the company was founded, by whom, and for what purpose. A history often describes the evolution of the company into its present form.

Mission Statement identifies the company's goals and principles of operation.

Corporate Philosophy explains the company's approach to the market, its management style, and the standards by which it does business with clients.

Facilities and Equipment describes the company's resources, manufacturing capabilities, and machinery.

Quality Control Measures highlights compliance with specific quality control guidelines or government protocols like ISO-9000.

A critical feature of a description of the company should be the use of details, preferably quantifiable details, about your company's operations. Using numbers where possible, tell the readers the size and output of your facilities. By name, if possible, tell them what kind of equipment you will devote to the project. Be specific about dates in your company's history. These data points will add a strong sense of realism to your description of the company.

Industry Experience

Proposal writers often prefer to round out the Qualifications section by stressing their company's experience and highlighting successful past projects. When discussing the industry experience of your team or company, you want to show a track record of success with similar projects. Or, at least you want to show that your company and personnel have experience in this particular industry. In some cases, a Qualifications section might list concise descriptions of similar projects in which your company satisfied the needs of similar clients. In other cases, you may just list out the companies with whom your team or company has done business in the past.

Again, details are important in a description of industry experience. Where possible, you should name people, projects, and any other concrete facts to support your claims about experience. These details will add a sense of realism into your description of these accounts. Vague and unsupported claims only sound like you are boasting or perhaps covering up your lack of qualifications. When supported with fact and details, though, these statements look like valid claims about your company.

Writing the Qualifications Section

Let us backtrack for a moment. Earlier, you identified a main strength about your team or company. This main strength will now become the claim around which you are going to invent the Qualifications section for your proposal. It will show why your team or company is uniquely qualified to handle the client's needs.

Opening

Like the other major sections in the proposal, the content of the Qualifications section should be organized into an opening, body, and closing. The opening of the Qualifications section, usually a short paragraph or two, will identify the purpose of the section and state a *main claim* (i.e., your main strength) about your company's qualifications. Specifically, in the opening you want to claim in some fashion that your company or team is "uniquely qualified" or "most qualified" for the project, because you possess a particular strength that sets you apart or above the competition. Of course, you do not need to use words like *uniquely* or *most,* but your main point for the section should be some kind of provable claim about the qualifications of your company or team. This kind of statement is not only the heart of the opening paragraph, it is the basis for the entire section.

For example, in her proposal to Earl Grey, the opening of Lisa Miller's Qualification section is rather short (Figure 6.3). Her heading "Background and Qualifications" identifies the subject of the section. Her first paragraph then mentions her purpose and main point, using her company's main strength to focus the Qualifications section.

Body

The body of the Qualifications section needs to back up the main claim you made in the opening. For instance, the opening of Lisa's Qualifications section claims that Insight Systems is "uniquely qualified to handle this project, because we provide flexible, low-cost communication networks that help growing companies stay responsive to shifts in their industry." Then, Lisa used the body of the Qualifications section to back up this claim. The body of the Qualifications section begins with biographies of Insight Systems' management. Supporting her claim in the opening paragraph, the biographies of Insight Systems' managers stress flexibility and innovativeness. Meanwhile, her description of Insight Systems' labor highlights the experience and education of Insight Systems' engineers and technicians, thereby showing how Insight Systems preserves flexibility and innovation in the industry.

FIGURE 6.3
Insight Systems' Qualifications Section

Background and Qualifications

At Insight Systems, we know this moment is a pivotal one for Earl Grey Designs. To preserve and expand its market share, Earl Grey needs to grow as a company, but it cannot risk overextending itself financially. For these reasons, Insight Systems is uniquely qualified to handle this project, because we provide flexible, low-cost communication networks that help growing companies stay responsive to shifts in their industry.

Management and Labor

With over fifty combined years in the industry, our management team offers the insight and responsiveness you will need to handle your complex growth needs.

Hanna Gibbons, our CEO, has been working in the telecommuting industry for more than 20 years. After she graduated from MIT with a Ph.D. in computer science, she worked at Krayson International as a systems designer. Ten years later, she had worked her way up to vice president in charge of Krayson's Telecommuting Division. In 1993, Dr. Gibbons took over as CEO of Insight Systems from its founder John Temple. Since then, Dr. Gibbons has grown Insight Systems into a major industry leader with gross sales of $15 million a year. Excited about the new innovations in telecommuting, Dr. Gibbons believes we are seeing a whole new kind of workplace evolve in front of our eyes.

Frank Roberts, chief engineer at Insight Systems, has 30 years of experience in the networked computer field. He began his career at Brindle Labs, where he worked on artificial intelligence experiments with analog computer networks. In 1985, he joined Insight Systems, bringing his unique understanding of networking to our team. Frank is very detail oriented, often working long hours to ensure that each LAN exactly meets the client's specifications and needs.

Lisa Miller, Insight Systems' senior computer engineer, has successfully led the implementation of thirty-three telecommuting systems in companies throughout the United States. Taking her computer science degree from Iowa State, Lisa has won numerous awards for her innovative approach to computer networking. She believes that clear communication is the best way to meet her clients' needs. *(continued on page 109)*

In her description of the history and facilities of Insight Systems, Lisa's Qualification section continues to stress flexibility and innovativeness. She pointed out that the company's founder emphasized flexible workspaces from the start. Also, she reinforced Insight Systems' reputation as an innovator by citing an article from a prominent business magazine and naming some prominent projects that they have already completed. Finally, Lisa pointed out that Insight Systems' office in Naperville is a model of the modern office. She decided not to go into detail about Insight Systems' facilities, because they were not relevant to the pro-

FIGURE 6.3
Continued

The resumes of our management team are included in Appendix B.

Our management team is supported by a progressive corps of high-technology employees. Insight Systems employs twenty of the brightest engineers and technicians in the telecommunications industry. We have aggressively recruited our employees from the most advanced universities in the United States, including Stanford, MIT, Illinois, Iowa State, New Mexico, and Syracuse. Several of our engineers have been with Insight Systems since it was founded. To keep our technicians on the industry's cutting edge, we maintain an ongoing training relationship with Simmons Technical Institute to ensure that our employees stay at the forefront of their fields.

Corporate History and Facilities

Insight Systems has been a pioneer in the telecommuting industry from the beginning; and it has stayed on the cutting edge of the field by continuously looking for innovative ways to improve its products and services. The company was founded in 1975 by John Temple, who believed that workplaces in the post-computer age would require more flexible communication options.

Since then, Insight Systems has become one of the "100 Companies to Watch" according to *Business Outlook Magazine* (May 2001). The company has worked with large and small companies from Vedder Aerospace to the Cedar Rapids Museum of Fine Arts to create telecommuting options for companies that want to maintain flexibility while keeping costs down and productivity high.

Insight Systems' Naperville office has been called a "prototype Information Age workspace" (*Gibson's Computer Weekly,* May 2000). A model of workspace efficiency, Insight Systems' office handles the needs of 50 employees in a 9000-square-foot office.

Experience You Can Trust

As members of a dynamic growing business ourselves, we at Insight Systems understand the challenges that face Earl Grey Design. The key to success is innovation, flexibility, and efficiency. Insight Systems will allow you to maintain these qualities as you continue to grow your business.

---

ject being proposed. However, if your Qualifications section needs to describe a manufacturing plant or important equipment, you should add in a detailed description of your facilities and machinery.

Closing

A closing paragraph, especially in smaller proposals, is often not needed in a Qualifications section. If the body seems to taper off into a logical ending point, then you can move on to writing the next section. But, if it looks like the body is still rather open-ended, you might want to include a concise closing paragraph to round out the discussion of the qualifications.

As with the closing of any section of the proposal, you should not introduce new information at this point. If you still have new information to add, make it part of the body of the section. The closing should simply reinforce and restate the main claim you made in the opening paragraph of the section. Essentially, the aim of the closing paragraph is to show the readers that your main claim has been proven in the body of the section. In Lisa's proposal, for example, the closing is very short. It simply reinforces the claim she made in the opening paragraph of the section. She may not have needed the paragraph at all, but she felt it helped her make a smoother transition into the next section of the proposal.

Creating a Persona

An important part of building character in a proposal is the development of a persona. In ancient Greece, the word *persona* meant "mask." Your persona is the public face that you show the world around you. For a speaker or writer, persona is the image that you want the audience to have of you.

On an individual level, of course, the advice to just "be yourself" is satisfactory. But how can a corporation just "be itself," and how can you reflect your company's persona in your proposal? Frankly, that's why companies pay large sums to public relations firms to create and maintain a specific persona in the public realm.

When writing a proposal, especially the Qualifications section, you should be conscious of the persona, or image, that you want the proposal to project. In many cases, you can simply turn to your own public relations materials. What is the slogan or key word that your materials project to the public? What is the recurring theme that seems to be reinforced in all your company's public correspondences?

If your company does not have a defined image or persona, mapping can help you create one for your proposal. Look at the results of your analysis of *what makes us different makes us attractive.* What is the key word that you think characterizes your company or team? Is your company *aggressive* or *conservative*? Is it *technologically advanced* or *experienced*? When you have settled on a key word, write it down on a sheet of paper and create a map around it. For example, let's say the persona you want to create is that of a "progressive" company. Putting progressive in the center of a sheet of paper, start coming up with synonyms and phrases that reflect progressive. Words like *advanced, cutting edge, new,* and *innovative* come to mind among others (see Figure 6.4). Mapping further, you can find more words and phrases that reflect the persona of your company.

When you are finished mapping out the persona you have in mind, you will have created a whole vocabulary of words that you can now carefully blend into your proposal's Qualifications section. As you keep using these key words, especially when you associate them with your company and personnel, you will cre-

FIGURE 6.4

Mapping out a Persona

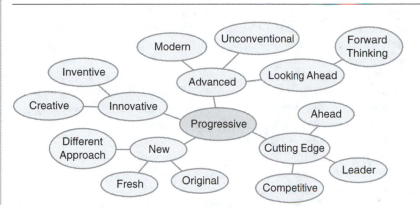

ate a persona by developing what rhetoricians call a *theme* in your writing. The best part about creating a persona in the Qualifications section is that the effects on the readers are subtle if not subliminal. After repeatedly seeing key words that bring up images of a progressive company, the readers will come to believe that your company is indeed innovative and advanced.

Creating a persona, however, is like adding spices to food. In moderation, using key words will tastefully bring out a particular persona in your Qualifications section. In excess, however, just like excess spices in food, the use of too many key words will overcome the real persona you are trying to enhance. Of course, a persona is always strongest when the key words are backed up by actions that reflect that persona. In other words, if your company is a rather stodgy firm, your attempts to build the "progressive" persona into your proposal will ultimately fail. After all, image eventually needs to measure up to reality. In the end, it is always best to assess the real persona of your company and then reflect that persona consciously in the Qualifications section of your proposal.

To Boilerplate or Not to Boilerplate

Before long, if you have not already, you will run into the word *boilerplate* when talking about proposals. Boilerplates are generic descriptions of the company, which are often pasted into proposals instead of project-specific Qualifications sections. In the rush to push the proposal out the door, some writers simply slap in their company's boilerplate rather than write an original description customized for the project and client.

The problem with boilerplates is that these generic files are often a hodge-podge of text fragments, sewn together from past proposals. They regularly contain information that is outdated or irrelevant to the project being proposed. And, all too often, the boilerplate has ballooned into a multipage monstrosity, because it has served as a catchall for clips about the company. Moreover, because they are generic, boilerplate Qualifications sections tend to use an impersonal, antiseptic tone that does not match the tone in the rest of the proposal. This antiseptic tone often undermines the attempts of the proposal to maintain the readers' enthusiasm for your plan.

Of course, most companies have built up assorted computer files of qualifications-related information, such as short biographies of key personnel, a corporate mission statement, a description of the company's facilities, and so on. It is fine to use these preexisting files to help you invent the Qualifications section. What you need to do, however, is fashion these disparate parts into a cohesive argument that is specific to the project you are proposing. Essentially, you need to *persuade* the readers that your team or company has the right people, facilities, equipment, and experience to handle their specific needs.

When deadlines approach, it is tempting to use the company's boilerplate with minimal adjustments. Try to avoid that temptation. The few hours spent customizing the Qualifications section to the project and client will be rewarded with a leaner, more focused section that stresses your company's unique strengths and qualities. Moreover, it will help you build trust with the client.

Last Word

One of the most common mistakes made by writers of proposals is underestimating the importance of the Qualifications section to the readers. You should always remember that proposals do more than simply offer plans and budgets. They also build relationships between people. So, it is important to recognize that the readers are not merely agreeing to a plan, they are agreeing to trust you. In the end, people hire people, not plans or budgets, so it is critical that you show the readers of your proposal why you are experienced, reliable, and responsive to their needs. The Qualifications section gives you the opportunity to build your character in the eyes of the readers.

CASE STUDY Who Is Qualified for the Work?

John, Karen, Thomas, and Sally were pretty excited about their plan, because they felt as though they were close to solving some of Elmdale Hill's problems. So, they decided to take a break from the project and agreed to work on the proposal the next week. The break was nice, but small doubts began creeping into their minds

about the project. The greatest obstacle to their plan, they soon began to realize, was that none of them had the experience or expertise to actually put together a merchants association.

When they met at the Elmdale Hill Café the next week, Karen came right out and confessed her concern about who would actually be able to make their plan a reality. She said, "I've been talking to some people about setting up nonprofit organizations like merchants associations, and they say the paperwork is a real bear. They started talking about a rat's nest of lawyers, accountants, taxes, and other things."

Thomas replied, "Actually, I thought of that too, so I started asking theater owners in other towns about merchants associations. One of them told me that his business district started a merchants association much like the one we have in mind. After a few failed attempts to create the group, his merchants association discovered a local accounting firm that specialized in setting up nonprofit organizations. He told me a CPA can help guide us through the whole process of setting up the merchants association as a nonprofit."

"I certainly like the idea of hiring some kind of expert," said Sally. "Here at Elmdale Hill, most of the business owners don't have the time or patience for a failed attempt to put together a merchants association. But we also don't have the money for a fancy consultant."

Thomas said, "The theater owner I talked to said it only cost them about $3000 to bring in a CPA to help organize their efforts. That sounds like a lot of money, but when it is divided up among the businesses in Elmdale Hill, it comes out to about fifty or a hundred dollars per business owner."

They all agreed to look into hiring a CPA to help them handle the financial and legal aspects of setting up a nonprofit. After interviewing a few CPA firms and comparing rates and estimates, they found a firm in town, Sanders and Associates, which seemed to offer the best all-around service for developing a nonprofit.

Sanders and Associates appointed one of its accountants, Gail Smithson, to work on the Elmdale Hill project. She looked over their proposal as it was written and suggested some improvements in the Plan section. Specifically, she began talking about the importance of writing a mission statement, a business plan, and a budget. She also talked about setting up bank accounts and preparing tax forms. If the business owners of Elmdale Hill agreed to start a merchants association, Gail said, she would be able to handle incorporating the merchant association as a nonprofit organization. She would also help them handle

much of the other paperwork, like writing mission statements, business plans, and budgets.

With Gail's professional advice, John, Karen, Thomas, and Sally felt much better about the whole process. They decided that their proposal to the other merchants should recommend hiring Sanders and Associates to help them handle the financial and legal aspects of putting together the Elmdale Hill Merchants Association. They decided to use a separate Qualifications section to advocate the hiring of Sanders and Associates.

As they sat down to begin drafting the Qualifications section, Karen said, "OK, I'm going to play devil's advocate here, because I know we're going to have some reluctant people out there who think that we can create this merchants association by ourselves. Or, they are going to want their own accountant to handle the project."

"Well, what makes Sanders and Associates the best accounting firm to do the job?" replied Thomas, "Why don't we hire another accounting firm or do it ourselves?"

They charted out various strengths and weaknesses on a sheet of paper, including their own if they tried to create the merchants association themselves (see Figure 6.5). In their strengths and weaknesses worksheet, they noted that Sanders and Associates had strong experience setting up nonprofits, including a couple other merchants associations in the state. Moreover, Sanders and Associates had a different rate for nonprofits than for-profit companies, making them less expensive. The other CPA firms in the area who handled nonprofits seemed to specialize in larger entities, like museums, galleries, and service clubs.

If they did the work themselves, there were a few advantages like saving money and the satisfaction of handling the project on their own. However, it soon became apparent that the time commitments would be too severe. Also, their lack of experience increased the risk of failure. "And," pointed out Thomas, "our fellow merchants won't see us as experts. They may be more inclined to trust someone from the outside who has handled these kinds of projects before."

They also called Sanders and Associates' main competitors. MegaCount Accounting was a large national chain that had experience with establishing nonprofit organizations. They even had in-house legal counsel, something Sanders

FIGURE 6.5

Elmdale Hill Strengths and Weaknesses Worksheet

Doing it Ourselves	Sanders and Associates	MegaCount Accounting	Elmdale Hill Bookkeepers
Strengths	*Strengths*	*Strengths*	*Strengths*
• Less expensive • More control • Satisfaction	• Experienced in nonprofit work • Not too expensive • Locally owned • Personal service • Increased chance of success • Small accounting firm	• Experienced in nonprofit work • Nationally known • Increased chance of success • Has in-house legal counsel	• Locally owned • Personal service • Good reputation in Elmdale Hill • Other merchants will support hiring them • Potentially a break on costs
Weaknesses	*Weaknesses*	*Weaknesses*	*Weaknesses*
• Lack of experience • Not seen as experts • Lack of time • Liability if things go wrong • Higher likelihood of failure	• Costs money • Adds extra layer of people involved • Some merchants think we can do it ourselves • Some merchants may want to hire their own accountant	• Large accounting firm • Lack of personal service • Not locally owned • Adds a few more layers of people involved	• No experience with nonprofits • Chance of success lowered a bit • Difficult to end relationship if they fail

and Associates did not offer. Nevertheless, they seemed to be better suited to large clients. When Sally visited their local office, she waited for a half-hour to see a sales representative, not even an accountant. Another competitor was the Elmdale Hill Bookkeepers, a popular accounting firm for many of the Elmdale Hill business owners. But the Elmdale Hill Bookkeepers did not have any experience with establishing nonprofit organizations. Sanders and Associates was their choice.

To answer the question "What makes the Sanders and Associates different?" or "What makes them the most qualified to handle the pro-

ject?" they wrote down a main claim for the Qualifications section: "Sanders and Associates has a track record of success helping organize business districts like ours. For a limited cost, they will bring their experience and know-how, allowing us to form the Elmdale Hill Merchants Association quickly and efficiently."

Using the materials Gail Smithson gave them at their visit, they began inventing the content of the body of the Qualifications section to back up their main claim. Specifically, they concentrated on the personnel, services, and prior experiences of Sanders and Associates to make their case. They then wrote up the Qualifications section for

FIGURE 6.6
Recommendation for Sanders and Associates

Hiring an Accounting Firm to Help

While collecting information about merchant associations, it became apparent to us that establishing a nonprofit organization is somewhat complicated. Therefore, we suggest the Elmdale Hill Merchants Association hire Sanders and Associates, an accounting firm that has a great amount of experience working with nonprofit groups. Sanders and Associates has a track record of success organizing business districts like ours. For a limited cost, they will bring their experience and know-how, allowing us to form the Elmdale Hill Merchants Association quickly and efficiently.

Sanders and Associates distinguishes itself from other firms with a strong dedication to quality and personal service. Recently, they helped Nob Hill set up a merchants association. We talked to a few Nob Hill business owners, and they were very pleased with Sanders and Associates' work on their behalf. Sanders and Associates has worked with over twenty other merchants associations around the state in the past ten years. We think this experience will help us navigate the difficulties of incorporation and the tax codes.

Should we agree to form a merchants association, Gail Smithson, a CPA at Sanders and Associates, has been assigned to handle the incorporation process. She received her CPA in 1985 after graduating from Northwestern University. She has fifteen years of experience as a CPA, and she considers nonprofits an area of expertise. From our discussions with Gail, we feel she would be an asset to our efforts to organize. She not only can handle all the paperwork and taxes, she can give us helpful advice about how to organize the merchants association itself.

Hiring Sanders and Associates might cost us a little more, but we believe this small cost will save us time and frustration. It will also increase our chances of succeeding in our attempts to establish the merchants association. Sanders and Associates' experience working with nonprofits will be an asset to our efforts.

---

the proposal. They decided to keep it short, putting the emphasis on Gail Smithson's credentials as a consultant and Sanders and Associates' experience in setting up small, nonprofit organizations. They believed it was important to tell their fellow business owners about what Sanders and Associates could do and why they were the right choice for the job. Also, they wanted to discuss some of the Sanders and Associates' previous successes with similar business districts to Elmdale Hill. That way, the other business owners would feel a little more secure about committing themselves financially to the project. Figure 6.6 shows a rough draft of the Qualifications section.

"Another part of the proposal finished," said Thomas as he corrected some typos in the draft. "Each part we write seems to bring the Elmdale Hill Merchants Association closer to life."

Sally sighed, "Every section we write, though, highlights just how much revision we're going to need to do when we put it all together. It seems like we're a long way from done."

Questions and Exercises

1. Find a proposal on the Internet that includes a stand-alone Qualifications section. Does the section prove that the bidding company is "uniquely qualified" for the job? Does the section have a clear opening, body, and closing? What topics did the authors choose to include in their Qualifications section? What information did they leave out? Why? Write a two-page memo to your instructor in which you analyze the content and organization of this Qualifications section. In your analysis, point out any strengths and suggest improvements.

2. On the Internet, locate the Web sites of three competing companies in an area with which you are familiar. For example, you might study bookstores, record shops, restaurants, computer manufacturers, and so on. In a table like the one shown in Figure 6.1, identify each of these companies' strengths and weaknesses. What is each company's main strength? What makes each company different from its competitors? Can you turn any weaknesses into strengths?

3. With a team, write a one-page Qualifications section for your company or university. Identify what makes your company or university unique or different from its competitors. What are some topics (e.g., mission, history, experience, management, employees, or facilities) that you believe need to be mentioned? What are some topics you would not mention? Why? Also, can you turn any of your company's or university's weaknesses into strengths?

4. Map out a persona for your company or university. If you had one positive word to describe your company, what would it be? Put this word in the middle of a sheet of paper and map out the persona associated with this word. Then, try to weave this persona into the Qualifications section you wrote for Exercise 2.

5. In your class, interview one of your classmates or colleagues. Write your instructor a one-paragraph biography of this person in which you discuss his/her education, experience, and special abilities. Also, add in a statement that personalizes the biography.

6. In this chapter, you were told to turn your company's weaknesses into strengths. At what point should concerns about honesty overcome the urge to make your company look more qualified? Where is the point at which trying to turn weaknesses into strengths becomes unethical? What are some ways you can determine when ethics are being infringed?

7. Study the Qualifications section from a real proposal. What persona, if any, is woven into this section? Underline some of the key words used in the Qualifications section. Do they show a common persona that the writers are trying to reinforce? If not, use mapping to develop a persona for this Qualifications section and seed the text with some key words that reflect that persona.

7 Introductions, Costs, and Benefits

Overview

This chapter discusses how to write introductions and conclusions for proposals. The chapter will meet the following objectives:

1. Show how introductions and conclusions frame, or set a context, for the body of the proposal.
2. Discuss the purpose of an introduction and how to invent its content.
3. Describe the "six moves" that make up the content of an introduction.
4. Show how a conclusion can be used to "amplify" the benefits of the proposal's plan.
5. Describe the "five moves" that make up the content of a conclusion.

Framing the Body of the Proposal

In many ways, introductions and conclusions are reflections of each other. An effective introduction defines the proposal's subject, purpose, and main point. It also stresses the importance of the subject. At the end of the proposal, the conclusion should close the proposal by restating the main point and discussing the costs and benefits of the plan. It should bring the readers back around to the beginning, restating the overall argument while stressing the advantages of taking action.

A good way to understand the different roles of the introduction, body, and conclusion is to remember the old speechmakers' adage: "Tell them what you're going to tell them. Tell them. And, tell them what you told them." In other words, a good introduction first lays out the argument in brief for the readers. Then, the body supports that argument with facts, reasoning, and examples. And finally, the conclusion restates the argument concisely, demonstrating that the main point of the argument has been proven. Cicero and other Roman rhetoricians called the introduction the "exordium" because here is where the document exhorts the readers to pay attention while it lays out the case to be argued. Conclusions were called "amplification" because here is where the document highlights and emphasizes the main point for the readers, driving the argument home.

The introduction and conclusion can also be seen as framing devices for the body of the proposal. The aim of the introduction is to create a mental framework for the readers, so they can conceptualize the whole argument at once. The body of the proposal fills in that framework with facts, reasoning, and examples. Then, the conclusion reframes the argument for the readers, again helping them comprehend the whole argument at once.

Because introductions and conclusions are similar, they will be discussed together in this chapter. First, you will learn how to write powerful introductions that invite the readers to sit up and pay attention to your ideas. Then, you will learn how to amplify your conclusion, stressing the importance of your proposal and driving your ideas home for the readers.

Setting the Stage: The Purpose of an Introduction

In his *Rhetoric,* Aristotle wrote, "The introduction is the beginning of a speech, corresponding to the prologue in poetry and the prelude in flute-playing; they are all beginnings, paving the way, as it were, for what is to follow" (1414b). As Aristotle suggested, a proposal's introduction offers the readers an overall sense of what will follow in the body of the work.

An effective introduction lays a foundation for the proposal in an abbreviated form. After reading the introduction, the readers should know exactly what the proposal is trying to prove. The introduction is especially important, because the beginning is where the readers are most attentive. Here is the best place to tell them what the proposal is about, what is being proposed, and why they should take notice. You should never underestimate the importance of the introduction, because it often makes or breaks a proposal. In so many ways, your introduction is your first impression on the readers. If you make a positive first impression, the chances are good that your readers will see you and your proposal as credible and trustworthy. A bad first impression, though, could negatively taint the rest of the document.

Why are introductions so hard to write? For one thing, the introduction plays a different role than the body. The body of the proposal provides the *content* for the readers. It offers them the facts, examples, details, and reasoning that they need to make a decision on the proposal. Quite differently, the introduction creates, or should create, the *context* for the information in the body. In other words, the introduction creates an overall framework into which the content will be placed.

For example, you have probably had the following experience. A co-worker walks up to you and begins telling you details without first providing a framework for understanding those details. She begins to rattle off data, facts, and other specifics. After a few moments of confusion, you stop her and say, "Whoa, what are you talking about?" "Why are you telling me this information?" Essentially, you are asking her to provide you with some contextual information for understanding the details she is telling you. Then, when she answers these questions about the context, suddenly all those details begin to make more sense. Now that you have a framework into which you can place the information, you can figure out how all those details fit into your work and life.

The introduction to a proposal is designed to offer this kind of mental framework for the readers, so they are prepared to understand the content you will provide in the body of the proposal. If you were to bypass the introduction and just toss the readers into the Situation section, they would more than likely be very confused. By the time they finally figured out what your proposal was doing, you would have already wasted a few important pages of information. Chances are pretty slim that readers would backtrack to re-read those pages.

Introductions are hard to write because they require you to already have a solid idea of the proposal's content, (i.e., the information in the body) *before* you write the introduction. In most cases, you will find that once you have drafted the body of the proposal, the introduction is actually very easy to write.

Inventing the Introduction

Fortunately, you have already done most of the preparation work necessary to write the introduction. When you defined the rhetorical situation in Chapter 3, you answered two key questions that will form the basis of the introduction. Specifically, on your rhetorical situation worksheet, you addressed these issues:

- What is the *subject* of my proposal?
- What is the *purpose* of my proposal?

Now that you have written the body of the proposal, it might seem like a long time since you initially defined your subject and purpose. At that time, you probably had a vague idea of what you were writing about and what you wanted the proposal to achieve. But now that you have written the body of the proposal, you should possess a much clearer idea of the subject and the purpose. You are now ready to begin inventing the content of the introduction.

Introductions usually tell the readers more than your subject and purpose. A typical introduction will include up to six moves:

Move 1: State the *subject* of the proposal.

Move 2: Identify the *purpose* of the proposal.

Move 3: State the *main point* that will be proven in the proposal.

Move 4: Stress the *importance* of the subject to the readers.

Move 5: Provide some *background information* on the subject.

Move 6: *Forecast* the organization of the proposal.

All six of these moves need not be made in an introduction. Statements about the subject, purpose, and main point are almost always included in the introduction of a proposal. Sentences identifying the importance of the subject, providing background information, and forecasting the structure of the proposal are helpful accessories that further assist the readers to understand what you are going to tell them in the body of the proposal.

Of course, these six moves are not necessarily made in this order, nor are they always made in separate sentences. Rather, *they should be accounted for* somewhere in the introduction. The moves themselves can be handled in a variety of different ways. To explain them further, let us look at these moves in more depth:

Move 1: State the Subject of the Proposal

The subject of the proposal is what you are writing about. In your introduction, you should clearly define the subject and what is included in the subject. In some cases, you may tell the reader what the subject does not include.

Move 2: Identify the Purpose of the Proposal

The statement of your proposal's purpose tells the readers what your proposal is supposed to accomplish. In one sentence, complete the phrase, "The purpose of this proposal is to . . ." If you cannot boil your purpose statement down to one sentence, the purpose of your proposal may not be clear to you or the readers. You wrote down a statement of purpose on your rhetorical situation worksheet. Right now might be a good time to see if your purpose changed as you wrote the Situation, Plan, and Qualifications sections.

The actual purpose statement in the introduction may or may not include a phrase like "The purpose of this proposal is to . . ." Nevertheless, a sentence should specifically tell the readers what the proposal will accomplish.

Move 3: State the Main Point that Will Be Proven in the Proposal

The main point of the proposal is the one idea above all that you would like the readers to take away from the proposal. In some cases, you might just come out and tell the readers your solution to the problem or how you will help them take advantage of an opportunity. For example, you might just say "We believe the best way to handle Baxter's flooding problem is to restore the wetlands surrounding the river." The body of the proposal would then prove that main point.

Sometimes, though, you may want your main point to be less direct, especially when you are proposing a rather innovative solution that the readers might reject before they possess all the facts. For example, you might write, "Controlling the flooding problem in Baxter will require an innovative, ecologically sensitive approach." This sentence is a bit vague, but it will provide a focusing claim that the rest of the proposal can support. A question can have the same effect: "In this proposal, we answer the question, 'How can we control Baxter's flooding problem in an ecologically sensitive way?'" Questions are more nebulous than statements; nevertheless, they provide the readers a focal point that will hold them over until the solution is revealed in the Plan section.

By stating your main point up front, you provide the readers with a primary claim or question that will focus their attention as they read the rest of the proposal.

Once the readers know your main point, they can then study the details of your proposal through the focus created by this statement. You are essentially saying, "Here's what we think should be done." The rest of the proposal leads the readers through the thought process that brought you to that main point.

Move 4: Stress the Importance of the Subject to the Readers

In the introduction, proposals need to hook the readers and capture their full attention. Therefore, somewhere in the introduction, you should tell the readers why the subject is (or should be) important to them—why they need to take action. You need to give your readers a good reason to pay attention.

The importance of the subject can be expressed in a positive or negative way. The positive approach stresses the opportunity available to the readers. Briefly, it shows them the advantages of taking action at this particular place and time. For example, you might say, "Controlling Baxter's flooding with proven ecologically sensitive methods will increase investment in the downtown area while making the river area a haven for birds, trees, and wildflowers."

The negative approach puts the readers on alert. You might write, "If you do not control the flooding in Baxter, it is likely that millions more dollars in damages will result, eventually driving out most of the businesses in the area." Of course, alarming the readers is a sure way to stress the importance of the subject, but you risk the readers becoming defensive or resistant to change. Therefore, make sure you use negative statements carefully in the introduction.

Move 5: Provide Some Background Information on the Subject

Typically, background information is made up of material that the readers already know. This information is designed to start the readers out on familiar ground, so they feel comfortable as they begin reading some of the new ideas you have to offer. Background information can be historical. For example, you might say,

> Flooding has been a recurring problem since the town of Baxter was founded in 1920. When Baxter was first incorporated, its downtown had only eight buildings, which were built far enough apart to allow open spaces and parks to soak up the occasional river overflow. However, as those open spaces were filled in with new buildings, overflow water had fewer places to go, creating the flooding problem we have now.

Of course, the proposal's readers probably already know most of this information, but it is familiar and safe to them. Background information gives the proposal's writers and readers a common base of information from which to start considering new ideas. Moreover, this background information allows the writer to show that the problem is a result of "change" and not anyone's fault. The inclusion of background information also hints that the writers have done their homework as they prepared to write the proposal, thus increasing their credibility.

Other forms of background information are available. Perhaps you might talk about the current state of the industry. Or, you might simply say something like, "At our meeting on January 30, we discussed some of your options for improving . . . ." Background information simply tells the readers something they already know, so they have a comfortable reference point from which to start considering new or different ideas.

Move 6: Forecast the Organization of the Proposal

Forecasting essentially outlines the body of the proposal for the readers by identifying the larger topics that the proposal will cover. By describing the content up front, forecasting helps the readers build a mental framework to understand the whole structure of the proposal.

Effective public speakers often use forecasting to build a mental framework for the topics they are going to cover in their speech. In their introduction, they tell the audience, "Today, I am going to talk about three important topics. First, I want to talk about . . . . Second, I will explain why . . . . And finally, I will discuss . . . ." The effect of this kind of forecasting on the audience is that they can now visualize the structure of the speech and follow the progress of the speaker as he works through the topics. As the speaker reaches transition points from one topic to the next, the audience can shift focus with the speaker, concentrating separately on each new topic.

In a proposal, forecasting has much the same effect on the readers. If your introduction briefly describes the structure of the proposal, the readers will be better prepared to consider each topic separately. The forecasting will provide them with a map of your proposal, so they have an overall idea of how you are going to lead them from the current situation, through your plan, through your qualifications, to the costs and benefits. As a result, the readers will know in advance how the argument will progress.

Working out the Six Moves on a Worksheet

As you invent the content for the introduction, it is helpful to begin by writing down a sentence or two for each of these moves. The worksheet in Figure 7.1 shows how you can phrase these moves as questions. Once you have written down answers to these questions, you should find yourself ready to write the introduction.

Writing the Introduction

When you were first learning how to write, you might have been told that there is only one way to write an introduction. First, you were told, an introduction begins with a sentence that grabs the readers' attention. Second, an introduction should end with your *thesis,* or main point. And finally, you were told that introductions need to be kept to only one paragraph. For the most part, this advice is not wrong, but it isn't necessarily right, either.

FIGURE 7.1
The Six Moves as Questions

Elements of the Introduction

What is the subject of this proposal? What is *not* the subject of this proposal?

What is the purpose of this proposal in only one sentence?

What main point is this proposal trying to make to the readers?

Why is this subject important to the readers?

What background information should the readers know before reading the proposal?

How will the body of the proposal be organized?

An introduction is far more fluid and flexible than you may have been led to believe. The six moves discussed in the previous section can be made in almost any order. Usually, proposals start out with some background information or a statement that stresses the importance of the subject to the readers. But there are other ways to begin a proposal. Many proposals start out with a statement of purpose. For example, "Our intent in this proposal is to . . . ." This first sentence is not going to shake the rafters, but it tells the readers up front what you are going to do. There are countless ways to start a proposal, so do not feel obligated to start with some kind of bang.

The statements of your purpose and main point are the most important features of the introduction, perhaps the whole proposal. Before reading the body of your proposal, the readers absolutely must have a clear idea of what you are trying to do (purpose) and what you are trying to prove (main point). So, you should not bury these statements somewhere in the middle of a paragraph in the introduction. They should appear at the beginning or end of a paragraph, where the readers are paying most attention. If you are not sure whether your purpose and main point are clear to the readers, you should make them painfully obvious. In these cases, use a sentence like, "The purpose of this proposal is to . . . ." And, if you want to make your main point absolutely clear, say something like, "Our aim is to prove to you that . . . ." It is better to be too blunt than too subtle about your purpose and main point.

Finally, an introduction should be concise. When readers begin a proposal, a mental timer starts in their heads. With their timer running, they immediately start asking questions like, "What is this proposal about? Why are these people writing to me? What is the point? Why should I care?" If you take too long to answer these questions, the readers will become frustrated or bored. To avoid frustrating the readers in the introduction, simply address the six moves and then hand the readers over to the body of the proposal. Poorly written introductions tend to have too much content, obstructing the readers' efforts to identify the subject, purpose, and main point of the proposal. If your introduction seems to run on too long, move any content (i.e., facts, examples, reasoning) to the body of the proposal. Put that content where it belongs—in the body—and limit the introduction to contextual information.

A good rule of thumb is to limit introductions to the first page of a single-spaced proposal. The number of paragraphs used in an introduction is not important, but typically a writer can only put about two or three paragraphs on a given sheet of paper. Of course, there are always exceptions, but if you notice that your proposal has a three- or five-page introduction, there is a good chance that the readers will lose their patience. Moreover, it is likely that all the extra content in your introduction has muddied your attempts to clearly state your subject, purpose, and main point.

Without a doubt, the introduction can be the hardest part of the proposal to write, but two strategies will make it much easier to write. First, write the introduction after you have written the body of the proposal. Doing so will save you hours of writer's block, because you will know exactly what needs to be said in the introduction. Second, write out the six moves before writing the introduction, addressing each move separately. Then, craft them into a concise introduction that sets a framework for the body of the proposal. If you do these two things, writing a proposal's introduction is simple.

The Introduction to the Earl Grey Proposal

Figure 7.2 shows the introduction of Lisa Miller's proposal to Earl Grey Design. Lisa wanted her introduction to grab the readers, because she knew the introduction would essentially make or break her proposal. Lisa's solution for the Earl Grey's office space shortage was likely different from her readers' expectations, so she assumed that they would never read her plan if her introduction made a bad first impression.

In the first paragraph of her proposal's introduction, Lisa provided some background information. The readers at Earl Grey were almost certainly familiar with all the details in this paragraph. Nevertheless, Lisa used these details to warm up the readers by telling them things they already knew. Moreover, this background information gave Lisa an opportunity to stroke the egos of the readers a bit—make them feel good about their company.

FIGURE 7.2
Proposal Introduction for Earl Grey Design

**Proposal to Earl Grey Design:
Telecommuting, Growth, and Flexibility**

Founded in 1979, Earl Grey is one of those classic entrepreneurial success stories in the architectural industry. With one thousand dollars of capital, Susan James and Thomas Weber began designing functional buildings for the Wrigleyville business community. Three years later, the company cleared its first million dollars in revenue. Today, Earl Grey is one of the leading architectural firms in the Chicago market with over fifty million dollars in annual revenue. The *Chicago Business Journal* has consistently rated Earl Grey one of the top-five architectural firms in the city, citing the company's continued innovation and growth in the industry.

With growth, however, comes growing pains. Earl Grey now faces an important decision about how it will manage its growth in the near future. The right decision could lead to more market share, increased sales, and even more prominence in the architectural market. However, Earl Grey also needs to safeguard itself against overextension should the Chicago construction market unexpectedly begin to recede.

To help Earl Grey make the right decision, this proposal suggests an innovative strategy that will support the company's growth while maintaining its flexibility. Specifically, we propose that Earl Grey implement a telecommuting system that allows selected employees to work a few days each week at home. Telecommuting will provide Earl Grey with the office space it needs to continue growing; yet, it will avoid the large investment in new facilities or disruption to the company's current operations.

In this proposal, we will first discuss the results of our research into Earl Grey's office space needs. Second, we will offer a plan for using a telecommuting network to free up more space at Earl Grey's current office. Third, we will review our qualifications at Insight Systems to assist Earl Grey with its move into telecommuting. And finally, we will go over some of the costs and advantages of our plan. Our aim is to show you that telecommuting is a way for Earl Grey to continue growing while maintaining the innovative spirit that launched this firm so many years ago.

In the second paragraph, Lisa identified the subject of the proposal—that is, managing Earl Grey's growth as a firm. She backed it up by stressing the importance of this subject to the readers. Specifically, she pointed out that the right decision would lead to further growth and influence, while the wrong decision might leave the firm vulnerable in a receding market. In this way, Lisa tried to stress the opportunity for growth while lightly hinting to the readers that inaction or wrong action could lead to negative consequences.

The third paragraph states the purpose and the main point of the proposal. For her purpose, Lisa wrote, "This proposal suggests an innovative strategy that will support the company's growth while maintaining its flexibility." Then, for her main point, she wrote, "We propose that Earl Grey implement a telecommuting network that allows selected employees to work a few days each week at home." Lisa was not subtle about her purpose and main point, because she believed the readers would consider her idea. With her purpose and main point stated up front, the readers could keep them in mind as they studied the details in the body of the proposal.

Finally, the last paragraph in the introduction forecasts the structure of the proposal. By outlining the body of the proposal for the readers, Lisa created a framework that the readers could use to visualize the rest of the proposal. They would know the topics covered and the overall logical progression of the text.

Overall, Lisa's introduction concisely lays out her argument for the readers. It prepares them for the body by making the introductory six moves while saving the content of the proposal for the body. Lisa did not need to make all six moves. For example, she could cut out the background information in the first paragraph or the forecasting in the last paragraph. But, she felt these paragraphs helped set a context for the body of the proposal. So, she decided to make these moves in the introduction.

Costs and Benefits: Concluding the Proposal

The best way to conclude a proposal is to stress the benefits of your plan. As mentioned earlier in this chapter, the conclusion is, in many ways, a reflection of the introduction. Just as readers are especially attentive at the beginning of a proposal, they are also highly attentive at the end. The conclusion is where you should bring the readers back to your main point while emphasizing the benefits of accepting your ideas.

The conclusion is where you are going to finally persuade your readers to say yes to your plan. Nothing new really happens in the conclusion of a proposal, except perhaps a short discussion of the costs. After all, when the readers reach this point in the proposal, they have already heard and considered your description of the current situation. They have already studied your plan and considered your qualifications. So, they know almost all the information they need to make a decision. At this point, it is your goal to *sell* them your plan by stressing its advantages. In the conclusion, you need to amplify your proposal by showing them the positive things that will happen if they say yes.

The only new information in the conclusion should be a short discussion of the costs of the project. As you might guess, for many readers the costs are a major focal point if not *the* focal point of any proposal. In some cases, the costs can be bitter medicine for the readers, because you are essentially telling them that they need to trade something valuable, usually money, for your plan and expertise. Fortunately, the costs can be strategically positioned in the conclusion, thereby sweetening the bitter medicine by stressing the benefits of accepting your ideas. That way, the readers will be able to weigh the costs directly against the benefits that your plan will bring.

Inventing and Writing the Conclusion

Conclusions are typically small compared to the other sections in the proposal. Nevertheless they are crucial toward finally persuading the client to say yes to your ideas. Proposal writers often use a gymnastics phrase, "stick the landing," to remind themselves that no matter how complicated the body of the proposal, the conclusion needs to land on both feet—with a smile.

The conclusion should be positive and forward-looking. It should never rehash the clients' problems, and it should never try to scare the readers into saying yes. Bringing up the clients' problems at this point just puts them in a bad mood. So, attempts to scare them at this point usually backfire. After all, no one likes to be browbeaten into agreeing with a plan (e.g., "Accept our plan or bad things will happen to you"). They want to feel as though accepting the proposal will make their lives better. So, with few exceptions, the proposal's conclusion should be positive in content and tone.

Like the introduction, the conclusion of the proposal can be built around specific moves. These moves are intended to stress the benefits of the plan while specifying its costs.

Move 1: *Transition* from the body of the proposal.

Move 2: State the *costs* of the plan.

Move 3: Highlight the *benefits* of the plan.

Move 4: Look to the *future.*

Move 5: Identify the *next step.*

Of course, all these moves do not need to be made in the conclusion. A combination of some or all of these moves will round out the proposal in a strong way. Let us look at these moves more closely.

Move 1: Transition from the Body of the Proposal

Transition points are found throughout proposals, but there is one particular transition that merits special attention—the transition from the body of the proposal to the conclusion. To illustrate the importance of this special transition, think of the public speeches you have heard over the years. When the speaker says, "In conclusion," or something to that effect, everyone in the audience perks up and starts listening. This kind of transition to the conclusion is a signal that the speaker is going to summarize the main points—that is, the important stuff.

In written documents, the importance of the transition is the same. As soon as you write "To sum up" or use a concluding heading like "Final Points," the readers will start paying closer attention to what you are writing because they know you are going to summarize the main points of the document.

The transition from the body to the conclusion should be obvious to the readers, because you want the readers to start paying close attention again. More than likely, after reading the body of the proposal and wading through the Qualifications section, the readers are at a low attention point when they reach the conclusion. They are tired, and the proposal has already given them numerous details to sort out and mull over. So the transition needs to be obvious to help wake them up.

There are three ways to make an obvious transition into the conclusion:

- Use an active heading that signals the conclusion and gently cues the readers that you going to bring the proposal to a close. A heading like "Concluding Remarks," "Our Recommendations," or "What are the Advantages of our Plan?" will usually prompt the readers to start paying closer attention.
- Start out the first sentence of the conclusion with a transitional phrase, such as "In summary . . ." "To conclude . . ." or "To wrap up . . ." Even these small phrases will bring the readers' attention back to your proposal, preparing them to consider your overall points.
- State or restate your proposal's main point. For example, a proposal's main point might be, "We believe a modernized manufacturing plant will provide Hanson Industries the flexibility and capacity to become the leader in the controls industry." Stated up front in the conclusion, this sentence will signal that you are bringing the proposal to a close.

The transition into the conclusion is a critical point in any proposal, so it should be handled with care. Once the conclusion has been signaled, you probably have a few paragraphs, at most a page or two, to make your final points. Public speakers often make the crucial mistake of saying "In conclusion . . ." or "In sum . . ." and then rambling on for ten more minutes. By the end of that ten minutes, the people in the audience are ready to fall out of their chairs. Once the speaker signals she is concluding, she probably has a minute or two to make her main points. Likewise, in a proposal, when you use a transition to signal the conclusion, you probably have about a minute or two of the readers' heightened attention. If you go longer, they will become frustrated, restless, and annoyed.

Move 2: State the Costs of the Plan

Obviously, the costs are the bottom line of any proposal. And yet, finding out how much a project will cost is typically not a high point for the readers—unless you are asking for less money than they expected. So, you need to find a way to present the costs in a positive light.

Various strategies are available for presenting the costs. In smaller proposals, costs can be concisely itemized in a short table, accompanied by a few explanatory comments in the body of the proposal. The table in Figure 7.3, for example, shows how major budget items can be summarized for the readers in a concise manner.

In larger proposals, writers will sometimes include a separate Budget section sandwiched between the Qualifications section and the proposal's conclusion. In these stand-alone Budget sections, the readers typically find an itemized table of costs and a detailed rationale for major and minor expenses. These large Budget sections can often run on for several pages.

FIGURE 7.3

A Small Table of Costs

The costs of the project are the following figures:	
Development of a prototype	$ 15,390
Retooling manufacturing line	89,600
New promotional campaign	32,200
Retraining of labor and staff	11,100
Contingency	10,000
TOTAL	$ 158,290

The problem with placing a large budget, tables and all, inside the body or conclusion of your proposal is that it kills the momentum of your argument, almost completely disrupting the story you are trying to tell. After all, by the time the readers sift through pages and pages of budgetary items, dollar figures, and justifications for various lines in the budget, they will more than likely forget your descriptions of the current situation, your plan, and your qualifications. As a result, when they reach the proposal's conclusion, all they will remember is how much money your project is going to cost them. In most cases, you do not want your clients thinking solely about the price tag when you are trying to persuade them to say yes to your company's project, service, or product.

There is a better way to handle the costs in a proposal. If possible, it is best to include only a brief synopsis of the project's overall costs in the conclusion of the proposal. Then, provide an itemized budget and a detailed rationale in an appendix. For example, a simple statement in the conclusion like, "As shown in our budget in Appendix B, we estimate the Goodman Restoration Project will cost $40,560,300," is sufficient for even the largest projects. This kind of simple sentence provides the readers with a bottom-line figure while directing them to a place where they can analyze the figures in greater depth. The advantage of this approach is that the readers avoid slogging through a detailed discussion of figures at this crucial point. But, if the readers want that detailed discussion, they can turn to the appendix where the figures are handled in depth. (In Chapter 8, we will discuss how to write stand-alone budgets for an appendix or a Budget section.)

If you think your proposal's conclusion needs more than one sentence about costs, then you might include a small table that breaks down the budget into its larger parts, much like the table shown in Figure 7.3. This kind of budget table sketches out the basic elements of the budget without breaking down the figures into itemized bits and pieces. You can then refer the readers to an itemized budget in the appendix that fills in the specific details behind these costs and offers a rationale for each expense.

When you handle the costs in the conclusion, state them in a straightforward, matter-of-fact way. Some proposal writers feel the strange urge to become apologetic, defensive, or phony-sounding when they mention how much the project will cost. They say, "We're sorry, but the cost of your new manufacturing plant will probably sound very expensive, but it's really not. We estimate it will cost . . . ." Or, they defensively state, "We have tried everything in our power to keep expenses to a minimum, but it looks like the project is going to cost . . . ." Even worse, they sometimes use a phony-sounding sales pitch: "And for the very, very low cost of $1,983,000, you can have the best manufacturing plant on the planet!"

These attempts to soften, defend, or put a positive spin on costs usually only end up backfiring, because they highlight your team or company's insecurities about the budget while needlessly drawing attention to the price of the project. Instead, when you mention how much the project will cost, just tell the readers the figure in a straightforward way. Apologizing, defending, or putting a phony-sounding sales spin on the costs will only have a negative effect on the readers.

One final note on costs. Something to keep in mind is that a proposal is a de facto contract, until it is superseded by a formal agreement or contract of some kind. In some cases, especially when the proposal is signed by the bidder and the client, the proposal *is* the contract for the project. So, if you promise that you can complete the project for a specific amount of money and the client accepts, then you are more than likely obligated to charge only that amount. Once the proposal is accepted, it is a binding contract in most cases. Therefore, costs in a formal proposal should be as exact as possible, and they need to be defensible in a court of law, if necessary.

Move 3: Highlight the Benefits of the Plan

In proposals as well as life, the best way to persuade people is to stress the benefits of your ideas to them. In a proposal, you need to show them the specific advantages of saying yes to your plan. The primary aim of a proposal's conclusion, therefore, is to stress the importance of your plan by summarizing and amplifying the benefits of your plan, urging the readers to accept your ideas.

In proposals, benefits tend to take three forms:

- **Hard Benefits**—deliverables, outcomes, and results
- **Soft Benefits**—quality, service, and satisfaction
- **Value Benefits**—common ideals and standards shared by client and bidder

Hard Benefits

Hard benefits are the quantifiable outcomes of the project that the readers can see, touch, or measure. These benefits can be found in your Plan section, when you discussed the deliverables of your project. The deliverables are the "hard" (i.e., seeable, touchable, measurable) results of your work for the client. You will notice that hard benefits work on two levels:

1. The clients receive *direct benefits* associated with possessing the deliverables highlighted in the Plan section (a building, PR campaign, a report).
2. *Consequent benefits* accompany these deliverables (more efficient employees, better relations with the community, understanding and insight).

For example, the direct benefits resulting from an implementation proposal might be tangible things like a new building, a new product, or a public relations campaign. These items are quantifiable objects that the readers can see, touch, or measure. These direct benefits also bring other consequent benefits to the client. A new building might make employees more efficient or allow the client's company to expand its services. A new product might mean more market share. A public relations campaign might result in a higher corporate profile or better ties to the community.

To identify the direct and consequent hard benefits, look back at your plan and list all the deliverables you promised the readers. Write those deliverables on the left-hand of a benefits chart like the one shown in Figure 7.4. Then, on the right-hand column of the hard benefits section, write down all the additional advantages to the readers of possessing that deliverable. Write down anything that comes to mind, placing yourself in the position of the readers. Ask yourself how each deliverable would make the readers' situation better than it was before.

Soft Benefits

Soft benefits are the intangible advantages of working with your team or company. These benefits include nonquantifiable qualities like trust, efficiency, satisfaction, and confidence. Overall, soft benefits cannot be held, seen, or even measured. Nevertheless, they are important benefits that your team or company will

FIGURE 7.4
Benefits Chart

Hard Benefits		Soft Benefits	
Deliverables (direct benefit)	*Added Benefits* (consequent benefit)	*Strengths*	*Added Benefits*
Value Benefits			

bring to the readers. To find these soft benefits, look back at the Qualifications section at the strengths you wrote down for your team or company. Pay special attention to your answer to the "what makes you different makes you attractive" question. Then, list these intangible benefits in the left-hand column of the benefits worksheet (Figure 7.4). In the right-hand column, write down all the advantages of these soft benefits for the readers.

Of course, you can make any claims you want about things like quality or satisfaction, but the best soft benefits are ones that highlight special qualities unique to your company. If your company has a reputation for high-quality work, then stressing quality in the conclusion would be a good idea. However, if your company has had some notable quality failures, then your attempts to sell the readers on quality will sound a little hollow. For this reason, when you are discussing the soft benefits in the conclusion, you should concentrate on what makes your company special or different from the competition.

Value Benefits

Value benefits refer to the common values held by the readers' and your team or company. Look back at the readers analysis worksheet you developed in Chapter 3 (Figure 3.2). In that worksheet, you wrote down the primary readers' motives, values, attitudes, and emotions concerning the project and your company or team. Under the *values* part of the worksheet, you should find some qualities that the readers value in themselves; therefore, it is pretty safe to assume they will value these qualities in the companies they hire to complete a project.

For example, let us say you are bidding for a contract with Grandview Manufacturing. After reading through their literature and talking with the Point of Contact, you find that the CEO of the company values on-time production above all else. In the past, Grandview has been burned by suppliers who were not able to meet deadlines. As a result of these missed deadlines, their just-in-time manufacturing methods were completely undermined. Now, the CEO of the Grandview Manufacturing is adamant that all contractors will meet strict deadlines, even if timeliness costs his company more money up front. So, in your conclusion, you might stress your company's commitment to prompt, on-time service.

The bulk of the conclusion will be taken up with a discussion of the hard, soft, and value benefits that your proposal is offering. In one way or another, you have already mentioned all these benefits in the body of the proposal, so there is no new information here. Rather, in the conclusion you are summarizing the benefits for the readers. By putting all these benefits together at this point, you will amplify the ending of the proposal—inviting the readers to say yes to your ideas.

Move 4: Look to the Future

Whether you are solving a problem or taking advantage of an opportunity, the bottom-line promise you are making to the readers is that their future will be better if they agree to your proposal. For this reason, many writers will include a

"Look to the Future" paragraph that illustrates for the readers the long-term advantages of the proposal's plan. For example, if you are proposing a new building, describe the company's employees working efficiently in its new state-of-the-art facility. If you are proposing a change in the personnel structure of the company, show the readers how your changes will create a more motivated, innovative work force that responds effectively to customers' needs.

If used, a "Look to the Future" should be short, at most one paragraph. Its aim is to simply show the readers that your plan leads to long-term results, not a short-term fix.

Move 5: Identify the Next Step

A good way to put the final touches on a proposal is to thank the readers, ask them to contact you with any questions, and tell them the next step. The next step is what you want the readers to do immediately when they are finished looking over your proposal. Should they call you? Should they set up a meeting with you? Will you be calling them or scheduling a visit? The readers should finish your proposal with a clear idea of what is needed to put the proposal into action.

Why is a next-step statement a good way to end the proposal? It is very common for readers to look over a proposal with approval, even excitement. Then, they file it away in some "good idea" stack or folder, because they do not know what needs to be done right now. The next-step statement is a trigger for the proposal. It tells the readers the small step they need to take right now to put the project into motion. Million-dollar proposals need a starting place. Sometimes that starting place is a simple phone call to set up a meeting.

Concluding the Earl Grey Proposal

Lisa Miller's proposal to Earl Grey Design was starting to take shape. She felt good about her description of the current situation and her plan for developing a telecommuting system to manage Earl Grey's limited office space. But she knew her conclusion would need to end the proposal on a strong note.

Figure 7.5 shows a rough draft of the conclusion she wrote for her proposal. In the first paragraph, Lisa decided to make two concluding moves. First, she signaled the transition into the conclusion with phrases like "To conclude" and "let us summarize." With these obvious concluding sentences, Lisa intended to recapture the readers' attention and urge them to pay closer attention. Second, at the end of this opening paragraph, Lisa restated her main point for the proposal: "We believe the best way to manage growth, while maintaining Earl Grey's financial flexibility, is to develop a LAN that will allow some of the company's employees to telecommute from home or from their worksite." Lisa hoped her repetition of the main point would create closure for the readers, driving home the most significant idea she wanted the readers to remember.

FIGURE 7.5
A Conclusion for the Earl Grey Proposal

The Benefits of Telecommuting and Project Expenses

To conclude, let us summarize the advantages of our plan and discuss the costs. Our preliminary research shows us that Earl Grey Design will continue to be a leader in the Chicago market. The strong economy, coupled with Earl Grey's award-winning designs, has bolstered the demand for your services. We believe the best way to manage growth, while maintaining Earl Grey's financial flexibility, is to develop a LAN that will allow some of the company's employees to telecommute from home or from their worksite.

Cost is the most significant advantage of our plan. As illustrated in Appendix A, implementation of our plan would cost $97,311. We believe this investment in Earl Grey's infrastructure will preserve your company's financial flexibility to react to the market's crests and valleys.

But the advantages of our plan go beyond simple costs. First, a telecommuting system will allow your current operations to continue without disruption. When the telecommuting system is ready to go online, your employees will simply need to attend an afternoon of training sessions on using the LAN and intranet. At these training sessions, we will also teach them time-tested strategies for successful telecommuting from home. Your management team can then gradually convert selected employees into telecommuters.

Second, employee morale will benefit from our telecommuting plan. With fewer employees at the office, there will be more space available for the employees who need to be in the office each day. Studies have shown that telecommuting employees report more job satisfaction, and they increase their productivity. We believe this improved employee morale is especially important in your field, because architects often feel more comfortable working in less formal environments. The flexibility of telecommuting will allow Earl Grey to recruit and retain some of the best people in the industry.

When the telecommuting system is in place, Earl Grey will be positioned for continued growth and leadership in the Chicago architectural market. The key to Earl Grey's success has always been its flexibility and innovativeness in an industry that seems to change overnight. Telecommuting will open up space at your current downtown office while maintaining the morale and productivity of your employees as your business continues to grow.

Thank you for giving Insight Systems the opportunity to work with you on this project. We are looking forward to the opportunity to submit a full proposal that describes our plan in greater depth. Our CEO, Dr. Hanna Gibbons, will contact you on May 15 to discuss the proposal with you and, if possible, set up a meeting.

If you have any suggestions for improving our plan or you would like to ask questions, please call Lisa Miller, our senior computer engineer, at 1-800-555-3864. Or, you can e-mail her at lmiller@insight_systems.com.

In the second paragraph, Lisa handled the costs. Because she was convinced her plan would cost less than the competitors' plans, she decided to phrase the costs as a benefit. Nevertheless, she stated the figure in a simple way, directing the readers to the appendix if they would want to study the costs of the proposal in greater depth.

In the third and fourth paragraphs, she continued to stress the benefits of the telecommuting plan. She mentioned hard benefits like the minimal disruption to Earl Grey's operations, increased morale, more office space, and increased productivity. These benefits were all quantifiable differences that would result from implementing the telecommuting system. She also mentioned some soft benefits, such as employee job satisfaction and comfort. These benefits would not be measurable, but they would be important quality-of-life issues for the readers. And finally, she worked in a few value benefits by stressing words like *success, flexibility, growth, innovativeness,* and *award-winning.* Lisa believed these words would highlight some of the common values that Earl Grey and Insight Systems shared.

In the fifth paragraph, Lisa offered a look to the future. She tried to show the readers at Earl Grey how the telecommuting system would create a better situation than their current one. She wanted to give them the impression that telecommuting would be a long-term solution in line with progressive thinking about the modern office.

Finally, in the last two paragraphs, Lisa told the readers the next step that would put the proposal into motion. She told the readers that Insight Systems' CEO, Hanna Gibbons would be contacting them to discuss the proposal and set up a meeting. Then, she ended the proposal with contact information in case the readers would have questions.

Overall, Lisa's conclusion makes the five concluding moves mentioned in this chapter. But, more importantly, her conclusion stresses the main point (her plan) and its importance (the benefits). In her proposal's conclusion, Lisa did not include any new information, except a brief mention of the costs. Instead, she amplified her main points, driving her argument home for the readers.

Last Word

Introductions and conclusions are partners in a proposal. The role of an introduction is to create a framework, or context, for the body of the proposal. It identifies the proposal's subject, purpose, and main point while stressing the importance of the subject. The role of the conclusion is to bring the readers back to the proposal's main point while again stressing the importance of the subject. An effective conclusion reframes the discussion, amplifying the benefits of saying yes to the plan.

Even when the conclusion is finished, the proposal writing process is not over. In the next chapter, we will discuss how to write budgets. In the remaining chapters, we will discuss the style and visual presentation of a proposal. When you are finished with the conclusion, however, you should feel some satisfaction. After all, you are on the home stretch in the proposal writing process.

CASE STUDY **Beginnings and Endings**

The Elmdale Hill Merchants Association, or the EHMA as John, Karen, Thomas, and Sally were beginning to refer to it, was beginning to look like it might just work. They were finished drafting the body of the proposal, so they turned to writing the introduction and conclusion.

They began by looking back at their notes about the rhetorical situation, especially their notes about the subject and purpose of the proposal. They were surprised at how much their ideas had matured in the last few weeks. When they wrote down their initial ideas on the subject and purpose, they had made some rather vague comments about "customer convenience and perception of convenience." The purpose they initially wrote down was "to develop a plan for improving the convenience and the customers' perception of convenience in the Elmdale Hill district."

"Wow," said John, "it seems like we have come a long way since then. We are probably going to need to refine these statements now that we know better what we are proposing."

They pulled out another piece of paper and wrote the six introductory moves down the left-hand side of the page (Figure 7.6). On the right-hand side of the page, they came up with some sentences that might address each of the moves.

Their proposal's subject and purpose became much more focused now that they had finished writing the body of the proposal. Specifically, their purpose statement stated directly that the proposal was intended to organize the Elmdale Hill business district into a merchants association. This subject and purpose still met their original goal to improve customer convenience, but their new subject and purpose implied a more realistic idea about how to do so.

Defining a main point turned out to be rather simple. "Essentially," John said, "we believe that the business owners in Elmdale Hill should band together to form a merchants association. That's our main point, isn't it?" The others agreed, offering some suggestions for refining John's statement. They added their main point to the worksheet.

Deciding how to stress the importance of the subject was not as simple, however. "I think we need to scare these people," said Karen, "Some of them are just sleepwalking into bankruptcy. They're in denial about their lost revenues."

But Sally was a little leery about scaring the readers. "I don't know, Karen. I think most of these people are just like us. They can see their bottom line losses over the last couple years. They just don't know what to do about it. We should start out on a positive note so we don't push them into further denial of the problem."

Thomas agreed with both Sally and Karen. He suggested that the introduction include an implied threat of some kind but also stressed the advantage of doing something about the problem. He dictated to John, "If we form a stronger community, we can increase our sales. If we do nothing, the Wheatmill Mall and the big chain stores are going to keep taking our customers."

Regarding background information, Thomas thought a historical start would be too boring for the readers. Instead, he suggested that they begin by showing how things had changed over the previous couple years. "Let's mention the Wheatmill Mall and some of the recent superstores that have come to the area." John thought they should also stroke the egos of the Elmdale Hill merchants a bit. "We should talk about how Elmdale Hill has always served a more discriminating, tasteful customer." They thought these statements would build up their readers a bit while reminding everyone about the kinds of customers they wanted to keep.

Finally, they wrote down forecasting statements on the worksheet. However, all four of them agreed that forecasting would probably not be necessary in their four-to-five page proposal.

With the six moves written out on the sheet, they drafted the introduction to the proposal (see Figure 7.7). Writing the introduction was not difficult, though they found themselves wanting to put in too many *content* details that should be handled later in the body of the proposal. Thomas took it upon himself to cross out any

FIGURE 7.6

Sketching out the Six Introductory Moves

Introduction	
Subject	Creating the Elmdale Hill Merchants Association
Purpose	The purpose of this proposal is to organize the Elmdale Hill business community, so we can improve customer convenience, strengthen our political standing, and improve the community's public image.
Main Point	To compete, the Elmdale Hill business owners need to create a stronger community by pulling together into a merchants association.
Importance of Subject	A merchants association would increase our sales. If we do not form a stronger community, we may continue to see a loss in sales.
Background Information on Subject	The Elmdale Hill merchants have been losing sales. The Wheatmill Mall and other chain stores are taking away our customers. Elmdale Hill has always served the customer who values quality and service.
Forecasting	This proposal will describe the current situation, offer a plan for creating a merchants association, and describe the qualifications of a CPA firm that can help us achieve nonprofit status.

extra content that was already handled in the body of the proposal.

While drafting the introduction, they decided to add the paragraph about the meeting, so the readers would not miss the invitation. They guessed that the other business owners would pay more attention to the proposal if they knew a meeting would be held.

With a good draft of the introduction finished, they turned to write the conclusion of the proposal.

Karen said, "This merchants association is going to take some money out of these folk's cash registers. So, in the conclusion, I think it is important that we show them how the advantages of our plan outweighs the money and time

needed to create and maintain a merchants association," said Karen.

Thomas replied, "I agree. I would want to know exactly what my membership in the association would buy me. I don't mean to be selfish, but when I am reading this proposal, I'm asking, 'what is in it for me?'"

Sally said, "That's why we're going to end the proposal by answering that exact question. We need to take all those good things we promised in the Plan section and put them right at the end. That way, the other merchants can weigh the costs directly against the benefits. If we do it right, the costs will look pretty cheap compared to the services offered by the merchants association."

FIGURE 7.7
A Draft of the Merchants Association Proposal's Introduction

Competing Better Together

Elmdale Hill has always been a haven for the discerning shopper. Our unique shops and attention to quality attracts customers who expect more from a business than the lowest common denominator in products, food, services, and entertainment.

But times are growing increasingly difficult for the Elmdale Hill business district. New competition from the Wheatmill Mall and several new chain stores and restaurants have taken a bite out of our sales. According to a recent informal survey, seven out of ten Elmdale Hill businesses did not do as well this year as the last year. Though it is too early to call our declining sales a "crisis," they do signal a need to take action to fend off new competition.

One proven way to increase sales is to form a "merchants association" that will coordinate our marketing efforts and consolidate our political strength. As individual businesses, we do not compete well against the megamalls and chains; but if we use a merchants association to focus our marketing efforts, we can target advertising and public relations in ways that will elevate the image and prestige of Elmdale Hill businesses. Moreover, by uniting as a community, we will have a stronger voice at City Hall, so we can collectively solve some of the social problems that have recently developed in our area.

In this proposal, we lay out the simple steps required to form an Elmdale Hill Merchants Association. On Monday, September 15, at 6:00 p.m., we will host a townhall meeting at the Star Catcher Theater on Central Avenue. You are invited to discuss this proposal at the town hall meeting and begin the process of creating an Elmdale Hill Merchants Association. If we all come together, we can strengthen our businesses and our communities.

John divided a sheet of paper into four columns. John and Sally began looking through their proposal's draft for the hard benefits they promised in the plan. Karen and Thomas began searching for some of the soft benefits. Both teams noted any value benefits they came across as they were searching for hard and soft benefits. Figure 7.8 shows how they filled out their benefits chart.

They were all surprised by the number of benefits mentioned in the body of the proposal. It seemed as though they were promising a solid return for the small investment in a merchants association.

Like the introduction, the writing of the conclusion was actually easier than they expected. To make a significant transition, they decided to begin the conclusion with a strong claim: "The businesses of Elmdale Hill face an important decision—one we should make together." Then, in the opening of the conclusion, they restated the main point of the whole proposal and the reason why they believe the merchants association was important.

FIGURE 7.8

Benefits Chart for Elmdale Hill Proposal

Hard Benefits		Soft Benefits	
Deliverables	*Added Benefits*	*Strengths*	*Added Benefits*
• Merchants Association	• More power, increased sales, better public relations	• Community oriented • Organized action	• Bring us together as a community • Structure and focus; feeling that something is happening
• Report that shows current economic situation in Elmdale Hill	• Better insight into our current situation and data to back up our statements	• Fighting off the mall and chain stores	• David vs. Goliath—beating back the tendency toward mediocrity
• Town hall meeting to discuss options	• Attention from press and government; buy-in from other merchants; feeling of community		
		• Pride and satisfaction	• Nicer to come to work
• A steering committee that will guide the creation of the Association	• Focused planning and goal setting; committed team of people	• Customer service	• Happier customers and better relations with community
• More political power	• Influence at City Hall and Police HQ		
• Better public image	• More customers, investment in area		
• Increased sales	• Better profits		

Value Benefits
Individuality Self-sufficiency High-quality service Attention to detail Unique, eclectic businesses

As they wrote the conclusion, however, they ran into one recurring problem. They kept phrasing statements in negative terms. For example, in an early draft, John wrote, "If we don't organize, there is a good chance the Elmdale Hill business district will be overrun with check-cashing stores, stripbars, and boarded-up shops."

Karen pointed out how those negative statements ended the proposal on a sour note. "John, we need to stay positive here. Let's concentrate on the good things that will happen if we form the merchants association. We already went over all the bad things when we discussed the problems. Our readers know what is at stake."

FIGURE 7.9
The Conclusion of the Elmdale Hill Proposal

Conclusion: The Advantages of a Merchants Association

The businesses of Elmdale Hill face an important decision—one we should make together. As we have argued in this proposal, in order to thrive in today's competitive environment, we need to organize ourselves into a merchants association. The costs to form and maintain a merchants association would be minimal (about $50 to $100 a month, as shown in Appendix A), but the benefits would be substantial.

Here are just a few of those benefits. First, a merchants association would allow us to work collectively on issues that concern the Elmdale Hill community. We would have more power with City Hall and the police. And, we would be able to present a positive image to the press and the public. Most important, however, our sales would increase as we enhanced our competitiveness against the megamalls and chainstores that have recently moved into our area.

The advantages of a merchants association also relate to our quality of life. We all take pride and satisfaction in our businesses and our community. By banding together into a merchants association, we can focus our efforts to fight off our megacompetitors who sacrifice quality and customer service for profit. We can continue to provide our customers with the kinds of unique products, services, and entertainment that make Elmdale Hill a special place to work, live, and visit.

Elmdale Hill is a great place to own a business. With a merchants association in place, who knows what the future will hold for us? Together, we can grow our businesses and bring in new businesses. Customers will see Elmdale Hill as a place where they can enjoy shopping, meet friends, and relax. Moreover, as business owners, we will have a sense of unity. We will be a supportive community that looks out for each other's interests.

On Monday, September 15, at 6:00 p.m, we will hold a town hall meeting at the Star Catcher Theater on Central Avenue. At the meeting, we will talk over this proposal. If the community supports this proposal, or at least the idea of a merchants association, volunteers will be nominated to form a committee to start developing the merchants association.

Thank you for your time and interest. We hope to see you at the town hall meeting. John Legler, owner of Milano's, will take your RSVP. He can also address any comments or questions you may have. Please call John at 555-4144.

The conclusion section ended up being six paragraphs. After an opening paragraph, they summarized the deliverables (hard benefits) in the second paragraph, and then they highlighted some of the soft benefits and value benefits in the third paragraph (see Figure 7.9). They then wrote a "Look to the Future" paragraph that illustrated a thriving Elmdale Hill business district benefit-ing from the promotion and guidance of the Elmdale Hill Merchants Association.

"OK," said Thomas, "we need to put some kind of trigger to get this whole thing in motion."

"Let's just ask them to RSVP for the town hall meeting. That little action on their part will get them to commit in a small way to the project. Once they're at the meeting, we'll persuade them to commit to the whole idea of a merchants association."

For some final touches, they thanked the readers and provided contact information. John volunteered to take the reservations for the meeting and let people call him with comments or questions.

Of course, they all knew there was plenty of work to be done, but they felt good about finishing a first draft of the proposal. They decided to kick back and enjoy the rest of the evening. The proposal seemed to be almost done.

Questions and Exercises

1. Look at a proposal you found on the Internet or at your workplace. In the introduction of the proposal, do the writers effectively frame the body of the proposal by clearly telling the readers the subject, purpose, and main point of the text? Does the introduction also stress the importance of the subject, offer background on the subject, and forecast the remainder of the proposal? Mark specific sentences where the writers make some or all of the six moves that are made in the introduction of a proposal. If some of these moves are missing, do you think the writers of the proposal had good reasons for leaving them out?

2. Now look at this proposal's conclusion. Does the proposal make a clear transition from the body to the conclusion? Where and how are the costs handled in the proposal? Were the authors hesitant or reluctant when they expressed the price of the project? Does the conclusion highlight hard, soft, and value benefits? Does it offer a look into the future for the readers? And finally, does it identify the next step, or trigger, that will put the proposal into motion? Mark specific sentences where the writers made some or all of the five moves common in a proposal's conclusion. If some of these concluding moves are missing, do you think the writers of the proposal had good reasons for leaving them out?

3. A common problem in most workplaces and campuses is obsolete computer facilities. Using a benefits worksheet like the one shown in Figure 7.4, list out the hard, soft, and value benefits that would be gained if your university or workplace upgraded its computer hardware or software. Compare the benefits you listed out with those listed out by others in your class.

4. For a practice or real proposal of your own, fill out a six moves worksheet like the one shown in Figure 7.1. Then, write an introduction for your proposal in which you try to address only these moves.

5. Then, write a conclusion for your practice or real proposal in which you address only the five moves described in this chapter. Pay special attention to the benefits described in the body of your proposal. Summarize those benefits in your conclusion.

6. Compare the introduction you wrote for Exercise 4 with the conclusion you wrote for Exercise 5. Does the introduction "tell them what you're going to tell them" and does the conclusion "tell them what you told them"? In other words, do the introduction and conclusion reflect each other in ways that frame the body of the proposal?

8 | Developing Budgets

Overview

This chapter will discuss the basic elements of a budget and show you how to write a stand-alone budget section or rationale for a proposal. The chapter will meet the following objectives:

1. Discuss the importance of a budget in a proposal.

2. Provide a vocabulary for talking about budgets.

3. Discuss the different elements of a budget.

4. Show how to write a budget rationale.

Budgets: The Bottom Line

Like it or not, budgets are often the most important part of any proposal, especially for the readers. After all, the bottom line *is* the bottom line, and some readers will scrutinize your budget with the eyes of a hawk. They will challenge the weak points in the budget, and they will try to cut away what they perceive to be fat. The more your readers cut out of your budget, the less flexibility you will have to complete the project. So, you want to be certain that your proposal's budget is sound and defensible.

Why are budgets so important? In short, proposals are about money. So, if the budget has problems, the whole proposal has problems. An unsound budget is one of the primary reasons why a proposal is rejected. Worse yet, if the budget does not anticipate all the costs for the project, the bidder (you) will usually swallow the cost overruns. That is never a pleasant experience. In the end, budgets are important because most proposals ultimately come down to money. You may have a sure-fire plan for solving the problem, but if your budget is unsound, those plans will never go far.

One way to safeguard against unsound budgets is to find a good accountant to help you handle the money issues in a proposal. Let's be honest. Most people have trouble following a budget in their personal lives. A budget for a project is even more complicated. To avoid these complications, a good accountant can help you anticipate some of the pitfalls of budget development. An accountant can also flag costs that you may have overlooked or forgotten to include. If you are already paying an accountant to handle the taxes for your business or you have accountants working at your workplace, you should plan to pay them a visit as soon as you have drafted the proposal.

This chapter is not designed to be a substitute for a good accountant. Instead, it will discuss some of the basics of budget development. That way, you can sketch out a rough budget before visiting your accountant. With this rough budget in hand, you can work with the accountant to create a formal budget that includes all the trimmings. In some cases, especially where the project is small, the concepts in this chapter will help you create a budget without an accountant.

Budget Basics

Like any profession, accountants have their own vocabulary. So, let us start by going over some of the basics of budget development.

Itemized and Nonitemized Budgets

Budgets can either be *itemized* or *nonitemized*.

Itemized Budgets

Itemized budgets break down the proposal's expenses to their smallest elements (within reason). It shows the readers exactly how much money is going to be spent on each part of the project. In an itemized budget, there is little or no "gray area," because you are trying to account for every dollar in the project. Itemized budgets often run several pages in a proposal.

Nonitemized Budgets

Nonitemized budgets on the other hand, tend to be less exact. They are used when the readers do not need to know exactly where each dollar will be spent. Instead, the readers need a rough breakdown of expenses to show them how you came up with the figures in the budget. Nonitemized budgets are shorter than itemized budgets because they tend to consolidate smaller costs into larger categories.

For a couple of reasons, it is usually best to develop an itemized budget whether you intend to include one in the proposal or not. First, an itemized budget helps you control your own costs if the proposal is accepted. An itemized budget will help you keep track of where the money is being spent, even if your clients are satisfied with a nonitemized budget in the proposal. As they say, the devil is in the details, especially when it comes to budgets. Itemization will help you find any hidden costs that will bleed money from your budget. Second, some clients will ask you very pointed questions about how specific figures were calculated. For example, if your budget lists a hundred-page training packet that costs $90, the readers may want to know exactly how you came up with that figure (after all, it would only cost them $5 for each packet if they ran it off on their own copier). If you created an itemized budget, you can point out in exact amounts how much expenses, such as labor and overhead, added to the production of the packet.

Fixed and Flexible Budgets

Budgets can also be *fixed* or *flexible.*

Fixed Budgets

Fixed budgets promise to provide the clients a particular product or service for a set price. In fixed budgets, that bottom-line price does not change, even if production costs rise or fall during the project. For example, when using a fixed budget, if the costs of the materials used to make a product suddenly rise, you cannot go back to the client and expect them to increase your budget to cover those additional expenses. On the other hand, if the price of your materials drop, thus decreasing your costs, then you can keep that windfall as profit. A fixed budget means the client's costs will not increase or decrease over the life of the project.

Flexible Budgets

Flexible budgets tend to be used in proposals that describe ongoing projects, especially internal company projects. This kind of budget is adjusted each month, quarter, or year to reflect changes in project costs. At the end of each reporting period, the projected costs in the budget are compared to actual costs, and adjustments are made for the next reporting period (see Donnelly 1984, p. 42). A flexible budget allows a company to regulate the costs of a project, modifying the budget to suit changes in objectives or the economy. In external proposals, flexible budgets tend to only work when there is a close relationship between a supplier and client. In these cases, the proposal and its budget are rewritten periodically to suit changes in costs.

If you are uncertain, you should talk to your readers and accountant about whether a fixed or flexible budget is appropriate for your proposal.

Fixed, Variable, and Semivariable Costs

An accountant will often begin a budget discussion by helping you identify the fixed, variable, and semivariable costs that will be involved in the project. Even with a fixed budget, some of your costs will fluctuate during the project. By identifying which costs are fixed, variable, and semivariable, the accountant can anticipate the behavior of these costs and estimate the appropriate figures for the budget (see Ramsey and Ramsey 1985, pp. 26–30). To save time (and money), you should try to break down your costs into these fixed, variable, and semivariable categories before you meet with an accountant.

Fixed Costs

Fixed costs are those expenses that will remain constant over the duration of a project. These costs might include the rent for facilities or equipment, yearly depreciation of facilities or equipment, and management's salaries and benefits. Fixed costs tend not to change with increases or decreases in production. In other words, even if your company increases production by 15 percent, the fixed costs will generally remain the same.

Variable Costs

Variable costs are expenses that change proportionally with increases or decreases in production. For example, if your company needs to increase production 5 percent, then variable costs like labor, materials, and energy costs will also increase by about 5 percent. An increase in production, after all, means you will need to buy more materials, hire more labor, and pay more energy costs.

Semivariable Costs

Semivariable costs are those expenses that fluctuate with production but not in direct proportion to production. For example, if you need to temporarily increase production by 5 percent to complete a project, you may need to pay your current hourly employees overtime at 1.5 times their normal rate. Also, if production increases 5 percent, the costs to repair your equipment may increase 15 percent. On the other hand, higher volume often means lower prices on materials, causing these costs to be lower. The difference between variable and semivariable costs is how they fluctuate with production. Variable costs rise and fall in step with production, while semivariable costs rise and fall in ways that are not in step with production.

For the most part, you should not lose any sleep over this three-part division of costs. The division of costs into fixed, variable, and semivariable costs is really only a convenient way for accountants to anticipate fluctuations that may occur as you take on a new project. Of course, the lines between these three categories are blurred. Mostly, the categories provide a starting point from which to identify which kinds of costs can be safely predicted and which need to be estimated.

Budgeting in Teams

Budgeting a project with a management team can be a real headache. The best way to talk over the budget with a team is to first decide whether your proposal needs a fixed or flexible budget. If the project has a clear conclusion date, your team will most likely need a fixed budget. If the proposal describes an ongoing program or operation, then your team may decide to develop a flexible budget with specific dates that identify when the budget will be reevaluated and adjusted.

Once you have decided what kind of budget you are creating, ask the team to list expenses. Then, sort these expenses into fixed, variable, and semivariable categories. For the variable and semivariable items, ask each team member write notes describing how these costs fluctuate with production. Where possible, also have team members provide examples describing how costs rise and fall with production. For instance, a team member might write, "Our suppliers charge us $30 per chip for 100 microchips. For each additional 100 chips, we receive a $1 per chip price reduction up to 500 chips. Therefore, if we buy 500 chips, they will each cost us $26 per chip."

Pulling together all these costs is a complicated process. Once all team members have submitted their projected costs, you can create a master file of costs that you will bring to your accountant. The explanations and notes provided by the team members will help you and the accountant devise an overall budget.

Inventing a Budget

Some clients, especially the federal government, will tell you exactly how they want you to break down project costs. In these cases, you should follow the guidelines they provide. If the clients do not provide any guidelines on the budget, however, you can start the budgeting process by dividing your costs into the following categories:

- Management and salaried labor
- Direct labor
- Indirect labor
- Facilities and equipment
- Direct materials
- Indirect materials
- Travel
- Communication
- Profit

Depending on whether you will include an itemized or nonitemized budget in your proposal, all of these categories may or may not be represented in the budget you submit with the proposal. Nevertheless, all costs for a project should be assigned to a category in your itemized budget. Let us look at these categories individually.

Management and Salaried Labor

As a fixed cost, the rates for management and salaried labor are calculated according to the percentage of their time that they are going to devote to the proposed project (see Figure 8.1). For example, let us say the project leader, who makes $120,000 per year, is going to spend 100 percent of his time on the project for six months. In the budget, you would identify him by name, write down his total yearly salary, and then multiply by .5 because he is spending half his time that year on the project. So, you would write down $60,000 for this manager on the budget sheet. Another manager who makes $120,000, however, is only going to devote a quarter of her time to the project over that six-month period. You would multiply her salary times .5 (for the 6 months) and .25 (for the quarter time) to come up with an amount of $15,000.

In most proposals, top managers are separately named in the budget and their costs are estimated individually. You may ask yourself, "How do I know how much time per week this manager is going to spend on this project?" After all, managers spend some weeks on one project and other weeks on another. Nevertheless, you should estimate how much time *on average* a manager is going to spend on each project. Use that average percentage to calculate how much that person's time will cost the client.

Costs for any other salaried personnel, like supervisors or team leaders, should be pooled together as *indirect labor.* These managers should not be listed by name in the proposal. Techniques for handling these managers in a budget are discussed later in this chapter with other indirect labor costs.

Other issues to keep in mind with management expenses are benefits, training, and any outside consultants or specialists that your managers will require to do their job. Benefits might include health insurance, vacation, and leave. The costs for these benefits should be calculated by your accountant. Training includes any special courses or learning tools your managers would need to successfully prepare for the project. Finally, if your managers need the help of outside consultants or specialists, you should build the costs of those consultants into this part of the budget. Consultants and specialists are usually compensated on a retainer or contract basis. When preparing the budget, you may need to designate a pool of cash out of which consultants or specialists will be paid if needed.

Direct Labor

Direct laborers are paid on an hourly basis. In a factory, direct laborers are the people assembling the product. In a store, the direct laborers are the people who run the cash registers, stock the shelves, and help people at the customer service desk, among other tasks.

Direct labor is calculated on an hourly basis. First you need to estimate how many hours an average hourly employee will spend on the project. Then, multiply those hours by the average amount your hourly employees make. Of course, employees are paid on a variety of different levels, especially in larger companies. Sometimes it helps to identify these levels in the budget and their respective pay scales. Then calculate the costs of the employees at each level separately (see Figure 8.1). For example, if you have ten "Level 3" employees working at an average $18.25 per hour, each hour worked by these ten employees will cost the client $182.50. In a project that is estimated to take 1000 hours, these employees will cost the client $182,500. Meanwhile, twenty "Level 2" employees working at an average $15.75 per hour for 1000 hours will cost $315,000.

If your direct labor requires any special training or you will need to hire new employees for a particular project, you should build those costs into this part of the budget. It might seem odd to charge a client for training your own employees, but that money needs to come from somewhere. If the client wants a special service, then they should be willing to pay for you to train and hire employees.

FIGURE 8.1

A Basic Budget Worksheet

			Total Cost
1. Management	Salary	Time Devoted to Project	
a. Project Manager (listed by name)			
Benefits			
b. Principal Managers and Supervisors (listed by name)			
Benefits			
c. Other Managers (indirect labor)			
d. Consultants			
e. Additional Management Training			
Total Management Costs			
2. Labor	Hours on Project	Cost per Hour	
a. Direct labor			
Level Three			
Level Two			
Level Three			
b. Indirect labor			
Level Three			
Level Two			
Level Three			
c. Hiring			
d. Training			
e. Labor Overhead			
Fringe Benefits Insurance Vacation Sick Leave Retirement			
Total Labor Costs			
3. Facilities and Equipment			Total Cost
Facilities			
a. Building Lease			

FIGURE 8.1

Continued

			Total Cost
b. Retooling Costs			
c. Depreciation of Facilities			
d. Insurance			
Equipment			
a. Computer Hardware and Software			
b. Tools			
c. Tables, Chairs, Desks			
d. Depreciation of Equipment			
Total Facilities and Equipment Costs			
5. Materials			
a. Direct Materials			
b. Indirect Materials			
c. Documentation (e.g., user manuals)			
Total Materials Costs			
6. Travel			
a. Air Travel (itemized by trip)			
b. By Car (estimated per mile)			
c. Lodging and Meals (per diem)			
Total Travel Costs			
7. Communication			
a. Phone			
b. Internet Provider			
c. Postage			
d. Documentation (e.g., reports)			
Total Communication Costs			
Pre-Profit Estimated Costs			
Profit or Fee			
Taxes			
Total Costs			

Direct labor also requires you to estimate *labor overhead*. Labor overhead includes fringe benefits, insurance, vacations, sick leave, and retirement. Overhead is typically calculated from standard formulas that an accountant will have available. Again, it is best to leave these calculations to the accountants.

Indirect Labor

Indirect laborers are the people who support the direct labor. Indirect laborers might include salaried supervisors, repair and janitorial services, and office and clerical support. In a budget, indirect labor is usually broken down into subcategories and charged on a salaried or hourly basis. The costs of salaried labor, especially for larger projects, is estimated similarly to the costs of management, meaning salaries are multiplied by the percentage of time these employees will spend on the project.

Hourly indirect labor is handled similarly to hourly direct labor. To calculate hourly indirect labor, estimate how many hours your repair staff, janitors, office, and clerical workers will devote to a particular project. In the budget, list these subcategories and their costs separately (see Figure 8.1).

As with direct labor, overhead should be calculated by an accountant and included with the costs for indirect labor.

Facilities and Equipment

The facilities and equipment section of the budget includes the fixed and semi-variable costs of the buildings and machinery that will be used, bought, or leased during the project. Facilities costs include any construction, renovation, or retooling of your factories or workspaces to accommodate the needs of the project. Also, expenses like insurance and maintenance supplies should be placed in this part of the budget.

Any machines, tools, office equipment, desks and chairs, computer hardware or software that are leased or purchased would also be handled under this part of the budget. The costs for larger pieces of equipment should be listed separately in the itemized budget, and smaller items should be grouped into subcategories (see Figure 8.1). In most cases, it is assumed that you (the bidder) will keep the purchased equipment and tools after the project is completed; nevertheless, you should clarify with the client who owns the equipment and tools after the project is completed.

In this section of the budget, you should also include the costs of depreciation for preexisting and purchased facilities and equipment that are used for the project. Depreciation is the lost value of facilities and equipment due to wear and aging during the project. Your company is entitled to charge that depreciation to the client. Depreciation is calculated according to a general formula that your accountant will have available. Like overhead, you should let the accountant handle these calculations for your budget.

Direct Materials

Direct materials include the materials that will make up the products or services you are developing for the client. For example, if you are proposing to produce a bike, direct materials might include metal for the frame, tires, tape for the handlebars, and so on. In an office environment, direct materials might include paper and supplies that go into the production of reports, manuals, videotapes, or CD-ROMs. In construction, direct materials might include lumber, fabric, pipes, or windows. Essentially, direct materials are the items that will be the client's property or disposed of after the project is completed.

In your budget, you should list out the direct materials that will go into the products and services. Then multiply the costs of these direct materials by the amount of products you will produce (see Figure 8.1).

One feature of direct materials that is often forgotten is the *documentation* for the product. If your deliverables include a user manual or Web site, make sure you include those costs in the direct materials part of the budget.

Indirect Materials

Indirect materials are the items that are used to turn direct materials into the product. For instance, cleaning supplies or lubricants for machinery are indirect material costs, because they are materials that are used while producing the product for the client. In an office, sometimes supplies like paper, pens, pencils, staplers, toner for the copy machine are put in this indirect materials category (see Figure 8.1).

The section handling indirect materials is often the forgotten part of a budget, and many companies have lost money because the indirect materials were not included. Items like paper, staples, and toner might sound like small things until you realize that these small things add up quickly, eating away your profit.

Travel

Travel costs are often hard to estimate accurately, especially airline travel costs. If you expect to travel for training, supervision, or meetings with the clients, you should build these travel costs into the budget. For travel by air, estimate how many trips will be needed. Then, contact a nationally recognized airline and ask their standard business rate for travel to and from the places you will need to travel. Avoid using an airline's sale prices to estimate travel costs, because the prices often increase before you need to fly.

Travel by train or bus is a bit easier to estimate because the rates do not fluctuate as wildly as airline rates. When estimating these costs, call up the bus or train company and ask for their standard business rate for travel to and from the places you will need to travel. Then, enter those total costs in the budget.

Travel by your car or your company's car is charged by the mile. Most organizations have a set rate for reimbursing mileage. Otherwise, the U.S. government publishes a standard rate that is a low but widely accepted figure. When you estimate the mileage for a project, make a generous estimate of how many miles you or your colleagues might be asked to travel during the project, keeping in mind that your actual mileage usually ends up higher than estimated mileage from Point A to Point B. Then, multiply those miles by the per-mile rate provided by your organization or the government. If you plan on renting cars, you should only plan to charge the clients the cost of the rental and the gas. With rental cars, you should not charge mileage.

Finally, if you need to stay at any hotels or other kinds of short-term lodgings, make sure you build those costs into the budget under travel. Again, to estimate these costs, call up the major hotel near the place you might stay. Ask for their standard *rack rate* for a night. The rack rate is usually higher than the rate they actually charge their guests, but this rate can be documented for the client. If you end up staying at the hotel for less than the standard room rate, you can use the savings to offset travel costs, which are usually more than you expected.

Communication

Another hidden project expense is communication costs. Almost certainly, you are going to be in contact with the client by phone, fax, letter, and the Internet. Even though these items may seem free to the average employee, they do cost your company money. Your accountant should be able to estimate how much a project's phone calls, faxes, postage, and Internet provider will cost your company. Otherwise, you may need to look at your records from past projects to help you estimate how much it will cost to communicate with the clients.

Communication also includes any costs to *disseminate* your findings. Sometimes, clients want any discoveries or breakthroughs sent out to journals, magazines, or universities. If the client wants you to communicate with others, build those costs into this part of the budget.

Profit

Finally, you or your company deserves to make a profit for providing your products or services to the clients. In proposals, profits are handled two ways. First, the profit can be built into the cost of the product or service. For example, let us say one unit of a company's product costs $50 to produce. The budget submitted to the client, however, charges $55 per unit. In this case, the bidder has chosen to use the product as the source of his profit, because each package/participant will yield $5 in profit.

The second way to handle profit, especially when you are providing the client with an itemized budget, is to simply include a "profit" line in the budget (see Figure 8.1). Indeed, if you are submitting a proposal to a government agency, you will often be required to disclose the profit you are making on the product or service. The profit then becomes an additional charge based on a flat rate or a percentage of the actual costs. An accountant should be able to help you develop a fair estimate of the profit you will receive.

There are advantages to both ways of calculating profit. Building the profit into the costs of the product or service is a hidden way to create a profit margin in a proposal. But you might find yourself defending the costs of your $70 per unit product when the client asks why it is so expensive to produce. The advantage of a separate profit line is that it clearly shows the clients how much money beyond the costs you would like to make for your products or services. However, the profit line is also an obvious addendum in a budget, making it a prime target for negotiation.

In most cases, profit is not expressed directly in the budget. Companies often consider their profit calculations to be "confidential" and are reluctant to submit them to the client. Also, some larger companies consider their profit margin nonnegotiable, even though everything in a proposal is ultimately open for negotiation.

Whichever way you choose to create a profit margin in your budget, you should remember two things when it comes to estimating your profit. First, your profit is the cushion in your proposal's budget. No matter how good you and your accountant are at estimating costs, the actual costs always end up being different. If they are higher, then those overruns will come out of your profit. If the costs are lower than you expected, you can add those savings to your overall profit. In the end, the profit can often be your safety net when your estimates are off. So, make sure the profit offers a sufficient cushion to handle overruns. Also, avoid cheating yourself out of a fair profit for your work. Sometimes bidders end up working for costs alone, leaving them nothing on which to grow their company.

Second, the profit is often the primary negotiating point between the client and bidder. Clients realize your company needs to make a profit; nevertheless, they are going to do their best to pay you as little as they can for your products and services. The profit in a budget is often the most obvious place to negotiate. After all, we may not be able to debate the costs of equipment or salaries, but profit is usually just a sum of cash calculated from a formula or flat rate. The clients will often ask you to reduce your profit percentage or your flat rate. It's up to you whether you will consider it.

Again, there is no substitute for a good accountant when you are developing a budget. An accountant can help you come up with the best way to express the profit in your budget.

Writing the Budget Rationale or Budget Section

In most cases, the budget should be written as a stand-alone section. As discussed in Chapter 7, some proposal writers prefer to sandwich a Budget section between the Qualifications section and the conclusion. Other proposal writers prefer to concisely mention the bottom-line costs of the project in the conclusion. Then, they move the larger discussion of the budget, a "budget rationale," to an appendix.

There are, of course, pros and cons to both approaches. A Budget section placed inside the body of the proposal ensures that the readers will look over your cost figures. On the other hand, these sections can run on for pages, bogging down the readers in numbers and perhaps causing them to forget the merits of your project. Placing the budget and a budget rationale in the appendix is a good way to avoid these problems. However, once in awhile, clients will complain that the budget is being "hidden" in the appendix.

Wherever you choose to include the budget, you should think of it as an argument that stands on its own. It is usually not sufficient to just say, "Here is our budget," as though the table of expenses speaks for itself. Rather, you should explain the reasoning used to come up with your figures.

Like any other section in a proposal, the Budget section or rationale has an opening, body, and conclusion. The opening paragraph identifies the subject of the section (the budget) and the purpose of the section (to present and discuss the costs of the project). It should also include a main point that the Budget section will prove. For example, you might claim, "By keeping expenses low, we offer the most efficient fabrication services in this industry." This kind of claim will focus your discussion of the budget, giving the section something to prove.

The body of the Budget section backs up that claim with a table of expenses and explanatory remarks that highlight the important parts of the budget. The aim of this budget rationale is to anticipate some of the readers' questions about the costs. Most clients are not as familiar with equipment, facilities, and materials as the bidders. So, a little explanation can go a long way toward helping the readers feel confident about the cost of the project. A table of budget figures like the one shown in Figure 8.1 is the heart of a Budget section or rationale. Your discussion of the budget should refer to specific lines in the budget table, at times illustrating how and why the figures were calculated in a particular way. Something to be avoided is simply dumping the budget table into an appendix with no explanatory information. Each larger section of the budget should receive at least one small paragraph of discussion.

The closing of a Budget section or rationale should simply restate the main point you made in the opening paragraph. The closing, usually only a sentence or two, is designed to round off the section and reinforce the soundness of your cost estimates.

As mentioned in Chapter 7, you should suppress any urges to be apologetic or defensive about the costs of your proposal. The budget is where you need to sound most confident. Otherwise, the readers will doubt the soundness of your figures, or they will detect a place where they can negotiate from a position of strength. The best approach is to just discuss the budget in a straight-forward way.

The Budget for the Earl Grey Proposal

The RFP from Earl Grey stated, "At this stage, exact cost estimates are not expected; however, pre-proposals should include a cost estimate. Earl Grey will negotiate for a final fee with the firm that submits the most feasible final proposal." Lisa

Miller knew this statement meant that Earl Grey was simply looking for a general idea of how much the project would cost. In the conclusion of her proposal, she would mention a bottom-line figure. However, she also wanted to include a non-itemized budget that would highlight some of the major expenses of the project.

With her team of engineers, Lisa went over the project as described in her Plan section. She had the engineers estimate the costs involved with their part of the project. She also asked them to break the costs down into fixed, variable, and semivariable costs to help her and the in-house accountant at Insight Systems anticipate how costs might fluctuate with any alterations to the plan.

Later that week, Lisa worked with the accountant to draw up a rough budget for the project. Figure 8.2 shows the nonitemized budget table she placed in Appendix A. The figure also shows how she provided concise explanations of the costs of her proposal.

Lisa's budget includes an opening, body, and conclusion like any section in the body of the proposal. The opening explains the purpose of the section and offers some background information. The body explains the more significant items in the budget table. And the conclusion rounds out the budget discussion by reinforcing the main point of the proposal and offering contact information.

Of course, this budget section could have just as easily been placed in the body of the proposal. After all, this appendix offers a small discussion of the budget, and it is not overly distracting. Nevertheless, Lisa sensed that the two principal architects at Earl Grey (her proposal's primary readers) were mostly interested in the plan and a bottom-line cost. Lisa wanted to include a breakdown of the budget, but she also wanted to avoid distracting the readers from her plan. If Earl Grey accepted her pre-proposal, she would write up an itemized budget that would break down the costs into greater detail.

The advantage of including a stand-alone budget like the one Lisa wrote to Earl Grey is that it provided a self-contained argument. The readers would be able to consider the money issues separately from the solution Lisa described in the Plan section.

Last Word

It would be hard to underestimate the importance of the budget in a proposal. Consider how you go about purchasing any product. You closely evaluate the merits of the product and take its drawbacks into account. But invariably, the last thing you think about before buying is the price. The last question you need to answer is, "Do I feel as though this item is worth the asking price?" The more information you have about the product, the less you will hesitate to say yes or no.

Readers evaluate proposals in much the same way. They look over the whole proposal, but in the end it all comes down to the money. The more information the readers have about how the budget was developed, the more likely they are to make a firm decision about whether your proposed plan suits their needs.

FIGURE 8.2

A Non-Itemized Budget for the Earl Grey Proposal

Appendix A: Budget

At Insight Systems, we pride ourselves on developing low-cost solutions for managing limited office space. In this appendix, we would like to go over some of the major costs of the telecommuting plan discussed in this proposal. These figures are estimates, as you requested in your RFP. We will provide a fully itemized budget with a formal proposal. Table A offers a summary of our estimated costs for the Earl Grey project.

Table A: Budget Summary

Item	Cost
Management and labor	$ 35,982
Equipment rental and purchase	5,250
Hardware and software	30,482
Materials	10,340
Travel	1,298
Communications	700
Costs before profit	$84,052
Profit (10% of before profit costs)	8,405
Taxes (gross receipts)	4.854
Total Costs	$97,311

As shown in Table A, management and labor are our primary costs. These costs represent two full-time managers, three computer engineers, two carpenters, and an electrician who will all be committed full time to the Earl Grey project.

Hardware and software make up the other significant expense in our budget. Where possible, we will utilize Earl Grey's existing computer infrastructure. However, additional hardware and software will be needed to upgrade your current infrastructure and create a LAN server.

Finally, our estimates for materials are dependent on the amount of carpentry required to hardwire the LAN system into your current operations. Our materials estimate in Table A is based on similarly sized projects we have handled in the past.

Overall, you should find that these costs are a small investment in your company's infrastructure that will help you manage your limited office space while allowing you to maintain financial flexibility. If you have any questions about these figures, please call Lisa Miller at 1-800-555-3864 or e-mail her at lmiller@insight_systems.com.

CASE STUDY   **Money Issues**

John was assigned the task of working out the budget for the Elmdale Hill Merchants Association proposal. To this point, he was excited about the proposal, but he was worried about the costs involved with putting together a nonprofit organization. After all, even though his restaurant was successful, he knew he could not afford to commit too much money to a merchants association. He was rather sure the other business owners would feel the same way. In the end, John had a hunch that money was going to be the main obstacle to putting together the association.

John made an appointment with Gail Smithson, the CPA from Sanders and Associates who was assigned to their project. Gail ended up being more enthusiastic about the proposal than John expected. She pointed out that her firm did not compete directly with the mall or large chain stores; however, many of her clients owned small businesses within the city. If their clients went out of business, eventually Sanders and Associates would feel the losses in their own bottom line.

After going over the proposal with Gail, John said, "We're a bit stumped on the budget. Do we need to hire a special manager to run the merchants association? Do we need to rent some office space? What kind of supplies should we buy? It just seems like there are too many things to consider at this point, and it all costs money."

Gail smiled. "John, you're not going about this the right way. Let's start from the beginning. What exactly is the purpose of your proposal?"

"To create a merchants association." John replied.

"That might be the long-term goal," Gail said, "but the actual creation of the merchants association is at least a couple steps down the line. Look more closely at your plan. Which actions in this plan require money right now?"

John looked closely over their plan. He listed a few items that might need money:

- Copying costs and postage for survey, reports, and ballots
- Printing posters for the organizational meetings

- Purchasing refreshments for the organizational meetings.

He soon realized that Gail was right. The aim of the proposal was not to immediately put together the whole Elmdale Hill Merchants Association. Instead, its aim was to create the *steering committee* of volunteers that would organize the business owners and incorporate the association as a nonprofit. Therefore, the budget John needed to create should handle the expenses associated with the steering committee's initial activities.

"All right," Gail said, "How much money is this committee going to need to do its job? Don't worry about the budget for the merchants association. The steering committee can work out that budget once they have a better idea about what kind of association is best for Elmdale Hill."

Gail and John began working through some of the elements of a budget. Gail pulled out her standard budget worksheet that she used with all her clients. At first, using a budget sheet to handle such a small budget seemed like overkill to John. After all, as a volunteer effort, items like "management" and "overhead" were not applicable to their proposal's budget. Nevertheless, the budget sheet helped them identify costs that John didn't expect. For example, they determined how much money would be needed for postage to send all these surveys and a postage-paid return envelope. They calculated how much long-distance calls and faxes would cost. And, they thought about the gas money needed for committee members to visit other towns with successful merchant associations.

Gail's generic budget sheet teased out some expenses that John didn't anticipate. John had assumed that he, Karen, Thomas, and Sally would just cover some of those costs themselves. But, he soon saw that those costs were adding up to several hundred dollars. John began to worry again. For one thing, he realized, the steering committee was going to need some additional funds if they were going to really do anything. Certainly, they couldn't expect the members of the steering committee to just foot the bill out of their own pockets. Who would volunteer for something that cost them money?

After crunching the numbers for awhile, John and Gail wrote up a tentative budget and budget rationale, shown in Figure 8.3. The budget not only covered the expenses of the organizational meeting, it also created a pool of money from which the members of the steering committee could be reimbursed for their expenses. Any extra money left over from the initial budget could be used to defray the accounting fees involved in incorporating the merchants association as a nonprofit organization.

The budget ended up with a $740 bottom line. "Wow, that added up quick," John said.

"It always does," said Gail, "That's why many good ideas don't go anywhere. People don't want to think about the money issues. But if you hadn't worked out even this simple budget, you and the steering committee would have grown increasingly frustrated by the money you were spending out of your own pockets. There is a good chance your merchants association would have never even taken its first steps."

"But where is this money going to come from?" said John.

Gail leaned back and said, "I've been giving that issue some thought myself. A couple nonprofit organizations I worked with before have asked for a 'donation' from people attending the organizational meeting. Even a ten-dollar donation from each person who attends the organizational meeting would probably give you enough funds for the steering committee. Then, at the meeting, you can ask for further donations. In your cover letter for the proposal, tell the other merchants that the money will be used to create a small treasury to reimburse the members of the steering committee. Most people will probably pay for that."

"Good idea. If we can get eighty people to attend, we have the funds we need to get this project rolling."

John had not yet decided where the budget would appear in the proposal. It was a short budget and rationale, so creating a Budget section inside the body of the proposal would probably work just fine. Nevertheless, he thought they might just attach the budget rationale to the proposal as an appendix, so money issues would not sidetrack the attention of the readers. He wanted the proposal's primary readers to think about the benefits of forming a merchants association, not the minimal costs of doing so.

FIGURE 8.3
A Draft Budget for the Merchants Association Proposal

Operating Budget for the Steering Committee

At this point, we can only predict the expenses for the steering committee. These expenses will be modest, as shown in Table X. The steering committee needs funds to print surveys, reports, ballots, and posters. They will need postage to send out those materials and some funds to cover any long-distance calls to other merchants associations. Refreshments at the two organizational meetings will also be paid for out of the steering committee's budget.

To create a nominal budget for the steering committee, we are asking attendees at the initial organizational meeting on September 15 to donate $10. Any additional donations toward this effort will be accepted gratefully at that time, also.

(continued on page 159)

FIGURE 8.3
Continued

Table X: Steering Committee Budget

Item	Cost
Printing	
Survey	20.00
Report (survey results)	30.00
Report (steering committee)	30.00
Ballots	20.00
Posters	50.00
Communications	
Postage (surveys, reports, ballots)	280.00
Long-distance calls	100.00
Refreshments	
Drinks (2 organizational meetings)	40.00
Snacks (2 organizational meetings)	70.00
Travel	
By Car (32 cents a mile)	100.00
Total Costs	$740.00

The overall costs of incorporating a merchants association, according to Gail Smithson at Sanders and Associates, will run from $2000 to $4000, depending on the kind of merchants association we choose to create. We estimate that charter membership in the Elmdale Hill Merchant Association will cost each business about $150, but the actual cost will depend on the decisions of the steering committee and the number of business owners who are willing to participate.

Questions and Exercises

1. Using your own personal finances, divide your expenses into fixed, variable, and semivariable costs. List out these costs in a budget table in which you list yourself as management or labor (depending on whether you receive a salary or are paid hourly). Then, write a one-page budget rationale to your parents, spouse, or friend in which you justify the major expenses in your budget.

2. Find a proposal on the Internet or at your workplace that includes an itemized budget. Where does the budget appear in the proposal? How does the placement of the budget influence the reading of the whole proposal? How does

the budget itemize costs? Does the proposal include a rationale that explains parts of the budget to the readers?

3. Write a budget for a practice or real proposal. First, decide whether you need a fixed or flexible budget. Second, list out your major costs, dividing them into fixed, variable, and semivariable categories. Third, place these costs in a budget worksheet, breaking them down according to the larger categories described in this chapter. And finally, write a short budget rationale in which you lead the readers through the highlights of your budget.

4. Ask your local Small Business Association representative about the budget requirements for a business plan to start a new business. Ask the representative what kinds of information investors or banks need in order to consider lending money. When you are finished, report your findings to your class.

9 Writing With Style

Overview

This chapter discusses the use of stylistic techniques to clarify your writing while making it more persuasive. In this chapter, the following objectives will be met:

1. Discuss the importance of style in a proposal.
2. Define style and the role of style in writing.
3. Show how to use the plain style.
4. Show how to use the persuasive style.

Good Style Is a Choice, Not an Accident

To this point in this book, we have been talking about inventing and organizing the content of a proposal. In the remainder of this book, we will discuss the style and design of proposals. Mistakenly, some people believe that style and design are not important to their proposal. After all, they say, the content of the proposal is the stuff that counts. The rest is just window dressing.

Actually, style does more than dress up the content of your proposal. It expresses your company's attitude toward the work. Style also reflects your character by embodying the values, beliefs, and the relationship you want to share with the readers (Laib 1993, 21). In a word, style is about quality. Style is about your company's commitment to excellence and attention to detail.

All proposals have a style, whether or not that style was consciously developed by the writers. Consequently, when writers do not pay attention to style, a proposal typically exhibits an erratic style that annoys or confuses the readers. Have you ever read a text that just didn't feel right? More than likely, you were reacting to the erratic style used in the text.

Good style is a choice you can and should make. This chapter will discuss two types of style that are prevalent in proposals. The *plain style* involves writing strong sentences and paragraphs that express your ideas clearly to the readers. The *persuasive style* is used to motivate the readers by appealing to their emotions and values. Both the plain and persuasive styles have their place in any given proposal. The challenge is to balance these two styles in ways that will instruct the readers and move them to action.

What Is Style?

If you are like most people, style is a rather murky concept. Some documents just seem to have a good style, while others do not. Consequently, you may have come to believe that good style is something some people have from birth. Good style might even seem accidental. You aren't sure how it happened, but your co-workers tell you that something you wrote is very readable, even eloquent.

What is style? Style works at a few different levels in a proposal. On the sentence level, good style might involve choosing the right words or forming sentences that are easy to read. On the paragraph level, style could involve weaving sentences together in ways that emphasize your main points and lead the readers comfortably through your ideas. At the document level, style involves setting an appropriate tone and weaving themes into your work that appeal to your readers' emotions and values. In his book *Technical Writing Style*, Dan Jones defines style the following way:

> Style affects or influences almost all other elements of writing. Style is your choices of words, phrases, clauses, and sentences, and how you connect these sentences. Style is the unity and coherence of your paragraphs and larger segments. Style is your tone—your attitude toward your subject, your audience, and yourself—in what you write. Style is who you are and how you reflect who you are, intentionally or unintentionally, in what you write (3).

Style does more than make the content easier to read and more persuasive. In many ways, it illustrates your clear-headedness, your emphasis on quality, and your willingness to communicate and work with the readers.

Style is not embellishment or ornamentation. Some people mistakenly believe that style is the spice sprinkled over a proposal to make the content more palatable to the readers. These writers throw in some extra adjectives and an occasional metaphor to perk up the bland parts of the proposal. But, just as spices are most flavorful when they are cooked into food, style needs to be carefully worked into the proposal. Indeed, a proposal that uses stylistic devices to embellish the content is merely hinting to the readers that the proposal lacks substance. Style enhances and amplifies content, but it should never be used to artificially embellish or hide a lack of content.

Classical rhetoricians like Cicero and Augustine discussed style in three levels: plain style, middle style, and grand style. The plain style is for instruction and demonstration, allowing the writer to lay out the facts or describe something in simple terms. The middle style is for persuading people to take action. When using the middle style, the writer highlights the benefits of taking action or doing something a particular way. The grand style is for motivating people to do something they already know they should do. For example, Winston Churchill, Martin Luther King, Jr., and John F. Kennedy regularly used the grand style to motivate their listeners to do what was right, even if people were reluctant to do it.

In proposals, there is little opportunity to use the grand style, because they tend to focus on instructing and persuading the readers. Proposals that use the grand style often seem too fanatical and excessive. So, in this chapter we will concentrate on using the plain and persuasive styles in proposals. A proposal that properly combines the plain and persuasive style will be both informative and moving for the readers.

Writing Plain Sentences

In a proposal, the plain style tends to be used when the writers need to instruct the readers about a situation or process. Specifically, the plain style is used mostly in the Situation section, where you are describing a problem or opportunity for the readers, and the Qualifications section, where you are describing your background and experience. In some cases, the Plan section might also be written in plain style, especially when your plan is rather straightforward.

As a student, you were more than likely advised to "write clearly" or "write in concrete language" as though simply making up your mind to write clearly or concretely was all it took. In reality, writing plainly is a skill that requires practice and concentration. Fortunately, once a few simple guidelines have been learned and mastered, style writing will soon become a natural strength in your writing.

To start, let us consider the parts of a basic sentence. From your grammar classes, you learned that a sentence typically has three main parts: a subject, a verb, and a comment. The subject is what the sentence is about. The verb is what the subject is doing. And, the comment says something about the subject. For example, consider these three variations of the same sentence.

Subject	Verb	Comment
The Institute	**provides**	**the government with accurate crime statistics.**

Subject	Verb	Comment
The government	**is provided**	**with accurate crime statistics by the Institute.**

Subject	Verb	Comment
Crime statistics	**were provided**	**to the government by the Institute.**

The content in these sentences has not changed. Nevertheless, the emphasis in each sentence changes as we replace the subject slot with different nouns. Sentence A is *about* the "Institute." Sentence B is *about* the "government." Sentence C is *about* the "crime statistics." By changing the subject of the sentence, we essentially shift the focus of the sentence, drawing our readers' attention to different issues.

This simple understanding of the different parts of a sentence is the basis for eight guidelines that can be used to write plainer sentences in proposals, as shown in Figure 9.1. We will discuss these sentence guidelines in more detail in the following pages.

FIGURE 9.1
Sentence Guidelines

Guideline 1: The subject should be what the sentence is about.

Guideline 2: Make the "doer" the subject. Subject is the "doer."

Guideline 3: State the action in the verb.

Guideline 4: Put the subject early in the sentence.

Guideline 5: Eliminate nominalizations.

Guideline 6: Avoid excessive prepositional phrases.

Guideline 7: Eliminate redundancy.

Guideline 8: Make sentences "breathing length."

Guideline 1: The subject should be what the sentence is about

At a very simple level, weak style often occurs when the readers cannot easily identify the subject of the sentence. Or, the subject of the sentence is not what the sentence is about. For example, what is the subject of the following sentence?

1. Ten months after the Hartford Project began in which a team of our experts conducted close observations of management actions, our final conclusion is that the scarcity of monetary funds is at the basis of the inability of Hartford Industries to appropriate resources to essential projects that have the greatest necessity.

This sentence is difficult to read for a variety of reasons, but the most significant problem is the lack of a clear subject. What is this sentence about? The word *conclusion* is currently in the subject position, but the sentence might also be about the *experts*, the *Hartford Project*, or *scarcity of monetary funds*. Indeed, many other nouns and nounlike words also seem to be competing to be the subject of the sentence, such as *observations, management, structure, conclusion, inability*, and *company*. These nouns and nounlike words bombard the readers with potential subjects, undermining their efforts to identify what the sentence is about.

When the sentence is restructured around *experts* or *scarcity*, most readers will find it easier to understand:

1a. Ten months after the Hartford Project began, our experts have concluded through close observations of management actions that the scarcity of monetary funds is at the basis of the inability of Hartford Industries to appropriate resources to essential projects that have the greatest necessity.

1b. The scarcity of monetary funds, our experts have concluded through close observations of management actions ten months after the Hartford

Project began, is at the basis of the inability of Hartford Industries to appropriate resources to essential projects that have the greatest necessity.

Both of these sentences are still rather difficult to read. Nevertheless, they are easier to read than the original because the noun occupying the subject slot is the focus of the sentence—that is, what the sentence is about. We will return to this sentence about Hartford Industries after discussing the other guidelines for plain style.

Guideline 2: Make the "doer" the subject

Guideline 3: State the action in the verb

In your opinion, which revision of sentence 1 above is easier to read? Most people would point to sentence 1a, in which *experts* is in the subject slot. Why? In sentence 1a, the experts are actually doing something. In sentence 1b, *scarcity* is an inactive noun that is not doing anything. Whereas experts take action, scarcity is merely something that happens.

Guidelines 2 and 3 reflect the tendency of readers to focus on who or what is doing something in a sentence. To illustrate, which of these sentences is easier to read?

2a. On Saturday morning, the paperwork was completed in a timely fashion by Jim.

2b. On Saturday morning, Jim completed the paperwork in a timely fashion.

Most people would say sentence 2b is easier to read because Jim, the subject of the sentence, is actually doing something, while the paperwork in sentence 2a is inactive. The active person or thing usually makes the best subject of the sentence.

Similarly, Guideline 3 states that the verb should contain the action in the sentence. Once you have determined who or what is doing something, ask yourself what that person or thing is actually doing. Find the action in the sentence and make it the verb. For example, consider these sentences:

3a. The detective investigated the loss of the payroll.

3b. The detective conducted an investigation into the loss of the payroll.

3c. The detective is the person who is conducting an investigation of the loss of the payroll.

Sentence 3a is easier to understand because the action of the sentence is expressed in the verb. Sentences 3b and 3c are increasingly more difficult to understand, because the action, *investigate,* is further removed from the verb slot of the sentence.

Guideline 4: Put the subject early in the sentence

Subconsciously, readers start every sentence looking for the subject. The subject anchors the sentence, because it tells the reader what the sentence is about. So, if the subject is buried somewhere in the middle of the sentence, the readers will have greater difficulty finding it, and the sentence will be harder to read. To illustrate, consider these two sentences:

4a. If deciduous and evergreen trees experience yet another year of drought like the one observed in 1997, the entire Sandia Mountain ecosystem will be heavily damaged.

4b. The entire Sandia Mountain ecosystem will be heavily damaged if deciduous and evergreen trees experience yet another year of drought like the one observed in 1997.

The problem with sentence 4a is that it forces the readers to hold all those details (i.e., trees, drought, 1997) in short-term memory before the sentence identifies its subject. Readers almost feel a sense of relief when they find the subject, because they cannot figure out what the sentence is about until they locate the subject. Quite differently, sentence 4b tells the readers what the sentence is about up front. With the subject early in the sentence, the readers immediately know how to connect the comment with the subject.

Of course, introductory or transitional phrases do not always signal weak style. But when these phrases are used, they should be short and to the point. Longer introductory phrases should be moved to the end of the sentence.

Guideline 5: Eliminate nominalizations

Nominalizations are perfectly good verbs and adjectives that have been turned into awkward nouns. For example, look at these sentences:

5a. Management has an expectation that the project will meet the deadline.

5b. Management expects the project to meet the deadline.

In sentence 5a *expectation* is a nominalization. Here, the perfectly good verb *expect* is being used as a noun. After turning the nominalization into a verb, sentence 5b is not only shorter than sentence 5a, it also has more energy because the verb *expect* is now an action verb.

Consider these two sentences:

6a. Our discussion about the matter allowed us to make a decision on the acquisition of the new x-ray machine.

6b. We discussed the matter and decided to acquire the new x-ray machine.

Sentence 6a includes three nominalizations *discussion, decision,* and *acquisition,* making the sentence hard to understand. Sentence 6b turns all three of these nominalizations into verbs, making the sentence much easier to understand. An additional benefit to changing nominalizations into verbs is the energy added to the sentence. Nouns tend to feel inert to the readers, while verbs tend to add action and energy.

Why do writers use nominalizations in the first place? We use nominalizations for two reasons. First, humans generally think in nouns, so our first drafts are often filled with nominalizations, which are nouns. While revising, an effective writer will turn those first-draft nominalizations into action verbs. Second, some people mistakenly believe that using nominalizations makes their writing sound more formal or important. In reality, though, nominalizations only make sentences harder to read. The best way to sound important is to write sentences that readers understand.

Guideline 6: Avoid excessive prepositional phrases

Prepositional phrases are necessary in writing, but they are often overused in ways that make writing too long and too tedious. Prepositional phrases follow prepositions (e.g., in, of, by, about, over, under) and they are used to modify nouns. For example in the sentence "Our house by the lake in Minnesota is lovely," the phrases *by the lake* and *in Minnesota* are both prepositional phrases. They modify the nouns *house* and *lake*.

Prepositional phrases are fine when used in moderation, but they are problematic when used in excess. For example, in sentence 7a the prepositions have been italicized and prepositional phrases underlined. Sentence 7b is the same sentence with fewer prepositional phrases:

7a. The decline *in* the number *of* businesses owned *by* locals in the town of Artesia is a demonstration *of* the increasing hardship faced *in* rural communities *in* the southwest.

7b. Artesia's declining number of locally owned businesses demonstrates the increased hardship faced by southwestern rural communities.

You should never feel obligated to eliminate all the prepositional phrases in a sentence. Rather, look for places where prepositional phrases are chained together in long sequences. Then, try to condense the sentence by turning some of the prepositional phrases into adjectives. In sentence 7b, for example, the phrase *in the town of Artesia* was reduced to the adjective *Artesia's*. The phrases *in rural communities in the southwest* were reduced to *by southwestern rural communities*. The resulting sentence 7b is much shorter and easier to read.

Guideline 7: Eliminate redundancy

In our efforts to stress our points, we often use redundant phrasing. For example, we might write *unruly mob,* as though some mobs are orderly, or we might talk about *active participants,* as though someone can participate without doing anything. Sometimes buzzwords and jargon lead to redundancies like, "We should collaborate together as a team" or "Empirical observations will provide a new understanding of the subject." In some cases, we might use a synonym to modify a synonym by saying something like, "We suggested important, significant changes."

Redundancies should be eliminated because they use two words to do the work of one. As a result, the readers need to work twice as hard to understand one basic idea.

Guideline 8: Make sentences "breathing length"

A sentence is a statement designed to be spoken in one breath. When a text is read out loud, the period at the end of each sentence is the reader's signal to breathe. Of course, when reading silently, we do not actually breathe when we see a period. Nevertheless, readers do take a mental pause at the end of each sentence. A sentence that runs on and on forces readers to mentally hold their breaths. By the end of an especially long sentence, readers are more concerned about getting through it than deciphering it.

The best way to think about sentence length is to imagine how long it takes to comfortably say a sentence out loud. If the written sentence is too long to say in one breath, it probably needs to be shortened or cut into two sentences. After all, you don't want to asphyxiate your readers. On the other hand, if the sentence is very short, perhaps it needs to be combined with one of its neighbors to make it a more comfortable breathing length. You also want to avoid hyperventilating the readers with a string of short sentences.

A Simple Method for Writing Plainer Sentences

To sum up the eight sentence guidelines, here is a process for writing plainer sentences. First, write out your draft as usual, not paying too much attention to the style. Then, as you revise, identify difficult sentences and apply the six steps shown in Figure 9.2.[1]

With these six steps in mind, let us revisit sentence 1, the example of weak style offered at the beginning of our discussion of plain style.

Original

1. Ten months after the Hartford Project began in which a team of our experts conducted close observations of management decisions, our final conclusion is that the scarcity of monetary funds is at the basis of the inability of Hartford Industries to appropriate resources to essential projects that have the greatest necessity.

Revision

1a. After completing the ten-month Hartford Project, our experts concluded that the Hartford Industries' budget shortfalls have limited support for priority projects.

---

[1] In his book, *Revising Business Prose,* Richard Lanham offers a simpler technique that he calls the "paramedic method." His method is less comprehensive than the one shown here, but it works well also.

FIGURE 9.2
Six Steps to Plainer Writing

1. Identify who or what the sentence is about.
2. Turn that who or what into the subject, and then move the subject to an early place in the sentence.
3. Identify what the subject is doing, and move that action into the verb slot.
4. Eliminate prepositional phrases, where appropriate, by turning them into adjectives.
5. Eliminate unnecessary nominalizations and redundancies.
6. Shorten, lengthen, combine, or divide sentences to make them breathing length.

In the revision, the subject (our experts) was moved into the subject slot, and then it was moved to an early place in the sentence. Then, the action of the sentence (concluded) was moved into the verb slot. Prepositional phrases like *to appropriate resources to essential projects* were turned into adjectives. Nominalizations like *conclusion* and *necessity* were turned into verbs or adjectives. And finally, the sentence was shortened to breathing length. The resulting sentence still offers the same content to the readers—just more plainly.

Writing Plain Paragraphs

As with sentences, some rather simple methods are available to help you write plainer paragraphs in proposals.

The Elements of a Paragraph

Paragraphs tend to include four kinds of sentences: a transition sentence, a topic sentence, a support sentence, and a point sentence. Each of these sentences plays a different role in the paragraph.

Transition Sentence

The purpose of a transition sentence is to make a smooth bridge from the previous paragraph to the present paragraph. For example, a transitional sentence might state "With these facts in mind, let us consider the current opportunity available." The *facts* mentioned were explained in the previous paragraph. By referring back to the previous paragraph, the transition sentence provides a smooth bridge into the new paragraph. Most paragraphs, however, do not need a transition sentence. These kinds of sentences are typically used when the new paragraph handles a significantly different topic than the previous paragraph.

Topic Sentence

The topic sentence is the claim or statement that the rest of the paragraph is going to prove or support. In a proposal, topic sentences typically appear in the first or second sentence of each paragraph. They are placed up front in each paragraph for two reasons. First, the topic sentence sets a goal for the paragraph to reach by telling the readers the claim you are trying to prove. Then, the remainder of the paragraph proves that claim with facts, examples, and reasoning. If the topic sentence appears at the end of the paragraph, the readers are forced to rethink all the details in the paragraph now that they know what the paragraph was trying to prove. For most readers, all that mental backtracking is a bit annoying.

The second reason for putting the topic sentence up front is that it is the most important sentence in any given paragraph. Since readers tend to pay the greatest attention to the beginning of a paragraph, placing the topic sentence up front guarantees they will read it closely. Likewise, scanning readers tend to concentrate on the beginning of each paragraph. If the topic sentence is buried in the middle or at the end of the paragraph, they will miss it.

Support Sentences

The support in the body of the paragraph can come in many forms. In Chapter 4, you learned that there are two ways to argue logically (i.e., using reasoning and examples). Sentences that use reasoning tend to make if/then, cause/effect, better/worse, greater/lesser kinds of arguments for the readers. Meanwhile the use of examples illustrates points for the readers by showing them situations or items that support your claim in the topic sentence. For the most part, sentences that contain reasoning and examples will make up the bulk of a paragraph's support sentences. Other support will come in the form of facts, data, definitions, and descriptions. In the end, support sentences are intended to prove the claim made in the paragraph's topic sentence.

Point Sentences

Point sentences usually restate the topic sentence at the end of the paragraph. They are used to reinforce the topic sentence by restating the paragraph's original claim in new words. Point sentences are especially useful in longer paragraphs where the readers may not fully remember the claim stated at the beginning of the paragraph. These sentences often start with transitional devices like *therefore, consequently,* or *in sum* to signal to the readers that the point of the paragraph is being restated. Point sentences are optional in paragraphs, and they should be used only occasionally when a particular claim needs to be reinforced for the readers. Too many point sentences will cause your proposal to sound too repetitious and even condescending to the readers.

Of these kinds of sentences, only the topic sentence and the support sentences are needed for a good paragraph. Transitional sentences and point sentences are useful in situations where bridges need to be made between paragraphs or specific points need to be reinforced.

Here are the four kinds of sentences used in a paragraph:

8a. How can we accomplish these five goals? (transition) Universities need to study their core mission to determine whether distance education is a viable alternative to the traditional classroom (topic sentence). If universities can maintain their current standards while moving their courses online, then distance education may provide a new medium through which nontraditional students can take classes and perhaps earn a degree (support). Utah State, for example, is reporting that students enrolled in their online courses have met or exceeded the expectations of their professors (support). On the other hand, if standards cannot be maintained, we may find ourselves returning to the traditional on-campus model of education (support). In the end, the ability to meet a university's core mission is the litmus test to measure whether distance education will work (point sentence).

8b. Universities need to study their core mission to determine whether distance education is a viable alternative to the traditional classroom (topic sentence). If universities can maintain their current standards while moving their courses online, then distance education may provide a new medium through which nontraditional students can take classes and perhaps earn a degree (support). Utah State, for example, is reporting that students enrolled in their online courses have met or exceeded the expectations of their professors (support). On the other hand, if standards cannot be maintained, we may find ourselves returning to the traditional on-campus model of education (support).

As you can see in paragraph 8b, a paragraph works fine without transition and point sentences. Nevertheless, they can make texts easier to read while amplifying important points.

Aligning Sentence Subjects in a Paragraph

Have you ever needed to stop reading a paragraph because each sentence seems to go off in a new direction? Have you ever run into a paragraph that actually feels bumpy as you read it? More than likely, the problem was a lack of alignment of the paragraph's sentence subjects. To illustrate, consider this paragraph:

9. The lack of technical knowledge about the electronic components in automobiles often leads car owners to be suspicious about the honesty of car mechanics. Although they might be fairly knowledgeable about the mechanical workings of their automobiles, car owners rarely understand the nature and scope of the electronic repairs needed in modern automobiles. For instance, the function and importance of a transmission in a car is generally well known to all car owners; but the wire harnesses and printed circuit boards that regulate the fuel

consumption and performance of their car are rarely familiar. <u>Repairs</u> for these electronic components can often run over 400 dollars—a large amount for a customer who cannot even visualize what a wire harness or printed circuit board looks like. In contrast, a <u>400-dollar charge</u> for the transmission on the family car, though distressing, is more readily understood and accepted.

There is nothing really wrong with this paragraph—it's just hard to read. Why? It is difficult to read because the subjects of the sentences change with each new sentence. Notice the underlined subjects of the sentences in this paragraph. These subjects are different, causing each sentence to feel like it is striking off in a new direction. As a result, each new sentence forces the readers to shift focus to concentrate on something new.

To avoid this bumpy, unfocused feeling, line up the subjects so each sentence in the paragraph stresses the same things. To line up subjects, first ask yourself what the paragraph is about. Then, restructure the sentences to align with that subject. Here is a revision of paragraph 9 that focuses on the "car owners" as subjects:

9a. Due to their lack of knowledge about electronics, some <u>car owners</u> are skeptical about the honesty of car mechanics when repairs involve electronic components. Most of our <u>customers</u> are fairly knowledgeable about the mechanical features of their automobiles, but <u>they</u> rarely understand the nature and scope of the electronic repairs needed in modern automobiles. For example, most <u>people</u> recognize the function and importance of a transmission in an automobile; but, the average <u>person</u> knows very little about the wire harnesses and printed circuit boards that regulate the fuel consumption and performance of their car. So, for most of our customers, a <u>400-dollar repair</u> for these electronic components seems like a large amount, especially when <u>these folks</u> cannot even visualize what a wire harness or printed circuit board looks like. In contrast, <u>most car owners</u> think a 400-dollar charge to fix the transmission on the family car, though distressing, is more acceptable.

In this revised paragraph, you should notice two things. First, the words *car owners* are not always the exact words used in the subject slot. Synonyms and pronouns should be used to add variety to the sentences. Second, not all the subjects need to be related to car owners. In the middle of the paragraph, for example, *400-dollar repair* is the subject of a sentence. This deviation from *car owners* is fine as long as the majority of the subjects in the paragraph are similar to each other. In other words, the paragraph will still sound focused, even though an occasional subject is not in alignment with the others.

Of course, the subjects of the paragraph could be aligned differently to stress something else in the paragraph. Here is another revision of paragraph 9 in which the focus of the paragraph is *repairs*.

9b. <u>Repairs</u> to electronic components often lead car owners, who lack knowledge about electronics, to doubt the honesty of car mechanics. The <u>nature and scope of these repairs</u> are usually beyond the understanding of most nonmechanics, unlike the typical mechanical repairs with which customers are more familiar. For instance, the <u>importance of fixing</u> the transmission in a car is readily apparent to most car owners, but adjustments to electronic components like wire harnesses and printed circuit boards are foreign to most customers—even though these electronic parts are crucial in regulating their car's fuel consumption and performance. So, <u>a repair</u> to these electronic components, which can cost 400 dollars, seems excessive, especially when the repair can't even be visualized by the customer. In contrast, a <u>400-dollar replacement</u> of the family car's transmission, though distressing, is more readily accepted.

In this paragraph, the subjects are aligned around words associated with repairs. Even though the subjects have been changed, the paragraph should still seem more focused than the original.

One important item you should notice is that paragraph 9a is easier for most people to read than paragraph 9b. Paragraph 9a is more readable because it has "doers" in the subject slots throughout the paragraph. In paragraph 9a, the car owners are active subjects, while in paragraph 9b the car repairs are inactive subjects. Much like sentences, the best subjects in a paragraph are people or things that are doing something.

The Given/New Method

Another way to write plain paragraphs is to use the *given/new method* to weave sentences together. Developed by Susan Haviland and Herbert Clark in 1974, the given/new method is based on the assumption that readers will always try to fit new information into what they already know. Therefore, every sentence in a paragraph should contain something the readers already know (i.e., the given) and something new that the readers do not know. To illustrate, consider these two paragraphs:

10a. Santa Fe is a beautiful place with surprises around every corner. Some artists choose to strike off into the mountains to paint, while others enjoy working in local studios.

10b. Santa Fe offers many beautiful places for artists to work, with surprises around every corner. Some artists choose to strike off into the mountains to paint, while others enjoy working in local studios.

Both of these examples are readable, but paragraph 10b is easier to read because the word *artists* appears in both sentences. Example 10a is a little harder to read, because there is nothing given that carries over from the first sentence to the second sentence.

Typically, the given information should appear early in the sentence and the new information should appear later in the sentence. Placed early in the sentence, the given information will provide a familiar anchor or context for the readers. Later in the sentence, the new information builds on that familiar ground. Consider this larger paragraph:

11. Recently, an art gallery exhibited the mysterious paintings of Irwin Fleminger, a modernist artist whose vast Mars-like landscapes contain cryptic human artifacts. One of Fleminger's paintings attracted the attention of some young school children who happened to be walking by. At first, the children laughed, pointing out some of the strange artifacts in the painting. Soon, though, the artifacts in the painting drew the students into a critical awareness of the painting, and they began to ask their bewildered teacher what the artifacts meant. Mysterious and beautiful, Fleminger's paintings have this effect on many people, not just school children.

In this paragraph, the beginning of each sentence provides something given, usually an idea, word, or phrase drawn from the previous sentence. Then, the comment of each sentence adds something new to that given information. By chaining together given and new information, the paragraph builds the readers' understanding gradually, adding a little more information with each sentence.

In some cases, however, the previous sentence does not offer a suitable subject for the sentence that follows it. In these cases, transitional phrases can be used to provide the readers given information in the beginning of the sentence. To illustrate,

12. This public relations effort will strengthen Gentec's relationship with leaders of the community. <u>With this new relationship in place</u>, the details of the project can be negotiated with terms that are fair to both parties.

In this sentence, the given information in the second sentence appears in the transitional phrase, not the subject. Transitional phrases are a good place to include given information when the subject cannot be drawn from the previous sentence.

To sum up at this point, there are two primary methods available for developing plain paragraphs: (1) aligning the subjects of the sentences and (2) using the given/new method to weave the sentences together. Both methods are useful in proposal writing and should be used interchangeably. In some cases, both methods can be employed in the same paragraph as the writer uses various techniques to weave the paragraph into a coherent whole.

When Is It Appropriate to Use Passive Voice?

Before discussing the elements of persuasive style, we should expose one important bogie monster as a fraud. Since childhood, you have probably been warned against using passive voice. In fact, you might even remember various people decreeing that passive voice was off-limits, period. It's bad for you, they said, never use it.

Indeed, passive voice can be problematic when it is misused. One problem is that passive voice removes the doer from the sentence. For example, consider this passive sentence and its active counterpart:

13a. The door was closed to ensure privacy. (passive)

13b. Frank Roberts closed the door to ensure privacy. (active)

Written in passive voice, sentence 13a lacks a doer. The subject of the sentence, the door, is being acted upon, but it's not really doing anything. The second reason passive voice can be problematic is the use of an extra *be* verb (i.e., is, was, were, has been). The extra verb might slow the readers down a bit.

Despite dire warnings about passive voice, it does have a place in proposals, especially highly technical or scientific proposals. Either of these conditions makes a passive sentence appropriate:

- The readers do not need to know who or what is doing something in the sentence.
- The subject of the sentence is what the sentence is about.

For example, in Sentence 13a, the person who closed the door might be unknown or irrelevant to the readers. Is it important that we know that *Frank Roberts* closed the door? Or, do we simply need to know the door was closed? If the door is what the sentence is about and who closed the door is not important, then the passive is fine.

Consider these other examples of passive sentences:

14a. The shuttle bus will be driven to local care facilities to provide seniors with shopping opportunities (passive).

14b. Jane Chavez will drive the shuttle bus to local care facilities to provide seniors with shopping opportunities (active).

15a. The telescope was moved to the Orion system to observe the newly discovered nebula (passive).

15b. Our graduate assistant, Mary Stewart, moved the telescope to the Orion system to observe the newly discovered nebula (active).

In both these sets of sentences, the passive sentence may be more appropriate, unless there is a special reason Jane Chavez or Mary Stewart need to be singled out for special consideration.

When developing a focused paragraph, passive sentences can often help you align the subjects and use given/new strategies. For example, does the use of passive voice in the following paragraph help make the paragraph more readable?

16a. The merger between Brown and Smith will be completed by May 2004. Initially, Smith's key managers will be moved into Brown's headquarters. Then, other Smith employees will be gradually worked into the Brown hierarchy to eliminate any redundancies. During the merger process, employees at both companies will be offered all possible accommodations to help them through the uncertain times created by the merger.

16b. Brown and Smith will complete their merger in May 2004. Initially, Bill's Trucking Service will move the offices of key managers at Smith into Brown's headquarters. Brown's human resources manager will then gradually move Smith's other employees into the Brown hierarchy to eliminate any redundancies. During the merger, vice presidents, human resources agents, and managers at all levels will offer accommodations to employees at both companies to help them through the uncertain times created by the merger.

Most people would find Paragraph 16a more readable because it uses passive voice to put the emphasis on *employees*. Paragraph 16b is harder to read because it includes irrelevant doers, like Bill's Trucking Service, and it keeps changing the subjects of the sentences, causing the paragraph to seem unfocused.

In scientific and technical proposals, the passive voice is often the norm because *who* will be doing *what* is not always predictable. For example, in Sentence 15b, we might not be able to predict in our proposal that Mary Stewart will actually be the person adjusting the telescope on a given evening. More than likely, all we can confidently say is that *someone* at the observatory will move the telescope on a particular day. So, the passive is used because *who* moves the telescope is not important. The fact that the telescope will be moved, on the other hand, is important.

Used properly, passive voice can be a helpful tool in your efforts to write plain sentences and paragraphs. Passive voice is misused when the readers are left wondering who or what is doing the action in the sentence. In these cases, the sentence should be restructured to put the doer in the subject slot of the sentence.

Persuasive Style

In Chapter 4, we discussed the importance of using logic, character, and emotion to persuade readers. Persuasive style uses character and emotion to motivate readers to say yes to your ideas. The persuasive style is designed to move them to take action, while the plain style is particularly useful for describing things or instructing the readers.

When used properly, the persuasive style can add emphasis, energy, color, and feeling to your writing. On the other hand, when used improperly, persuasive style can sound excessive to readers. There is a fine line between persuading the readers with powerful imagery and emotion, and turning them off with the "hard sell." Persuasive style is best used at strategic points in a proposal when you are trying to emphasize or amplify specific ideas. As a rule of thumb, this style is best used in areas of the proposal where you expect the readers to make decisions.

There are, of course, many ways to be persuasive or amplify your arguments. In proposals, though, the following four persuasion techniques are helpful toward giving your writing more impact:

- Elevating the tone
- Using similes and analogies
- Using metaphors
- Changing the pace

Let us consider each of these techniques separately.

Elevating the Tone

Tone is essentially the resonance or pitch that the readers will "hear" as they are looking over your proposal. Most people read proposals silently to themselves, but all readers have an inner voice that vocalizes the words as they move from sentence to sentence. By paying attention to tone, you can influence the readers' inner voice in ways that persuade them to read the proposal with a specific emotion or attitude. You can also use tone to establish a sense of character that will reassure the readers about your, your team's, or your company's credibility. Tone puts a human face on the text, if only momentarily, to appeal to the readers on an emotional and character level.

Writers will often choose to elevate the tone at strategic places in the proposal, like introductions, openings, closings, and conclusions. For the most part, the plain style, which is used in the bulk of the proposal, sets a rather neutral, professional tone. As you near the closing paragraph of larger sections or the conclusion of the proposal, however, you should gradually "elevate" the tone of your writing to express a particular emotion or character. Effective public speakers use this tone elevation technique all the time. Their speech may start out with a good amount of energy, but it soon settles into a rather plain style. When the speaker nears important transition points or the conclusion, he elevates the tone. Hearing this elevated tone, the listeners know the speaker is nearing an important point, so they listen more closely.

One easy way to elevate tone in written texts is to first decide what feelings of emotion or character you want to heighten at important points in the proposal. Then, map out those feelings on a piece of paper. For example, let us say we want to convey a sense of excitement as the readers are looking over the proposal. We would first put the word 'excitement' in the middle of a sheet of paper. Then, as shown in Figure 9.3, we would map out the feelings associated with that emotion.

FIGURE 9.3

Mapping a Tone that Shows Emotion

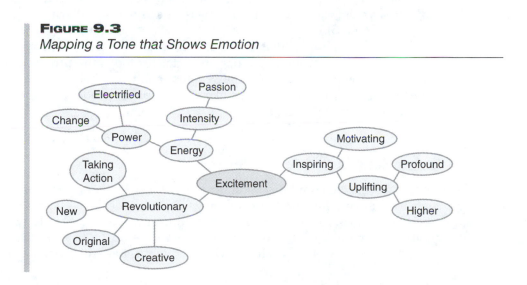

FIGURE 9.4

Mapping a Tone that Shows Character

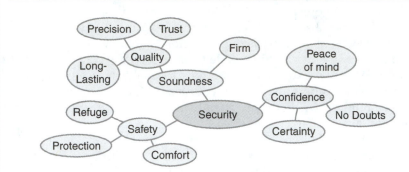

To put this tone of excitement in your proposal, weave these words into the text at strategic moments. Subconsciously, the readers will detect this elevated tone in your work, and their inner voice will begin reinforcing the sense of excitement you are trying to convey.

Similarly, if you want to add in a particular sense of character, map out the words associated with that character trait. For instance, let us say you want your proposal to convey a sense of 'security.' A map around security might look like the diagram in Figure 9.4.

If you weave these words associated with *security* into strategic places in the proposals, the readers will perceive the sense of security that you are trying to convey.

The best places to weave in specific tones are in the introduction and conclusion of the proposal and the openings and closings of its larger sections. These are the places where the readers tend to make decisions about whether or not to accept the proposal.

Of course, writers can overdo the use of a particular tone. To avoid this problem, decide on one emotion and one character for the entire proposal. Multiple emotional or character tones will only confuse and overwhelm the readers. Also, use these words only sparingly. Just like adding spices to food, you want to avoid overseasoning your proposal.

Using Similes and Analogies

Similes and analogies are rhetorical devices that help writers define difficult concepts by comparing them to simpler things. For example, let us say a proposal we are writing needs to describe a "semiconductor wafer" to people who know almost nothing about semiconductors. A simile could be used to describe the wafer this way: "A semiconductor wafer is like a miniature Manhattan Island crammed on a silicon disk that is only three inches wide." In this case, the simile ("X is like Y") not only clarifies the concept by putting it into familiar terms, it also creates a visual image that helps the readers understand the complexity of the semiconductor wafer.

Analogies are also a good way to help the readers visualize difficult concepts. An analogy follows the structure "A is to B as X is to Y." For example, a medical analogy might be, "Like police keeping order in a city, white blood cells seek to control viruses in the body." In this case, both parts of the analogy are working in parallel. *Police* is equivalent to *white blood cells* and *keeping order in the city* is equivalent to *control viruses in the body.*

Similes and analogies are primarily used to provide the readers with a quick, visual understanding of something unfamiliar by comparing it to something familiar. A good rule of thumb is to reduce the use of similes and analogies when the readers are experts. Use them more often when the readers are less experienced with your subject.

Using Metaphors

Though comparable to similes and analogies, metaphors work at a deeper level in a proposal. Specifically, metaphors are used to create or reinforce a particular perspective that you want the readers to adopt toward your subject or ideas. For example, a popular metaphor in Western medicine is the "war on cancer." If we were writing a proposal to request funding on a cancer-related subject, we might weave this metaphor into our proposal. We could talk about *battles with cancer cells, new weapons against cancer,* and the *front line of cancer research.* By employing this metaphor throughout the proposal, we would reinforce a particular perspective about cancer research. A metaphor such as *war on cancer* would add a sense of urgency to our proposal, because it suggests that cancer is an enemy that must be defeated, at almost any cost. Of course, cancer research is not really a war. And yet, we accept this metaphor with little question or dispute.

Metaphors are very powerful tools in proposal writing because they tend to work at a subconscious level. In other words, the use of the *war on cancer* metaphor should not be obvious to the readers. Instead, the metaphor is used in key places throughout the proposal to gradually shift the readers' point of view, turning cancer into an enemy in their minds.

But what if a commonly used metaphor, like the *war on cancer,* is not appropriate for our proposal? In these cases, we can create a new metaphor and use it to invent a new perspective for the readers. For example, perhaps we want our readers to view cancer as something to be managed, not fought. Our new metaphor, *managing cancer* would allow us to talk about *negotiating* with cancer cells or using drugs that *mediate* between cancer cells and regular cells. We might speak of patients as *managers* who set goals and priorities that their body will aim to reach. Doctors might become *consultants* who offer patients advice on managing their illness. This new metaphor, creates a quite different perspective than the *war* metaphor. We can use this new metaphor to shift the readers' perspective, urging them to think differently about how they will handle their illness.

To use metaphors in proposals, you should first look for the existing metaphors that are widely used in your field. For example, perhaps you notice that "drugs are a disease in our city" is prevalent in the media. You can then use this metaphor to create a theme in your proposal. Extending the metaphor, you might say, "Our city needs treatment," or, "We need to control the illness first, then we can begin recovering." By playing off the original metaphor, you can create more metaphorical phrases that reinforce the perspective you want.

In some cases, new metaphors need to be created from scratch. For instance, a proposal that is arguing for the construction of a new office building might use a metaphor like, "Harmon Industries needs a new home." This *home* metaphor could then be used to invent a theme in which words associated with homes, like *comfort, security, garden,* and *family,* are woven into the text. In this case, we could use this *home* metaphor to shift the readers' perspective from "the office building is the workplace" to "the office building is our home."

Changing the Pace

You can also regulate the readers' pace as they work through your proposal. Longer sentences tend to slow the reading pace down, while shorter sentences tend to speed up the pace. By paying attention to the length of sentences, you can increase or decrease the intensity of your writing. For instance, let us say you believe a problem is urgent and needs to be handled right away. The best way to increase the intensity in your proposal would be to use short sentences while you describe that problem. As the pace increases, the readers will naturally feel impelled to do something, because they will sense the problem is rapidly growing worse. On the other hand, if you want the readers to be cautious and deliberate, longer sentences will decrease the intensity of the proposal, giving the readers the sense that there is no need to rush.

Sentence length is a great way to convey the intensity you want without saying something like "This opportunity is slipping away!" or "We really need to take action now!" Sentence length can also soothe anxious readers by slowing down the pace a bit.

Last Word

After reading through this chapter, some people may wonder about the ethics of using stylistic devices to influence the readers. Most people would not question the use of plain sentences and paragraphs to help the readers to understand the ideas in a proposal. But, the use of persuasive style might sound a bit like manipulating the readers.

To be candid, you *are* manipulating the readers when you are trying to persuade them. That's what proposals do. The challenge is to match your proposal's style to the readers' needs. Plain style is best for instructing the readers, giving them the facts in a straightforward way. Persuasive style is used to motivate the readers to take action. Motivating people is ethical if you are urging them to do what is best for them. When persuasive style is used properly, it matches tone, choice of words, and pace to the situation that the readers face. It stresses important ideas at important points in the proposal.

CASE STUDY   Revising for Clarity and Power

Sally always preferred revising to drafting. When drafting a text, she would find herself feeling at a loss for words, struggling to put her ideas down on paper. But, once the words were on the page, she enjoyed revising them into smooth, powerful arguments. So, when the first draft of the Elmdale Hill Merchants Association proposal was finished, Sally told the others she would take charge of revising it. The others were more than happy to hand that task over to her.

She began revising by looking at the proposal on the sentence and paragraph levels. Stylistically, some of the sentences were difficult to read, because they did not use appropriate subjects and action verbs. Similarly, several of the paragraphs were a struggle to read, because they didn't use solid topic sentences and the sentences were not woven together well. But Sally knew these stylistic problems were typical for a first draft.

In particular, one paragraph from the Situation section caught her interest (from Figure 4.9). The paragraph originally read—

A more serious publicity-related problem is the increasingly negative portrayal of Elmdale Hill in the local media. Because we are not actively projecting a positive public image of ourselves, the media only reports the negatives. As a result, the few criminal acts committed in this neighborhood seem to receive significant coverage without any counter-response. Meanwhile, the positive aspects of Elmdale Hill are rarely known outside the district, because we lack a uni-fied voice and we have no source for keeping the media informed about the people and events that make Elmdale Hill a fun place to live, work, and shop.

She noticed that each sentence in the paragraph used a different subject, and the subjects of some sentences were not always easy to identify.

So, she began revising the paragraph by asking what the paragraph was about. She decided the paragraph was about negative press. She then restructured the sentences in the paragraph to focus on this subject.

The media's negative portrayal of Elmdale Hill is another publicity-related problem. This lack of positive press exists because Elmdale Hill has not actively worked to project a positive image to the public. As a result, the public only hears about the rare criminal acts committed in this neighborhood, giving them a bad impression of the area. Meanwhile, positive news stories about Elmdale Hill area are few, because we have no source for keeping the media and the public informed about the people and events that make Elmdale Hill a fun place to live, work, and shop. (Underlines show subjects of sentences.)

On the sentence that resisted subject alignment (sentence 3) she used the given/new technique to make it blend better with the sentences around it.

Sally decided that the overall organization of the paragraph was fine. A transitional sentence started off the paragraph by referring back to the previous paragraph. The second sentence was the topic sentence, because it provided a claim that the paragraph would prove. The remainder of the paragraph used logical reasoning to support the topic sentence. Sally concluded that the paragraph was doing just fine without a point sentence, so she did not add one.

After Sally finished revising all the paragraphs in the proposal to make them more readable, she decided to amplify certain parts of the proposal with persuasive style. First, she began thinking about the tone she wanted the proposal to convey. She found herself returning to the word *urgent* as a possible tone for the whole document.

Putting the word *urgency* in the middle of a sheet of paper, she mapped out some words associated with this concept (Figure 9.5).

With her map finished, Sally wove some of these words into the introduction, opening paragraphs, closing paragraphs, and the conclusion of the proposal, creating a sense of urgency for her readers.

Finally, Sally decided she wanted to use a metaphor that would reinforce a particular perspective in the minds of the proposals' readers. It seemed a bit old-fashioned—maybe even cliché—but she wanted to weave the metaphor "The Elmdale Hill businesses are members of a family" into the proposal. This *family* metaphor seemed to capture the warmth and together-ness that she wanted to readers of the proposal to adopt.

Thinking about this metaphor, she began to list out some words and phrases that fit it:

- pulling together in times of crisis
- looking out for each other
- helping each other
- "sister" businesses
- holding family meetings
- putting our house in order
- tightening our belt
- saying only nice things about each other
- going on outings together
- nurturing young businesses
- protecting each other from outsiders
- leaning on each other
- building and maintaining relationships
- familiarity

Of course, Sally knew the Elmdale Hill businesses weren't really a family. They were a collection of stores, restaurants, and theaters that happened to be in the same area. Nevertheless, by weaving the family metaphor into her proposal, she hoped to change her readers' perspective from the uninspiring "Elmdale Hill is a business district" to something warm, familiar, and friendly. If the merchants accepted her family metaphor, they might be more inclined to go out of their way for each other.

FIGURE 9.5

Setting a Tone of Urgency

When Sally was finished revising, the proposal included basically the same content as before. However, her attention to sentences and paragraphs had made the text much clearer and more readable. Meanwhile, her attention to tone and the inclusion of the family metaphor gave it more depth and energy. The final Elmdale Hill proposal appears in Chapter 12 of this book. There, you can see the other revisions Sally made to the style of the proposal.

Questions and Exercises

1. Using the six steps outlined in Figure 9.2, revise the following sentences to make them more readable:

   a. According to our survey that we conducted last Friday after the president gave his speech on crime on campus, the collection of data offers a demonstration on how much of importance this issue is to women of college age.

   b. The meeting over the project for Guilford simply gave us confirmation that we may find it necessary to pursue the hiring of an engineer who can program in the computer languages of FORTRAN and C++.

   c. Due to concerns about the large amounts of flammable items in close proximity to the location of the fire, it was necessary that an investigation of the blaze in the southwest corner of the building be conducted by an inspector from the fire department.

2. Find three sentences that are hard to read. Use the six steps outlined in Figure 9.2 to make these sentences easier to read. Then, in a memo to your instructor, describe the steps you followed to improve the sentences' readability.

3. Use subject alignment and given/new techniques to make the following paragraph more readable:

   Because clear writing is equated with sincerity and trustworthiness by most readers, style is important in proposal writing. The soundness and honesty of an argument will be questioned by the readers, if the meaning of proposal is hard to interpret. After all, they wonder, perhaps the argument in the proposal is not clear to the writers if their ideas cannot be expressed in plain language. Even worse, important assumptions or facts might be hidden in the twists and turns of the sentences and paragraphs, they might suspect. On the other hand, the writers show the readers that they know what is needed and how to provide it when they submit a plainly written proposal. In my experience, the clients are more easily won over by writers who submit a plain proposal rather than a proposal that is hard to read.

4. On campus or in your workplace, find a couple paragraphs that seem difficult to read. First, align to subject in each paragraph to see if this technique improves readability. Then, use given/new strategies to revise each paragraph.

Which method works better? Would a combination of subject alignment and given/new be more appropriate in some cases?

5. Study the style of a proposal found on the Internet or in your workplace. What is the tone used in the proposal? Does the proposal use any similes or analogies to help the readers visualize difficult concepts? Can you locate any metaphors/themes that are woven into the text? How might the techniques of persuasive style discussed in this chapter be used to improve this proposal?

6. A common metaphor in our society is the "war on illegal drugs." With a team, think up some common phrases that demonstrate this metaphor in use. What does this metaphor imply about people who use and sell drugs? What police tactics does the metaphor suggest? What does the metaphor imply about our interactions with countries who export illegal drugs? If we wanted to handle the drug problem from a different perspective, what might be some other appropriate metaphors? How might these metaphors imply different approaches to illegal drugs?

7. While revising some of your own writing (perhaps your Situation or Plan sections from earlier chapters), try to create a specific tone by mapping out an emotion or character that you would like the text to reflect. Weave a few concepts from your map into your text. At what point is the tone too strong? At what point is the tone just right?

8. Using the same text from Exercise 7 revise the text by shortening all the sentences. How do these shorter sentences change the pace of your writing? Now, revise the text by lengthening the sentences. How do these longer sentences change the pace of your writing?

10 | Designing Proposals

Overview

This chapter discusses how to develop a persuasive visual design for a proposal. The chapter will meet the following objectives:

1. Discuss the importance of design in a proposal.
2. Discuss the application of gestalt theory to design.
3. Define four principles of design for crafting effective page layouts.
4. Describe the use of a five-step "design process" for inventing, revising, and editing pages.

"How You Say Something . . ."

The old saying, "How you say something is what you say," is truer now than ever in proposal writing. Not long ago, document design was considered a luxury in proposals, not a necessity. More recently, though, the availability of desktop publishing software has heightened the importance of design in all documents. Readers *expect* proposals to be visually interesting and engaging. They expect proposals to make a positive first impression. And, they expect the design of a proposal to help them read the document more efficiently by highlighting important ideas. These days, people cringe when a proposal with little or no design crosses their desk, because they quickly realize that their needs as readers were not anticipated by the writers.

Design is more than simply making a proposal look nice. An effective design increases the readability of the text by highlighting important information and allowing the readers to process the text in a variety of different ways. Moreover, the design of a proposal establishes a particular tone for the document—an image. Much as clothing and body language establishes an image for a public speaker, a proposal's design signals the attitude, competence, and quality of the bidders to the clients. Of course, the content is still the most important feature of a proposal. Even the best design will never hide a weak understanding of the situation or a flawed plan. However, design can make a positive impression on the readers while emphasizing your ideas. It can incline the readers favorably toward your document before they even read a word.

In the field of rhetoric, a branch called "Visual Rhetoric" studies the persuasive effects of design on readers of documents. In this chapter and the next, we will apply some of the principles of visual rhetoric to designing proposals.

How Readers Look at Proposals

Occasionally, readers will study a proposal from front to back, starting at the introduction and ending with the conclusion. In most cases, though, people read proposals at different levels, skimming some sections and paying closer attention to sections that directly affect their interests. Most readers, for example, make an initial surface-level scan of the proposal. They look at the executive summary, read the introduction, and then scan each major section's headings and opening paragraphs. Their aim is to gather an overall sense of the structure and argument of the proposal.

Readers will then start to pay closer attention to the sections of the proposal that affect them most. Accountants responsible for money issues will pay attention to sections that handle the costs and the budget. A technical expert will look closely at the details of the plan to see if it is feasible. Decision makers will check whether the proposal correctly describes their current situation and offers a feasible plan to address that situation. They will also pay more attention to any descriptions of the bidders' qualifications.

Eventually, some of the readers may study the proposal from front to back, especially if they are deciding whether to accept it. While they are reading front to back, they will want the proposal to use visual techniques to highlight the main points of each section.

The challenge of good design is to permit the readers to choose how *they* want to read the proposal. The proposal should be designed in a way that helps them process the text at different levels, while making the text usable in a variety of different possible contexts. Good design gives the readers easy "access points" where they can enter the text from a variety of different places for a variety of different reasons.

Four Principles of Design

Good design is not something to be learned in a day. Nevertheless, you can master some rather basic principles of document design that will help you make better decisions about how your proposal should look. In this section, we will discuss four rather simple principles of design that were derived from *gestalt psychology,* an area that has deeply influenced the graphic arts (Bernhardt 1986; Moore and Fitz 1993). The basic assumption of gestalt design is that humans do not view their surroundings passively (Arnheim 1964, 28). Rather, they instinctively look for relationships among objects, creating wholes that are more than a sum of their parts.

FIGURE 10.1

The Whole Is More than a Sum of the Parts

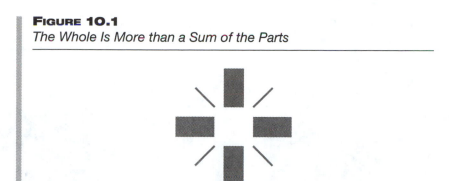

For example, in Figure 10.1, most people see a square, and they might even see an X in the middle of the square. According to gestalt design, viewers see a whole that is more than the sum of the parts in the graphic.

Like this diagram, design in a proposal allows readers to also visualize larger relationships among parts. Visual design can help them draw the natural connections among these parts to see the proposal as a greater whole.

The four design principles we will discuss in this chapter are **balance, alignment, grouping,** and **consistency**. These principles are based on gestalt psychology, especially Kurt Koffka's work in the area. The actual gestalt principles are a bit hard to remember, and not all of them pertain to designing a text. As a synthesis of gestalt theory, the four principles in this chapter are designed to provide a simpler handlist of terms with which you can master document design for proposals.

Design Principle 1: Balance

On a balanced page, the design elements offset each other to create a stable feeling in the text. To illustrate, imagine a page is balanced on a point. Each time we add something to the left side, we need to add something to the right side to maintain balance. Similarly, when we add something to the top of the page, we need to add something to the bottom. Figure 10.2, for instance, shows an example of a balanced page and an unbalanced page.

The text on the right is unbalanced because the items on the right side of the page are not offset by items on the left. Meanwhile, the page is top-heavy because the text is bunched up toward the top of the page. The page on the left, however, feels stable because the design elements have been balanced evenly on the page. Whereas readers would find the unbalanced page uncomfortable to read, they would have little trouble looking over the balanced page on the left.

One thing to note, however, is that a balanced page is not necessarily a symmetrical page. In other words, as shown in the left page in Figure 10.2, the two halves of the page do not need to mirror each other, nor do the top and bottom need to be identical. Instead, the sides of the page should simply offset each other to create a sense of balance.

FIGURE 10.2
Balanced and Unbalanced Pages

When balancing a page layout, graphic designers will talk about the "weight" of items on a page. What they mean is that some items on a page attract the readers' eyes more than others. A picture, for example, has more weight than printed words because readers' eyes tend to be drawn toward pictures. Likewise, colored text or graphics weigh more than black and white, because readers are attracted to color. An item placed on the right side of the page will have more weight than an object placed on the left side, because Western readers tend to read from left to right. In other words, an item on the right side of a sheet of paper creates more tension (has more weight) than something on the left.

Here are some general guidelines for weighting the elements on a page:

- Items on the right side of the page weigh more than items on the left.
- Items on the top of the page weigh more than items on the bottom.
- Big items weigh more than small items.
- Pictures weigh more than written text.
- Graphics weigh more than written text.
- Colored items weigh more than black and white.
- Items with borders around them weigh more than items without borders.
- Irregular shapes weigh more than regular shapes.

When designing a standard page for a proposal, the challenge is to create a layout that allows you to keep the text as balanced as possible. In some cases, graphic designers want to lay out unbalanced pages, because unbalanced pages create a sense of tension and unease in the readers. Writers of proposals, however, have little use for an unbalanced page design that makes the readers feel tense and uneasy.

Using Grids to Balance a Page Layout

A time-tested way to devise a balanced page design is to use a page "grid" to evenly place the written text and graphics on the page. Grids divide the page vertically into two or more columns. The examples in Figure 10.3 show some standard grids and how they might be used.

In most cases, as shown in Figure 10.3, the columns on a grid do not translate into columns of written text. The grid is simply used to structure the text evenly, allowing columns of text or larger pictures to overlap one or more columns.

Why use a grid in the first place? It might be tempting to merely expand the margin on the right or left side in an ad hoc way. The problem with this approach is that readers subconsciously sense the page's irregular spacing. As gestalt design implies, the readers will subconsciously look for regular patterns or shapes. If no grid is used, the readers will try to imagine a grid anyway, thus creating more reading tension than necessary. Furthermore, in the long run, a grid-based page design offers more flexibility. An ad hoc layout may work for a couple pages, but as charts, margin text, and graphics are added, the page design will grow increasingly difficult to manage.

One solution, of course, is to use a simple one-column design. In a one-column format, graphics and text are usually centered in the middle of the column (see Figure 10.4).

There is, of course, nothing wrong with a one-column grid. A one-column grid tends to be rather traditional and word dominant, and it provides limited flexibility on the placement of graphics. For example, as shown in Figure 10.4, few options exist for the placement of a graphic on the right page. Nevertheless, this page design is easy to use.

Other Balance Strategies

With the advent of desktop publishing, we now have the ability to use design features that were once limited to large publishers. In proposals, writers now use design features like pullouts, margin comments, and sidebars to enhance the reading of the body text.

Pullouts   Quotes or paraphrases can be *pulled out* of the body text and placed in a special text box to catch the readers' attention. Essentially, pullouts are used to break up large blocks of text and create access points for the readers. Magazines, for example, frequently use pullouts when a picture or graphic is not available to break up a page of words. A pullout should draw its text from the page on which it appears. Often, the pullout is framed with rules or a box, and the text wraps around it (see Figure 10.5).

Margin Comments   Key points or highlight quotations may be summarized in the margin of the proposal. When a grid is used to design the page, one of the margins often leaves enough room to include an additional list, offer a special quote drawn from the body text, or provide a simple illustration. In a large proposal, margin comments might even be used to remind the readers where

FIGURE 10.3
Grids and their Uses

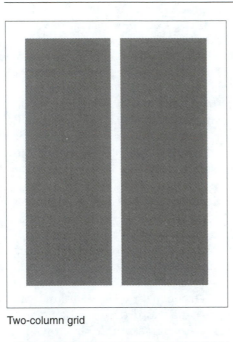

Two-column grid

Three-column grid

FIGURE 10.3
Continued

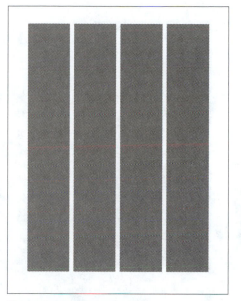 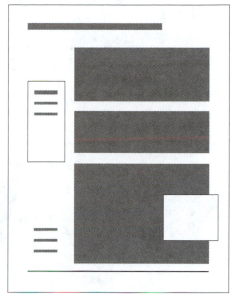

Four-column grid

FIGURE 10.4
A One-Column Page Design

 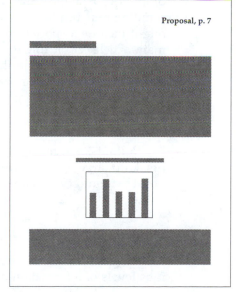

One-column grid

FIGURE 10.5
Other Visual Techniques Used to Balance Pages

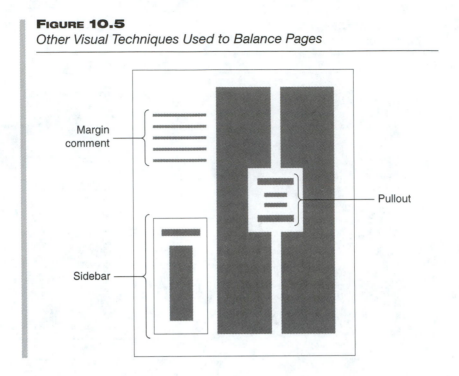

they are in the proposal by restating the outline of the proposal and highlighting the main points of the section they are about to enter (see Figure 10.5).

Sidebars Examples that reinforce the text but are not essential to its understanding may be placed in a sidebar. In a magazine article, for example, a sidebar might include a special profile of an important person who is mentioned in the main article. Or, it might provide a "story within the story" that illustrates an important point made in the body text. In proposals, sidebars could be used to explain a process in more detail or describe a previous project that was a success. Sidebars should never contain essential information that the readers require. Rather, they offer supplemental information that enhances the readers' understanding.

Pullouts, margin comments, and sidebars can be used to balance a text and break up large blocks of words. Meanwhile, they enhance the reading of the proposal by reinforcing main points and providing supplemental information.

Design Principle 2: Alignment

Alignment is the use of vertical "white space" to help the readers identify the various levels of information in a proposal. The simplest alignment technique is the

FIGURE 10.6

Using Lists as Alignment Tools

use of an indented list to offset a group of items from the body text. An indented list signals to the readers that the listed items are intended to supplement the text in the surrounding paragraphs. In Figure 10.6, for example, the page on the left gives no hint about the hierarchy of information in the text, making it difficult for a reader to scan the text. The page on the right, meanwhile, uses indented lists to clearly signal the hierarchy of the text. The indented material is easily recognized as supplemental information.

In a proposal, blocks of text can be aligned to show the hierarchy of information. Examples or explanatory information can be indented to signal that they are to be considered separately from the body text. Figure 10.7 illustrates how information can be indented to signal various levels in the text.

Essentially, alignment uses white space to create vertical lines in the text. The readers will mentally draw the vertical lines into the page, seeing aligned elements as belonging to the same level of importance.

Design Principle 3: Grouping

Even the most patient readers have difficulty trudging through large, undivided blocks of text. Grouping techniques help break the text down into smaller parts that are more comprehendible, especially for scanning readers. The principle of grouping

FIGURE 10.7
Alignment that Shows Hierarchy of Information

is based on the assumption that readers comprehend better when information is divided into smaller chunks. A large block of text, perhaps a one-column page with no headings and no indentation, seems uninviting to a reader and difficult to read. Grouping allows you to break up the page by providing the readers more white space and giving them a variety of access points at which to enter the text.

The simplest type of grouping is paragraphing, because paragraphs break a larger stream of written text into blocks of ideas. There are more advanced ways, however, to group information on a page, including using headings, rules, and borders.

Using Headings

The primary purpose of headings is to signal new topics to the readers, but they also cue the readers into the overall organization of the proposal. With a quick scan of the headings in the document, the readers should be able to easily identify how the information in the proposal is organized.

In a larger document like a proposal, headings should highlight the various levels of information for the readers. A first-level heading, for example, should be sized significantly larger than a second-level heading. In some cases, first-level headings might use all capital letters (all caps) or small capital letters (small caps) to distinguish them from the font used in the body text. To make the first-level heading stand out, some writers even prefer to put them inside the left-hand margin or "hanging" into the left-hand margin (see Figure 10.8).

FIGURE 10.8
Levels of Headings

FIRST-LEVEL HEADING

This first-level heading is 18 pt. Times, boldface with small caps. Notice that it is significantly different from the second-level heading, even though both levels are in the same typeface. This heading is also *hanging*, because it is placed further into the margin than the regular text. Use consistent spacing above and below each head (e.g., 24 pts. above and 18 pts. below).

Second-Level Heading

This second-level heading is 14 pt. Times with boldface. Usually, less space appears above and below this head (perhaps 18 pts. above and 14 pts. below).

Third-Level Heading
This third-level heading is 12 pt. Times italics. Often no space appears between a third-level heading and the body text, as shown here.

Fourth-Level Heading. This heading appears on the same line as body text. It is designed to signal a new layer of information without standing out too much.

Second-level headings should be significantly smaller and different than the first-level headings. Whereas the first-level headings might have used all caps, the second-level headings might capitalize only the first letter of each word (excluding articles and short prepositions) (e.g., "Marketing for the MTV Generation"). First- and second-level heads are often made boldface. Third-level headings might be italicized or placed on the same line as the body text itself. Figure 10.8 shows various levels of headings.

Early in the proposal writing process, you should decide how the proposal will use headings. Headings are powerful tools for breaking information down into groups; however, when used improperly they can create unneeded chaos in a proposal. They need to be used consistently throughout the document.

Using Horizontal and Vertical Rules

In page design, horizontal and vertical rules are straight lines that can be used to carve the proposal into larger blocks. Rules should be used judiciously in a proposal, because they can impede the progress of the reader through the text. Too many rules make the document look like its been chopped up into small bits

FIGURE 10.9
Using Rules to Divide a Page into Groups

and pieces. But, when used properly with headings or to set off an example, horizontal and vertical rules can help the readers identify the larger groups of information in a proposal.

Figure 10.9 illustrates how rules can be used to divide a page into larger parts.

As shown in Figure 10.9, the horizontal and vertical rules carve the text into larger chunks, ensuring that the readers will see them as groups. On the other hand, rules can restrict how the reader views the page by framing off text into isolated blocks of information.

Using Borders

Like rules, borders are also used to group text into units. Borders, however, tend to be even more isolating than rules, because they enclose text completely, setting it off from the rest of the information on a page. Borders are best used to set off examples, graphics, pullouts, and sidebars that supplement the body text. For example, Figure 10.10 shows how a border can be used to set off an example or sidebar on a typical page.

Borders are helpful tools for grouping information. However, like rules, they can be overused. If borders are used sparingly in a proposal, they will draw the readers' attention to the information inside the border. When borders are used too often, however, the readers will grow immune to their grouping effects, and they will tend to skip reading the information inside.

FIGURE 10.10

Using Borders to Group Information

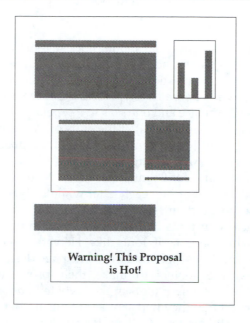

Design Principle 4: Consistency

The final design principle, consistency, simply suggests that each page in the proposal should be designed similarly to other pages in the document. Specifically, each page should follow a predictable pattern in which design features are used uniformly throughout the proposal. For example, the typefaces used in the proposal should be consistent. Lists should use consistent numbering schemes for sequential lists and consistent icons for nonsequential lists. Meanwhile the same grid should be used throughout the proposal as a template.

There are four techniques available for giving each page a consistent look: headers and footers, typefaces, labeling, and lists.

Headers and Footers

Even the simplest word processing software can put a header or footer consistently on every page. As their names suggest, the header is text that runs across the top margin of the page, and the footer is text that runs along the bottom of the page. In many proposals, headers and footers include the title of the proposal and perhaps the bidding company's name. They also invariably include a page number. Page numbers are critical in proposals, because they help the readers refer to various parts of the proposal with ease. If there are no page numbers available, the readers find themselves struggling to tell others where to look in the proposal, instead of merely telling other readers "go to page X."

Headers and footers can also include design features like a horizontal rule or even a company logo. If these items appear at the top or bottom of each page of the proposal, the document will tend to look like it is following a consistent design.

Typefaces

As a rule of thumb, a proposal should not use more than two different typefaces. Computers have given us access to hundreds of different typefaces from Arial to Zingbats, but you do not need to use them all in your proposal. Instead, most page designers will choose two typefaces that are very different from each other, usually one *serif* typeface and one *sans serif* typeface. A serif typeface, like Times or Bookman, has small tips (serifs) at the ends of main strokes in the letters. A sans serif font is one that does not include these small tips. This body text is set in 10 pt. Palatino—a serif font. Figure 10.11 shows the difference between a serif font (Palatino) and a sans serif font (Helvetica). Notice how the letters in Palatino include the additional tips on each letter while Helvetica does not.

There are no hard rules for typeface usage, just guidelines. To readers in North America, serif fonts like Times or Palatino tend to look more formal and traditional, while sans serif fonts like Helvetica seem informal and modern. Because sans serif fonts look modern, some page designers will use them in headings, headers, and footers to make their proposal look more progressive. Designers often prefer serif fonts in the body text, because North American readers usually report that they find sans serif fonts harder to read at length.

To complicate matters further, international readers like those from the United Kingdom are accustomed to sans serif fonts like Helvetica appearing in the body text. They, consequently, find sans serif fonts easier to read at length.

Your choices of typefaces, of course, are up to you. Whatever your choice of typefaces, however, you should use them consistently throughout the proposal.

FIGURE 10.11
Serif and Sans Serif

This paragraph uses the Palatino typeface. Serif typefaces are often used in traditional-looking texts, especially for the body text. Studies have suggested inconclusively that serif typefaces like Palatino are more legible, but there is some debate as to why. Some researchers claim that the serifs create horizontal lines in the text that make serif typefaces easier to follow (White, p. 14). These studies, however, were mostly conducted in the United States, where serif fonts are common. In other countries, such as Britain, where sans serif fonts are often used for body text, the results of these studies might be quite different.

This paragraph uses Helvetica, a sans serif typeface. A sans serif typeface tends to look more modern and progressive to most readers. However, sans serif text tends to be harder to read at length, at least for readers in the United States. Generally, sans serif typefaces are best used in titles and headings.

Labeling of Graphics

Graphics, such as tables, charts, pictures, and graphs, should be labeled consistently throughout the proposal. In most cases, the label above a graphic will include a number (e.g., Table 5) and a title (e.g., Forecast of Future Sales). In some cases, though, the number and title might appear below the graphic. Again, the important thing is to be consistent. You should always choose a consistent typeface for labeling and then locate the labels consistently on each graphic. In Chapter 11, we will further discuss how to use graphics in proposals.

Sequential and Nonsequential Lists

The design of lists is a decision that should be made up front while planning a proposal. In proposals, lists are useful for showing a sequence of tasks or a group of similar items. However, when lists are not used consistently in a proposal, they can also create substantial confusion for the readers.

A simple way to design lists is to remember that they tend to fall into two basic categories: sequential and nonsequential. Sequential, or numbered, lists are used to present items in a specific order. For instance, in a proposal, sequential lists might handle a list of tasks or they might rank various objectives. In these lists, numbers or letters are used to show the order or hierarchy of the items. Nonsequential lists, on the other hand, use bullets, checkmarks, or other icons to show that the items in the list are essentially equal in value.

Lists are handy tools for making information more readable, and you should look for opportunities in your proposal to use them. When you include a list, though, make sure you are consistent in your usage of sequential and nonsequential lists. In sequential lists, numbering schemes should not change in the proposal except for good reason. For example, you might choose a numbering scheme like 1), 2), 3). If so, do not number the next list 1., 2., 3., and others A., B., C., unless you have a good reason for changing the numbering scheme. Similarly, in nonsequential lists, use similar icons when setting off lists. Do not use bullets with one list, checkmarks with another, and pointing hands with a third. These inconsistencies only confuse the readers while making your proposal seem unpolished.

To avoid these problems with lists, decide up front how your proposal will use lists. Choose one style for sequential lists and another for nonsequential lists and stick with those two styles throughout the proposal.

The Process of Designing a Proposal

Balance, alignment, grouping, consistency. Once you know these four basic principles, designing a proposal becomes much easier. These four principles form the basis of a "process" that you can use to design almost any text. In their book, *Designing Visual Language,* Charles Kostelnick and David Roberts (1998) suggest that a design process "includes several kinds of activities, beginning with invention, followed by revision, and ending with fine-tuning" (23). Like writing, Kostelnick and Roberts point out, designing a text is a fluid process in which the designer cycles among the different parts of the process until the design is completed.

Following a design process becomes especially important when you are working with a team on a proposal. Your team should start out by making some or all of the design decisions *before* team members go off to write theirs part of the proposal. With design issues settled up front, each team member can then conform his or her part to the overall design of the proposal, making assembly of the proposal much easier at the end. Moreover, each team member can help find or create visual items like the graphics or sidebars that will make up the proposal's design. If your team waits until the proposal's due date to consider the design of the proposal, chances are good that you will need to resort to the lowest common denominator—that is, little or no design.

To create effective layouts for proposals by yourself or with a team, you can follow this five-step process:

1. Consider the rhetorical situation.
2. Thumbnail a few example pages.
3. Create a design stylesheet.
4. Develop a few generic pages.
5. Edit the design.

Step One: Consider the Rhetorical Situation

Start out the design process by revisiting your understanding of the *rhetorical situation*, which you developed at the beginning of the proposal writing process. Specifically, you should pay attention to the unique characteristics of the primary readers and the physical context in which they will read the proposal.

Different readers will respond to a document's design in various ways, so you want your proposal to align with the primary readers' values and attitudes. For instance, if the primary readers are rather traditional, the proposal should use a conservative design that includes a simple layout, a classic font like Times, and limited amounts of graphics. If the readers are more progressive or trendy, the design can be a little more creative. In this case, perhaps you might use more graphics. You might consider using an unusual font for the headings, or perhaps you might add a splash of color. If you know the topic is an emotional one for the readers, positive or negative, perhaps some photographs might reinforce or defuse those emotions by showing the people or issues involved in the proposal.

Second, the context in which the proposal will be used is also important. Pay special attention to the physical factors that will influence the reading of the proposal. For example, if you know that the readers will look over the proposal in a large board meeting, then you will want to make the text as scannable as possible with clearly identifiable headings, plenty of lists, and a generous use of graphics to reinforce the proposal's main ideas. You might also add pullouts or margin comments to state your main points in ways that pop off the page. On the other hand, if you think each proposal will receive a close reading, perhaps fewer

FIGURE 10.12
Thumbnails

 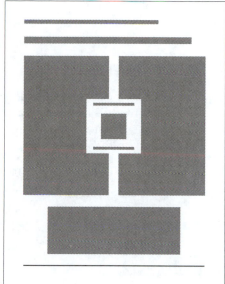

graphical elements and more paragraphs would give the text a more detailed, grounded feel.

Step Two: Thumbnail a Few Example Pages

With the readers and context in mind, sketch out a few possible page layouts that would suit the rhetorical situation. Graphic artists will often start designing pages by sketching a few "thumbnails" freehand or on a computer (see Figure 10.12). Thumbnails take a few moments to draw, but they will allow you to look over possible designs before you commit to a particular page layout—saving you time in the long run.

While thumbnailing designs, pay special attention to the balance of the page. Will the page use two, three, or four columns? Where will graphics appear on a page? Will there be space for margin comments, pullouts, or sidebars? How large will the headings be on the page? Where will a header or footer be placed? Most designers sketch a few different possible layouts and then decide which one seems to best suit the rhetorical situation. If you are working with a team, provide the other team members with a few different possible layouts and let them choose the best one.

Once you have developed a basic pattern for the body pages, thumbnail a few possible cover pages for the proposal. Allow yourself to be bold with the cover.

Nothing puts readers in a positive mood better than an active, professional cover (the "everything centered" cover is a real yawner). You can add energy to your cover by increasing the size of the text, moving the text to the left or right side of the page, adding in a graphic, and so on. All these features will give momentum to the proposal while reassuring the readers that the proposal is not going to be boring.

Step Three: Create a Design Style Sheet

Style sheets are records of your design decisions. After sketching out some thumbnails or creating a page layout, you should write down some of your decisions about various design elements of the document. These features can be handled on five levels:

Line Level	font, font size, and use of italics, bolding, and underlining
Paragraph Level	spacing between lines (leading), heading typefaces and sizes, indentation, justification (right, center, left, full), sequential and nonsequential lists, column width
Page Level	columns, headers and footers, rules and borders, use of shading, placement of graphics, use of color, pullouts, sidebars, page numbers, use of logos or icons
Graphics Level	captions, labeling, borders on graphics, use of color, fonts used in tables, charts, and graphs
Document Level	binding, cover stock, paper size, color, weight, and type (glossy, semi-gloss, standard), section dividers

Sometimes, making all these design decisions can be a daunting task. Nevertheless, in a larger proposal, a style sheet actually saves time, because writers can refer to it when they have a question about specific design issues. When working with a team of other writers, you can simplify the writing process considerably by asking each writer to follow the style sheet as closely as possible. That way, when the whole proposal comes together, the final draft will require far less editing of the design.

Style sheets are living documents that can be modified as the proposal is developed. Certainly, a style sheet is never something to be slavishly followed. Rather, it should be modified as the writing of the proposal creates new challenges for the design.

Step Four: Develop a Few Generic Pages

Graphic designers will tell you that the best time to design a document is before the words are written. In most cases, however, writers start thinking about design after they have completed an outline or drafted a few pages of the proposal. At this point in the writing process, they can bend and shape the text into a generic page layout. They can create a *template* that can be used to structure all the pages in the proposal.

With your thumbnails sketched and a style sheet created, use some or all of the proposals' content to create a template that each page in the proposal will follow. As you add content to your design, you will likely discover that some of your earlier style decisions need to be modified to fit the needs of a real document. Mark these modifications down in your style sheet.

Each page should follow the same basic pattern as the other pages. Avoid the temptation to make small alterations to accommodate the demands of individual pages. Instead, if one page's design needs to be changed, you might need to go back and alter the overall template to accommodate these modifications. By creating a few generic pages, you can find places where alterations are needed *before* you start designing the whole proposal.

Step Five: Edit the Design

Like writing, editing is an important part of design. After you have completed designing the text and adding the written text and graphics, you should commit some time exclusively to revising and editing the proposal's design. While adding text and graphics, you more than likely stretched your original design a bit. Now it is time to go back and correct some of the smaller inconsistencies that came about as you put the text together.

To help you edit, look back at the rhetorical situation, your thumbnails, and your style sheet. Does the final design fit the readers and the context in which they will read the proposal? Does the final design reflect the visual qualities you wanted as you sketched out your thumbnails? Are there any places where the final design needs to be revised to fit the style sheet? Or, does the style sheet need to be modified to fit decisions you made as text and design were meshed together? In the end, make sure the final, edited design fits the rhetorical situation with which you started the writing process.

Last Word

In the struggle to pull a proposal together, often at the last minute, there is a tendency to see design as a luxury that can be ignored in a pinch. It's the content, not the design that is important, right? In reality, though, how you say something is what you say. If you hand in a proposal that uses a one-column format with double spacing and underlined headings, the readers are going to wonder whether you, your team, or your company have the creativity and commitment to quality required for their project. After all, how a proposal looks says a great amount about how your company does business. In the long run, it is worth the effort to spend the few hours required to design an attractive, functional proposal.

CASE STUDY: **Creating a Look**

Thomas was thinking about the proposal's design long before they had completed the rough draft. If owning a movie theater had taught him one thing, it was the importance of how something looked. His customers seemed to put a high value on the look of his theater, the design of the posters that advertised new movies, and even the uniforms Thomas and his employees wore each night.

So he decided to design the proposal himself. Looking over the notes he had written about the rhetorical situation, he began to think about what kind of design would suit the primary readers of the proposal and contexts in which they would consider the proposal's ideas. Specifically, he knew that the primary readers were the other business owners in the Elmdale Hill district. Most of them were like Thomas—working hard to keep their businesses afloat. They would only have limited time and energy to read a proposal.

Most of them were also enterprising and progressive. Many business owners had left high-paying jobs in traditional corporations to start their own restaurant, book store, clothing store, etc. They were people who liked to feel different than others—like they were out on their own. Thomas also realized, though, that these people were worried about their businesses. He wanted to create a design that would reflect the seriousness of the subject while also appealing to the progressive entrepreneurial spirit that motivated the proposal's primary readers.

From his rhetorical situation worksheets, Thomas also recognized that the readers' context would be important to the design of the proposal. The primary readers would probably first look over the proposal during slow times at their businesses. Thomas could even visualize them at the cash register, sneaking glances at the proposal between customers. Others would take the proposal home to study it after business hours. Either way, the design of the proposal would need to accommodate a scanning reader who was not going to have the time or energy to commit full attention to the text.

The readers would also need to use the proposal at the organizational meeting described in the proposal. Thomas knew the design must highlight important points, so the business owners could use them as talking points in the meeting.

With these readers and contexts in mind, Thomas began thumbnailing a few possible pages for the proposal (Figure 10.13). He decided to use a two-column page, because that layout would decrease the width of each column, making the text easier to scan. It would also allow him to add in some pullouts to highlight important points and ideas in the proposal. He also wanted to include a box on the first page—maybe every page—that would highlight details about the organizational meeting.

Thomas decided that the first page would double as a cover page. He also didn't want the cover page to seem too formal, because he thought a formal cover page would invite the readers to save the proposal for later when they had more time—and more than likely never read it. Instead, he believed, a title on the top of the first page might invite the readers to start scanning the text immediately.

When he finished thumbnailing some pages, Thomas began developing a simple style sheet. He knew a small proposal like this one did not need an extensive style sheet; however, he wanted to jot down a few of his ideas for fonts, type sizes, and graphics. That way, John, Karen, and Sally could conform their parts of the proposal to a standard design. Figure 10.14 shows the style sheet that he started with.

From prior experience, Thomas knew his decisions in the style sheet would need to be modified as the text was put into the proposal. But, creating a style sheet took only a couple minutes, and it gave him a good idea of how the final proposal would look.

With his thumbnails and style sheet in hand, Thomas began creating a couple generic pages using the rough draft of the proposal they had written to this point. As he designed the generic pages, it became obvious that he needed to col-

FIGURE 10.13

Thumbnails for Elmdale Hill Proposal

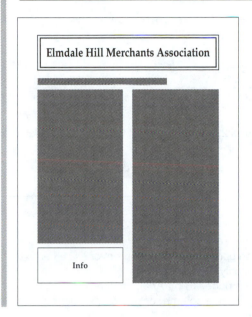

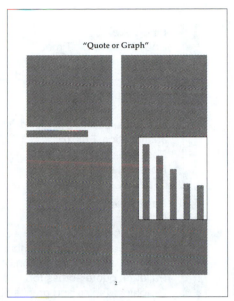

lect a little more information before he could completely design the proposal. First, he wanted to add some quotes from other merchants across the top of each body page. For example, he wanted to include a quote like, "I'm feeling added pressure due to the Wheatmill Mall," or, "Advertising on my own is too expensive." He felt these quotes on each page would add a human dimension to the proposal while reinforcing the themes in the written text. Second, Thomas needed some charts, tables, and graphics for the body pages. Karen had already volunteered to make these graphics, but Thomas knew he needed to tell her about the fonts, labels, and borders he wanted her to use.

Thomas kept designing and redesigning the proposal as the proposal was written and edited. The final design required some compromises and modifications to his original ideas. Nevertheless, when he looked back on the original rhetorical situation they laid out at the start, he felt his design met the readers' needs. You can see Thomas's final design for the Elmdale Hill proposal in Chapter 12.

FIGURE 10.14
Thomas's Style Sheet

Line Level
Body Text: 12 pt. Times
Italics: Use with titles and to emphasize

Paragraph Level
Leading: Single Space
Headings: Level 1, 16 pt. Arial; Level 2, 12 pt. Arial bold; Level 3, 12 pt. Arial italics
Justification: Full
Sequential lists: 1. 2. 3.
Nonsequential lists: boxes

Page Level
Columns: Double
Header: none
Footer: centered page number on each page, including cover
Borders: around information box only, 1 pt. lines
Pullouts: quote across top of each page, 18 pt. Arial, centered
Graphics: Tables and graphs fit into one column, or go across both columns at
top or bottom of page.

Graphics Level
Font: Arial 10 pt.
Labeling: Title and number across top of graphic in 12 pt. Arial bold
Borders: 1 pt. border around each graphic, if needed
Captions: none

Document Level
Binding: Plastic Comb
Cover stock: Same as body paper
Paper: 25 lb, off-white standard (Ivory), 8.5 x11 in.

Questions and Exercises

1. Choose three full-page advertisements from a magazine. How did the designers use balance, alignment, grouping, and consistency to design these advertisements? How is the rhetorical situation (subject, purpose, readers, context, objectives) reflected in the design of these pages?

2. Analyze the design used in a proposal. Write a memo to your instructor in which you discuss how the proposal's design uses the principles of balance, alignment, grouping, and consistency. Then, note where the proposal strays

from these principles. Based on your observations, do you think the proposal's design is effective? How might it be improved?

3. Many proposals are now being placed on the Internet or in CD-ROM format. Find a proposal on the Internet. How did the writers handle the proposal's on-screen design? How does the design of an online proposal differ from paper-based proposals? What are some strategies writers might follow to make proposals more readable on a computer screen?

4. For a practice or real proposal of your own, go through the five-step design process discussed in this chapter. Study the rhetorical situation from a design perspective, then thumbnail a few pages for your proposal. Write out a basic style sheet. Develop some generic pages for your proposal. And finally, add content into your design.

5. Study the page layouts used in other kinds of documents (newsletters, posters, books). Can any of these designs be adapted for use as models for designing proposals? Why might you try different designs that break away from the more traditional designs used in proposals?

6. Look at the designs of the example proposals in Chapter 12. How do these significantly different designs change the tone and readability of the text?

Using Graphics

Overview

This chapter discusses the use and design of graphics in a proposal. The chapter will meet the following objectives:

1. Discuss the importance of graphics in a proposal.
2. Offer four guidelines for using graphics appropriately.
3. Illustrate the proper use of graphs, tables, and charts.
4. Discuss the proper use of photography and drawings.

The Need for Graphics

Given the ease with which today's computers create graphics, there really is no good excuse for a proposal that lacks visuals like graphs, charts, tables, and even pictures. We live in an increasingly visual society, meaning that people rely more heavily on what they can see, not what they read. In many cases, graphics not only enhance the story you are trying to relate in your proposal, but also tell a large part of the story itself.

For example, consider the paragraph shown in Figure 11.1. The data points in this paragraph soon become a jumble of numbers that are difficult to process and almost impossible to remember. And yet, the simple table that follows this paragraph presents this same data in a highly accessible format.

Figure 11.1 illustrates how graphics can provide the readers with a great amount of information at a glance. Graphics help you avoid bogging the readers down in data, keeping them reading instead of giving them an excuse to just skip ahead to parts of the proposal where they will not be overwhelmed by numbers. Graphics also help you and the readers compare numbers and identify trends. In Figure 11.1, for instance, the figures in the paragraph are difficult to compare. However, when the figures are put into the table, the numbers are easy to compare. Later in this chapter, you will see how graphs and charts can be used to show trends in the data.

There are also other benefits to graphics. First, a graphic will often stop a reader from scanning the proposal. When scanning readers come across an interesting visual, they will typically look into the written text to find an explanation for the data being displayed. The graphic in this case serves as an "access

FIGURE 11.1
Text vs. Table

Example Text

According to the 2000 Sales Figures Report (p. 21), adults from ages 20–29 were responsible for purchasing an average of 30 meals per person per year, spending an average of $6.50 per visit, and accounting for 35 percent of our total sales. Meanwhile, teenagers (ages 10–19) purchased 120 meals per person per year, spending an average of $5.15 per visit and accounting for 40 percent of our total sales. Children under 10 years accounted for 10 percent of our overall sales, purchasing 50 meals per person per year at an average of $2.10 per visit. Adults ages 30-39 bought an average of 15 meals per year, spending $4.17 per visit and accounting for 10 percent of our overall sales. And finally, adults ages 40 years and above accounted for only 5 percent of our total sales, spending only an average of $3.94 per visit and purchasing only 10 meals per person per year.

Example Table

Table 24 Sales of Meals by Customer Age

Customer Age	Average Number of Meals per Year	Average Dollars Spent per Visit	Percent of Total Sales
under 10	30	$2.10	10
10–19	120	$5.15	40
20–29	30	$6.50	35
30–39	15	$4.17	10
over 40	10	$3.94	5

Source: 2000 Sales Figures Report, p. 21

---

point" at which the reader can re-enter the text. Second, graphics break up large blocks of written text, providing the readers with a periodic rest while reading the proposal. Third, and perhaps most important, graphics visually reinforce your argument in the proposal. In our visual age, readers tend to trust what they can see, so a well-placed graphic can often bolster the proposal's argument with a simple glance.

Guidelines for Using Graphics

Graphics capture the readers' attention. When used properly, they reinforce and clarify your message, often slicing through the numerous details and numbers to create a powerful image in the readers' minds. Spatially, they can highlight relationships among data points, organizations, and people. When used improperly, however, graphics introduce unnecessary clutter to your proposal, distracting the readers' attention away from the important parts of the written text. For these reasons, it is important to use graphics wisely.

There are four guidelines you can follow when using graphics in a proposal. A graphic should do the following:

- Tell a simple story
- Reinforce the written text, not replace it
- Be ethical
- Be labeled and placed properly

Let us consider each of these guidelines more closely.

A Graphic Should Tell a Simple Story

When you glance at a graphic in a proposal, you should immediately know what "story" it is designed to tell. In a line graph, for example, a rising line might indicate an increase in sales. In a bar chart, a tall column next to a short column might show that one factory produced more product than another factory. In a pie chart, a large slice might indicate where the majority of the last year's budget was spent. These kinds of graphics tell a simple story that the readers can immediately recognize.

When planning a graphic, first ask yourself what story you want the graph, chart, table, or picture to tell. Do you want to illustrate a trend in sales? Do you want to compare levels of growth among test subjects and a control? Do you want to show how the budget should be divided? Once you have articulated the story you want the graphic to tell, write it down in one sentence. For instance, you might write, "This graph will show how different amounts of water affect the growth of hybrid Roma tomato plants." Once you have written down the story you want to tell, you can then identify the appropriate way to illustrate that story. The graph in Figure 11.2 demonstrates how a graphic can tell a simple story about tomatoes.

If a graphic does not tell a *simple* story, the readers will often not be able to figure out what message it is trying to convey. Readers tend to glance at graphics, not study them in depth. So, if the graphic's story is not immediately apparent, the graphic will just waste their time and it will waste space in your proposal.

A Graphic Should Reinforce the Written Text

A graphic can be used to clarify and reinforce, but it cannot replace the written text. Instead, the written text and the visual text should play off each other. The written text should refer the readers to the graphic, and the graphic should reinforce what is said in the written text. The two should work hand-in-hand. For example, the written text might claim, "The chart in Figure 5 illustrates Carson Industries' rise in productivity over the last ten years. We believe this rise, in part, demonstrates that our new flextime program is having a positive effect on employee morale." The written text in this case accomplishes two goals. First, it refers the readers to the figure, using the figure as a supportive example. Second, the written text clearly identifies the story the graph is designed to tell.

FIGURE 11.2
A Graph that Tells a Simple Story

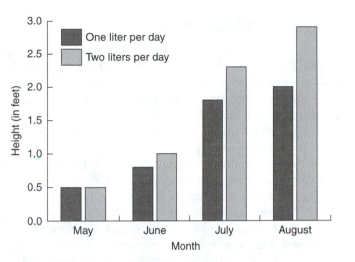

Graph 10: Average height of G-10456a hybrid
Roma tomato plants receiving different
amounts of water per day.

If a graphic does not directly support written text, it should not be included in the proposal. Sometimes, when a proposal is being revised, the written text that references a particular graphic is edited out of the proposal. At these moments, it might be tempting to just keep the graphic in the proposal anyway, even though it no longer reinforces the written text. In the end, though, these excess graphics only distract and confuse the readers. The readers will wonder why you wasted space (and their time) with a graphic that was not even important enough to mention in the text.

Along these lines, graphics should never be used to simply decorate a text. Not long ago, pie charts and clip art were novelties in proposals, making them interesting for that reason alone. But today, excess pie charts and clip art have become annoying eyesores in proposals, especially when they are being used to merely add decoration or color. Used appropriately, pie charts can be helpful, as we will discuss later in this chapter. But when pie charts are used as decoration, they suggest a dumbed-down proposal that lacks substance. Junk pie charts waste the readers' time and insult their intelligence. If a pie chart is only being used to decorate the text, the proposal is better off without it.

It is tempting to advise you not to use clip art at all. When desktop publishing first came into the workplace, clip art was an original way to enhance the message and tone of a proposal. But now, most readers are tired of those little pictures of people shaking hands, pointing at whiteboards, and climbing ladders. In most cases, clip art is just decorative fluff that takes the readers' attention away from your proposals' argument.

A Graphic Should Be Ethical

In the effort to strengthen a proposal's message, there is always a temptation to use graphs, charts, and tables to hide facts or exaggerate trends. For example, it might be tempting to use a table to hide important data points that do not support the proposal's argument. In a line graph, it might be tempting to leave out data points that resist attempts to draw a smooth sloping line. Or, perhaps the scales on a bar chart might be altered to suggest more growth than is actually the case.

A good rule of thumb with graphics—and a good principle to follow in proposal writing altogether—is to always be absolutely honest with the readers. The readers are not fools, so attempts to use graphics to stretch the truth are easily detected. Moreover, dishonesty in a proposal has a way of coming back to haunt the bidders later. After all, a proposal is just the beginning of a relationship, not the end. The bidder may win the contract by misleading the readers, but later a price will be paid when those deceptions are discovered. In the long run, honest words and graphics keep you out of trouble.

Kostelnick and Roberts (1998) warn that unethical graphics can erode the credibility of an entire document (pp. 300–302). Even if the readers only suspect deception, they will grow suspicious of the graphic, the document, and the writers themselves. Also, in his book, *The Visual Display of Quantitative Information* (1983), Edward Tufte offers an insightful discussion of ethical and unethical uses of graphics. His discussion of visual ethics provides helpful tips about staying honest when using graphics.

A Graphic Should Be Labeled and Placed Properly

Proper labeling and placement of graphics helps the readers move back and forth between the written text and the visual displays. Each graphic in a proposal should be sequentially numbered and labeled with an informative title. For example, the graph in Figure 11.2 includes a number (Graph 10) and a title (Average height of G-10456a hybrid Roma tomato plants receiving different amounts of water per day). This labeling allows the reader to quickly locate the graphic in the proposal.

Other parts of the graphic should also be carefully labeled:

- The x and y axes of graphs and charts should display standard units of measurement.
- Columns and rows in tables should be labeled so the readers can easily locate specific data points.
- Important features of drawings or illustrations should be identified with arrows or lines and some explanatory text.

Captions are not mandatory with graphics, but a sentence or two of explanation can often help reinforce the story the graphic is trying to tell. Also, captions should include names of any sources if the data or graph was taken from another text.

When placing a graphic, try to put it on the page where it is mentioned or, at the furthest, on the following page. Readers will rarely flip more than one page to look for a graphic. Even if they *do* make the effort to hunt down a graphic that is pages away, the effort will take them out of the flow of the proposal, urging them to start skimming the text. In almost all cases, a graphic should appear after the point in the text at which it is mentioned. When a graphic appears before it is mentioned, it often confuses the readers because they lack the context to interpret what the graphic is trying to show.

Using Graphics to Display Information and Data

A variety of different graphics are available for displaying information and data. Each graphic allows you to tell a different story with the information you are presenting.

Line Graphs

In proposals, line graphs are typically used to show trends over time. The y-axis (vertical) displays some kind of measured quantity like income, sales, production, and so on. The x-axis (horizontal) is divided into even time increments like years, months, days, or hours. For example, Figure 11.3 shows a line graph that plots the population changes in mountain lions and bighorn sheep over a five-year period.

As you can see, the line graph allows the readers to easily recognize the trends in animal populations. The drawback of line graphs is their inability to help the readers gather exact figures. For instance, in Figure 11.3, can you tell exactly how many mountain lions were sighted in 1997? Line graphs are strongest when the trend is more important than the exact figures behind that trend.

Bar Charts

Like line graphs, bar charts can be used to show trends over time. Bar charts are also well suited to show increases in volume. For example, Figure 11.4 demonstrates how a bar chart can plot a volume.

The advantage of a bar chart over a line graph is that the vertical columns suggest a physical quantity. In other words, the columns allow readers to make easier comparisons among data points because one column is physically larger or smaller than the others. A line graph, in contrast, only plots vertical points without providing a sense of the volume that is being measured.

Something you should also notice is that the y-axis in a bar chart must always start at zero. If the y-axis does not start at zero, the differences among columns will be exaggerated artificially, giving the readers the impression that the differences in amounts are greater than they really are. In almost all bar charts, it is unethical to start the y-axis at any number other than zero.

FIGURE 11.3
A Line Graph

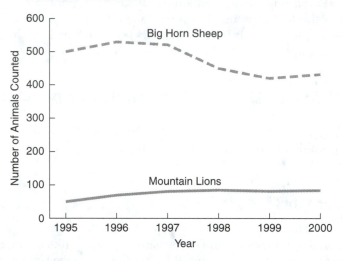

Figure 17.2: Relationship between Populations of Mountain Lions and Big Horn Sheep in the Manzano Mountains

FIGURE 11.4
A Simple Bar Chart

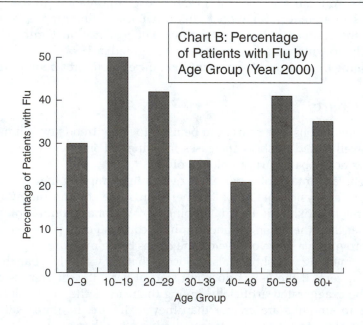

Chart B: Percentage of Patients with Flu by Age Group (Year 2000)

FIGURE 11.5
A Basic Table

Table 2: Observations of Perching Birds at
Peterson Pits during Month of June

Birds Sighted from 6:00–9:00 a.m.	1997	1998	1999	2000
Robins	370	380	420	443
Purple Finches	284	293	305	321
Cardinals	84	92	100	113
Blue Jays	79	92	105	103
Goldfinches	27	33	25	37

Source: A. Lawler, (2001) "Habitat Restoration Strengthens Perching Bird Populations" *Central Iowa Ornithology Quarterly 73*, p. 287–301.

Tables

Tables offer the most efficient way to display a large amount of data in a small amount of space (Figure 11.5). The number and title of the table should appear above the table. Along the left column, the *row titles* should list the items being measured. Along the top row, the *column titles* should list the qualities of the items being measured. Beneath the table, if applicable, a citation should identify the source of information.

In proposals, tables tend to be used two ways. First, they are used in Situation sections to provide baseline data that offers a numerical snapshot of the past or present situation. Figure 11.5, for example, might be used to show the current situation regarding bird populations in Story County, Iowa. Second, tables are used to present budgets, breaking down costs into cells that can be easily referenced.

Pie Charts

As stated earlier, pie charts are often overused in proposals. Nevertheless, a good pie chart can be used to demonstrate how a whole was cut into parts. In proposals, pie charts are often used to illustrate how sales, income, or expenses have been divided. For example, the two pie charts in Figure 11.6 show the estimated sources of income and expenses for a nonprofit organization.

When labeling a pie chart, you should try to put category titles and specific numbers in the graphic itself. For instance, in Figure 11.6, each slice of the pie charts is labeled and includes a measurement to show how the pie was divided. Without these labels, these pie charts would not be nearly as helpful to the readers.

FIGURE 11.6
Pie Charts

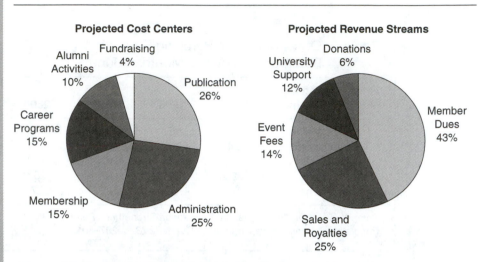

Figure 15: Proposed Alumni Association Budget, 2000–2001

One thing to remember about pie charts is that they use a large amount of space to display only a limited amount of data. The pie charts in Figure 11.6, for instance, use half a page to plot a mere six and five points, respectively. If you decide to use a pie chart, make sure the story you are illustrating is worth that much space in your proposal.

Organizational Charts

In proposals, organizational charts are used to illustrate the relationships among people, companies, and divisions (Figure 11.7). Usually, these charts are placed in the Qualifications section of a proposal or an appendix, though occasionally they may be used in the discussion of the plan. Essentially, they are designed to show the chain of command in a project or organization.

Organizational charts can be helpful, especially when there are many people and divisions involved in a project. In proposals for smaller projects, however, organizational charts often waste too much space. When deciding whether to include an organizational chart, ask yourself whether the chart has a specific purpose. Will it help the clients figure out who at their company will interface with people at your company? Will it help participants determine who answers to whom in a project? If your organizational chart does not have a clear purpose, then you should move it to an appendix or not use it at all.

FIGURE 11.7
An Organizational Chart

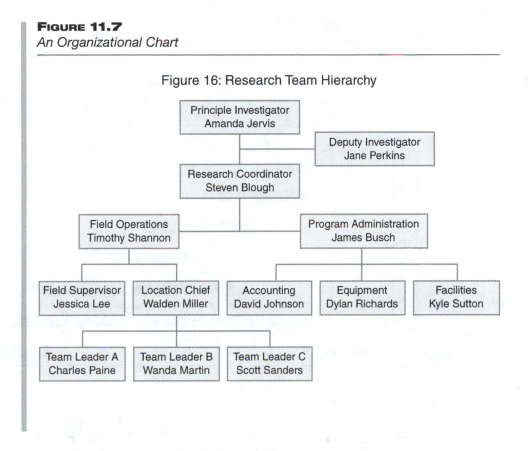

Figure 16: Research Team Hierarchy

Gantt Charts

Gantt charts have become quite popular in proposals, especially now that project-planning software regularly includes graphing tools to create these charts. Gantt charts, like the one in Figure 11.8, are used to illustrate a timeline, showing when various phases of the project will begin and end.

There are two primary benefits to including a Gantt chart in a proposal. First, the chart shows how different stages of a complex project will overlap and intersect. Second, it gives the readers an overall sense of how the project proceeds from start to finish. The Gantt chart in Figure 11.8 demonstrates both of these benefits.

Readers are beginning to expect Gantt charts in proposals, especially in highly technical proposals. These charts are typically used to reinforce the discussion of the proposal's plan, offering a visual sense of how the project will progress.

FIGURE 11.8
A Gantt Chart

Table 23: Project Schedule

		March	April	May	June	July	Aug.	Sept.	Oct.	Nov.	Dec.
		Review Meetings Each Monday									
Activity	Planning	▬									
	Design		▬▬								
	Prototypes			▬▬							
	Testing				▬▬▬						
	Production			factory prep. ▬▬▬				full production ▬▬▬▬▬			
	Promotion		plan campaign ▬▬	promo. materials ▬▬▬				sales reps out ▬▬	convention ▬▬		
	Delivery									▬▬	

Pictures

Digital cameras and scanners are making the placement of photographs in proposals easier than ever. When used properly, pictures can visually reinforce claims made in the written text. But, like those slides of your last vacation, photographs rarely capture the essence of what you are trying to show. In many cases, photographs leave the readers wondering what story the writers are trying to illustrate. To use a photograph appropriately, make sure it tells a clear story, and never use photographs to merely decorate the proposal. If you decide to include photographs, the readers should be able to determine exactly what story the photograph is trying to illustrate.

Photographing People

When photographing people, a good rule of thumb is to only include people doing what they actually do in the workplace (people rarely huddle in a cubicle, pointing at a computer screen). If you need to include a picture of a person or a group of people standing still, take them outside and photograph them against a simple but scenic background. Photographs taken in the office tend to look dark, depressing, and dreary. Photographs taken outdoors, on the other hand, imply a personality of openness and free thinking.

If you need to photograph people inside, put as much light as possible on the subjects. If your subjects will allow it, use some facial powder to reduce the glare off their cheeks, noses, and foreheads. Then, take their picture against a simple backdrop to reduce background clutter that may distract the readers from the subjects of the photograph. If you are photographing an individual, take a picture of their head and shoulders. People tend to look uncomfortable in full-body pictures.

Photographing Equipment

When taking pictures of equipment, try to capture a close-up shot of the equipment at work. If the equipment has moving parts, try to focus the picture on those parts doing something. After all, a machine sitting alone on a factory floor looks pretty boring. A machine in action implies progress. If, however, you need to show a machine doing nothing, put a white dropcloth behind it to block out the other items and people in the background. Again, make sure you put as much lighting as possible on the machine so it will show up clearly in your photograph.

Drawings

Line drawings are often superior to pictures for illustrating machines, buildings, and designs. Whereas pictures usually include more detail than needed, a drawing limits the graphic to only the basic feature of the subject. A drawing allows you to show close-ups of the parts in a machine, the details of a building, or the schematics of electronic components. Drawings also allow you to show "cut aways" of buildings or machines, illustrating features that are not visible from the outside. Figure 11.9 shows a drawing that might appear in a proposal written by Lisa Miller for her pre-proposal to Earl Grey Designs.

Unless you are an artist yourself, it is probably a good idea to hire a professional illustrator to handle your drawings in a proposal. Before meeting with the illustrator, sketch (thumbnail) the drawing you have in mind. Then, when you meet with the illustrator, explain what story you want the drawing to tell or what point you want it to make. With this information, the illustrator will better be able to draw a graphic that suits your proposal's needs.

The primary drawback of using drawings is the time and expense required to create them. You should plan to use drawings only when they are absolutely needed to make an important point in the proposal.

Other Kinds of Graphics

Of course, there are countless other ways to visually present information and data. The graphics discussed in this chapter are only the most prevalent ones used in proposals. In special cases, you may find yourself needing radar plots, maps, flowcharts, blueprints, scatterplots, pictographs, logic trees, screen shots, and other graphics not typically found in proposals. Also, each of the graphics discussed in this chapter can be altered to suit different needs. A bar chart alone, for example, can employ a variety of formats, such as a horizontal bar chart, stacked-bar chart, 100-percent bar chart, and deviation bar chart.

FIGURE 11.9
A Drawing

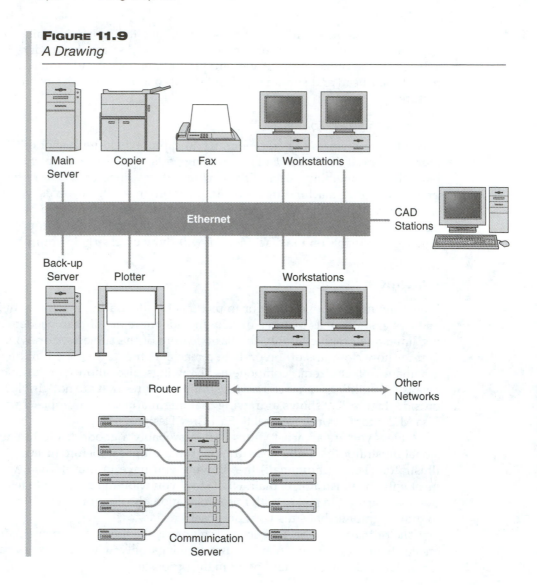

If you need to create a more specialized graphic, there are books available to walk you through their development. Tufte's *The Visual Display of Quantitative Information* (1983) is especially informative, and Kostelnick and Roberts offer a thorough discussion of graphics in their book *Designing Visual Language* (1998). See the References at the end of this book for more information on these texts.

Last Word

Graphics are often the sign of a professional, quality proposal. As you are writing the proposal, you should look for places where a graphic might be used to reinforce the message in the written text. In most cases, it is best to create each graphic *as* you are writing the proposal, or find someone else to do the graphics while you are composing. Why? Invariably, if you wait until the last moment to create the graphics, you will run out of time and end up including no graphics at all. In today's competitive environment, the absence of graphics in a proposal can often be the difference between a successful and unsuccessful proposal.

When writing a proposal, we must keep in mind that our society is becoming increasingly visual. Readers often do not have the time or patience to read a proposal word for word. So, they often scan the proposal looking for the main points. Graphics can be used to reinforce those main points, help the readers make comparisons among ideas, and illustrate trends. The old adage that "a picture is worth a thousand words" won't allow you to replace a thousand words of your proposal with a graphic. However, a graphic can be used to clarify or drive home an important point with a simple glance from the readers. They are powerful tools that you should plan to use in your proposals.

CASE STUDY: **Inventing Visuals**

Karen liked making graphs and charts. Maybe it was just the frustrated artist in her, trying to escape her otherwise business-oriented life. Maybe she understood illustrations better than piles of data. Whatever her reasons, she volunteered to handle the graphics in the proposal. Karen knew these visuals would be important, especially since many of the primary readers, other business owners in Elmdale Hill, would probably only scan the proposal. The graphics would need to bring them into the text.

Karen had two problems. First, for her, making graphs, charts, tables, and drawings was tedious work. Fortunately, her shop's spreadsheet software included a graphing tool that would help her turn data into visual displays. Her second problem was a bit more serious. At the moment, she didn't have any data to graph. The survey described in the proposal's Plan section would eventually generate some data, but those numbers would only be available *after* the proposal had been sent out and approved. Karen needed some numbers *before* the proposal would be sent out.

So, she began thinking about the stories she wanted her graphs to tell. On a sheet of paper, she wrote down a few trends she wanted to illustrate:

- Show a decrease (or increase) in sales in the Elmdale Hill district.

- Show crime levels in the district.
- Demonstrate that merchants associations can improve sales.

Creating a graphic to show the first trend, a decrease or increase in sales, would be a challenge. Karen needed real numbers—not just hearsay about declining sales—but she knew most of the business owners in Elmdale Hill would be reluctant to share their sales figures with her. So, she decided to conduct a small, unscientific survey to generate some numbers she could use. Her survey included the four questions shown in Figure 11.10.

On a morning break, Karen and John walked through the Elmdale Hill business district, handing a survey to each merchant. Karen knew her survey would not meet the standards of a professional pollster. Nevertheless, it would generate some helpful data for their proposal.

Overall, the other merchants seemed to welcome her survey. A few of them filled it out on the spot. Others dropped it in her mailbox after closing time. A couple of days later, she and John used another morning break to pick up the remainder of the surveys. About 80 percent of the merchants responded, and a few declined.

Karen tabulated the responses to the survey questions and entered them into her spreadsheet program. She decided to display the responses as

FIGURE 11.10
Karen's Unscientific Survey

Dear Elmdale Hill Business Owner,

My name is Karen Sanchez, owner of New Fashions clothing store on Central Avenue. A few other business owners and I are exploring the idea of creating a merchants association in Elmdale Hill. We are currently writing a proposal to all the Elmdale Hill merchants explaining our ideas.

To gauge the health of the Elmdale Hill business district, I have created a simple survey that should give us some insight into overall sales. If you could take a few moments to fill out the survey, you will help us write a more informed proposal. We don't need names or specific financial information.

Thank you for your help. I will visit your business in the next couple days to pick up the survey. Or, you can drop it off at my shop at 587 Central Ave. Please call me at 555-1192 if you have any questions.

Please answer the following questions by marking the appropriate box:

Questions:	Substantial Increase	Small Increase	Small Decrease	Substantial Decrease
1. Which answer best describes your sales this year?	☐	☐	☐	☐
2. Which answer best describes your sales over the last five years?	☐	☐	☐	☐
3. Which answer best describes your expected sales over the next five years?	☐	☐	☐	☐
4. In your opinion, which answer best describes how sales are doing in the whole Elmdale Hill district?	☐	☐	☐	☐

a horizontal bar chart, which illustrated the answers to each response (Figure 11.11).

Karen then turned to the second story she wanted to illustrate—crime rates in Elmdale Hill. Collecting crime statistics was easier than she expected. She talked to the president of the Elmdale Hill Neighborhood Association. The association's neighborhood watch committee had been receiving crime statistics from the local police every two years. The police statistics were broken down into four areas (i.e., violent crime, burglary, petty theft, and vandalism), charting the incidents of these crimes. Karen added this data into her spreadsheet program and created the line graph shown in Figure 11.12.

Karen noticed that her line graph confirmed her suspicions that crime had not increased significantly over the past ten years. In fact, petty theft and burglary had been declining. Vandalism seemed to be the only problem that was increasing significantly.

Finally, Karen wanted to graphically illustrate that merchants associations boost sales in business districts like Elmdale Hill. Unfortunately, she discovered that data on this subject was hard to obtain. She contacted a few of the existing merchants associations in the state, but all they could provide were graphs that showed their own trends in sales. Karen soon realized she would not be able to create a graph that showed, in general, that merchants associations improve sales. So, she decided to plot a graph showing the sales trends of the Market Square Merchants Association, a merchant association in a business district similar to Elmdale Hill. Figure 11.13 shows the graph she created.

Once she had the data, it took Karen only a couple of hours to develop these graphs. She felt the time was well spent. Not only would these graphs visually reinforce the written text in the proposal, they would also give the readers quick insight into the current situation in Elmdale Hill and the potential benefits of starting a merchants association.

FIGURE 11.11
Karen's Bar Chart

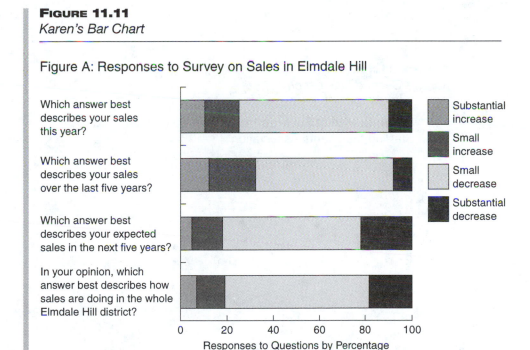

Figure A: Responses to Survey on Sales in Elmdale Hill

FIGURE 11.12
Karen's Line Graph

Figure B: Elmdale Hill Crime Trends Since 1990

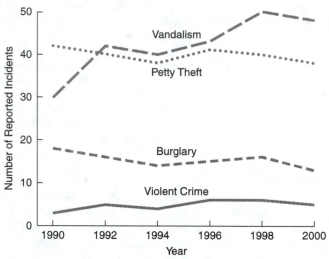

Source: 2001 Elmdale Hill Neighborhood Watch Report

FIGURE 11.13
Karen's Second Line Graph

Figure C: Market Square's Increase in Sales after Starting Merchants Association

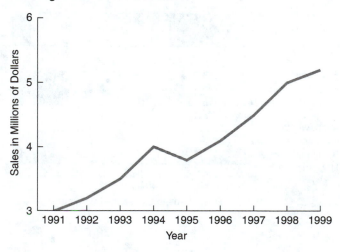

Questions and Exercises

1. Find a graph, chart, or table in a printed document. Does the graphic tell a simple story? Does it reinforce the written text, not replace it? Is it ethical? Is it labeled and placed properly? Find one or more graphics that do not follow the guidelines discussed in this chapter. Are they still effective? How could you improve each graphic?

2. Find a document that includes minimal or no graphics. Looking through the document, can you find instances where a graphic might have helped reinforce or clarify the written text? Create a graph, table, or chart that might be included in this document.

3. Create a simple survey that asks questions about a local problem. Ask some people to fill out your survey. Then, use the data you gathered to create various different types of graphs, tables, or charts.

4. Look at pictures in your local newspaper. Can you articulate what story they were designed to tell, even if they were not accompanied by written text? Also, look for pictures that do not tell clear stories. How could the author have used better pictures to suit the needs of the document and its readers?

5. Use the data in Figure 11.5 to create a couple of different kinds of graphs. Try making a bar chart and a line graph. How do these different graphs allow you to tell a different story with this data. Which graph do you think is more effective?

12 | Putting the Proposal Together

Overview

This chapter will discuss the development of front and back matter while describing how to revise proposals. The chapter will meet the following learning objectives:

1. Discuss the importance of rethinking and revising proposals.
2. Show how to write the front matter of a proposal.
3. Show how to write the back matter of a proposal.
4. Describe through the revision process.

Seeing the Proposal as a Whole Document

To this point in this book, you have learned how to invent, organize, stylize, and design your proposal, using rhetorical principles that are both ancient and modern. As you near the end of the proposal writing process, it is time to take stock of your proposal as a whole document. You need to ask yourself whether your proposal achieves its purpose and addresses the needs of the readers. These kinds of questions can be difficult to ask, especially when a good draft of the proposal is sitting in front of you. But, a committed effort to finish off the proposal at this point is usually the difference between the successful proposal and the one that came close.

In this chapter, we are going to discuss how to pull the entire proposal package together. The proposal itself is the core of the package. Nevertheless, you will likely also include additional materials like a letter of transmittal, an executive summary, a table of contents, and appendices. These materials are called the *front matter* and *back matter* of the proposal. Also, at this stage in the process, you should think about revising the proposal at least one more time. Your proposal probably looks rather finished. But don't stop now. Here is where you can add that extra polish that will convince the clients that you have the right plan to address their needs.

This chapter also includes two final versions of proposals that have been used as case studies throughout this book: the Elmdale Hill Merchants Association Proposal, and Insight Systems' proposal to Earl Grey Design. In these final drafts, you can see how the writers revised their proposals into their final forms.

Inventing Front Matter

Front matter consists of the materials that appear before the introduction of the main proposal. Like the introduction, the front matter is intended to set a context or framework for the proposal. Items in the front matter include some or all of the following items:

- Letter of transmittal
- Cover page
- Executive summary
- Table of contents

These materials are not mandatory in a proposal—nothing is—but they are often useful accessories that help the readers work more efficiently through your ideas. The inclusion of these front matter items also shows an attention to detail that the readers will appreciate.

Letters or Memos of Transmittal

The purpose of a letter of transmittal (or a memo of transmittal for internal proposals) is to introduce the readers to the proposal. Even though a proposal may not need a letter or memo of transmittal, there are a couple reasons why you should include one anyway. First, letters and memos are intended to be personal correspondences, unlike proposals which tend to sound more formal and less personal. On this personal level, a letter or memo of transmittal allows you to shake hands with the readers before they start looking over your ideas. Letters and memos are usually lighter in tone than proposals, setting the readers at ease before they start considering your ideas.

A second reason why letters and memos of transmittal are important is their ability to steer your proposal into the right hands. In large companies and organizations, even the most important documents end up on the wrong desk, in the wrong mailbox, and ultimately in the wrong trash can or recycle bin. By identifying the proposal's readers and purpose up front, a letter or memo of transmittal can steer your proposal into the right hands. If the wrong person receives your proposal, the letter or memo of transmittal will help them send it to the exact person who should receive it.

Writing a Letter or Memo of Transmittal

Like other documents, letters and memos have an introduction, body, and conclusion:

Introduction   The introduction of a letter or memo of transmittal should offer some background information and state the purpose of the proposal. Specifically, you should mention the RFP to which the proposal is responding or the meeting at which the proposal was requested. This kind of opening will help the readers remember exactly why the proposal is being sent to them. Then, you should tell the readers the purpose of the proposal itself. You can even include the same purpose statement used in the proposal's introduction, though most writers prefer to paraphrase that sentence to avoid the feeling of repetition. An introduction to a letter or memo of transmittal should run, at most, a few sentences.

Body The body of a letter or memo of transmittal should highlight and summarize the important points of the proposal. You might describe your plan in miniature if you think it will grab the readers' interest. You might also mention some of the key benefits of your plan or briefly describe your, your team, or your company's qualifications. Try not to run on in the body of the letter or memo. A letter or memo of transmittal should be concise, saving the details for the proposal itself. As a rule of thumb, the body of this letter or memo should run about two or three paragraphs.

Conclusion The conclusion should thank the readers for their time and tell them who to contact if they have any questions or need further information. You might also tell the readers that you will be in touch with them by a specific date to follow up on the proposal. The conclusion should be concise, perhaps two or three sentences.

Stylistically, letters and memos of transmittal should be simple and personal. The tone should be upbeat and friendly, yet respectful. A judicious use of *you* and *we* will make a personal connection between the readers and yourself. Meanwhile, you should avoid using business letter clichés like "enclosed please find," "pursuant to our agreement," or "as per your request." These clichés tend to undermine the personal nature of a letter or memo, unnecessarily putting the readers on guard. This kind of hackneyed business language will only make your letter or memo sound distant and aloof—an unfortunate tone to use if you want the readers to trust you. Instead of using clichés, simply write the letter as though you are talking to another human being. After all, you *are* talking to another human being, not a corporation. In a face-to-face conversation, you would never use these tired clichés and strange phrases, so you should avoid using them in a letter or memo.

In most cases, a letter or memo of transmittal should be limited to one page. Avoid the temptation to start arguing for your plan at this point. Instead, keep this letter or memo concise and positive. Let the proposal do the heavy lifting.

Lisa Miller's Letter of Transmittal to Earl Grey Design

A few chapters ago, Lisa Miller completed the first draft of her proposal to Earl Grey. While she was waiting for comments on the draft from her boss and the other engineers at Insight Systems, she decided to write a cover letter for the proposal (Figure 12.1).

FIGURE 12.1
Lisa Miller's Cover Letter to Earl Grey

Insight Systems ■

15520 Naperville Rd., Naperville, Illinois 62000-1234 (630) 555-1298
www.insight_systems.com

April 21, 2001

Grant E. Moser, Office Manager
Earl Grey Design
300 S. Michigan Ave., Suite 1201
Chicago, Illinois 60001

Dear Mr. Moser,

Thank you for the opportunity to submit a pre-proposal in response to Earl Grey's "Request For Proposals for Managing Office Growth" (May 29, 2001). Our pre-proposal outlines a strategy that will help your firm preserve its current award-winning office on Michigan Avenue while supporting your continued growth in the Chicago architectural market.

Our plan for managing your growth is simple. We suggest Earl Grey implement a telecommuting network that allows some employees to work from home or on-site. Telecommuting has several advantages. First, it will allow your company to maintain financial flexibility in the ever-uncertain Chicago market. Second, implementing a telecommunication network will create minimal disruption to Earl Grey's current operations. Third, telecommuting will preserve Earl Grey's already high employee morale, helping you retain and recruit top-level architects and staff.

We also look forward to building a lasting relationship with Earl Grey. Insight Systems has been a leader in telecommunication for more than twenty years. We have the right combination of innovation and experience to address Earl Grey's immediate and long-term needs.

Thank you for your time and consideration. Lisa Miller tells me she enjoyed meeting you and touring the Earl Grey office. I am looking forward to meeting you myself in the near future. If you have any questions or need further information, please call me at 1-800-555-9823, ext. 001. Otherwise, Lisa Miller can be reached by phone or e-mail (lmiller@insight_systems.com).

Sincerely,

Hanna Gibbons, Ph.D.
Chief Executive Officer, Insight Systems

Lisa decided to write the letter from her boss, Hanna Gibbons, directly to Grant Moser, the Point of Contact for the RFP. Of course, she knew others at Earl Grey would read this letter of transmittal, especially the principal architects at the firm, Susan James and Thomas Weber. But, she had a hunch that a personalized letter to Mr. Moser might incline him more favorably toward her proposal. In her experience writing proposals, Lisa had found that POCs often have influence over the primary readers, even if they are not the decision-makers themselves. If Mr. Moser did have some influence, Lisa hoped her letter would help win him over to her company's side.

Lisa kept the body of the letter short. In the second paragraph, she decided to stress the benefits of her plan rather than summarize her proposal at length. A long discussion of telecommuting would have just made the letter sound complicated, so she simply mentioned her plan and then stated some of its strengths. Then, in the third paragraph, she briefly pointed out Insight Systems' experience in the area. Again, though, she kept the discussion concise. She did not want to bog the readers down in details at this point.

The conclusion of the letter was meant to leave a positive image in the minds of Mr. Moser and the primary readers. At the end, the letter thanks the readers and looks to the future. It also provides them with contact information in case they have questions or need more information.

Overall, Lisa's letter of transmittal did not add anything new to the proposal. Nevertheless, it set a personal tone that she hoped would carry over a positive feeling into the reading of the proposal itself.

The Cover Page

The cover page of a proposal, like the letter of transmittal, is intended to identify the subject of the proposal and set a particular tone. The cover page typically includes the following items:

- Title of the proposal
- Name of the client's company
- Name and logo of the company submitting the proposal
- Date on which the proposal was submitted

Cover pages can be simple or elaborate. Like the rest of the proposal, the design of the cover page should fit the character of the project and the readers. For example, the cover page on the left in Figure 12.2 is intended to set a conservative tone for a proposal. It's use of a traditional serif font and a balanced page offers a feeling of security. The cover page on the right is a bit more progressive with its use of a sans serif font and a somewhat unbalanced page layout.

Is a cover page mandatory? Of course not. But a cover page is an easy way to set a professional tone for the proposal. Like the cover of a book, cover pages provide a distinct starting point at which the readers will begin assessing the merits of your ideas.

FIGURE 12.2
Two Different Cover Pages

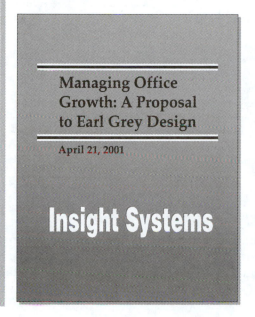
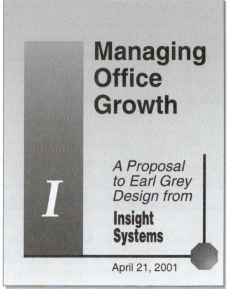

Executive Summary

In our fast-paced culture, executive summaries are often expected in proposals, especially large proposals. The purpose of an executive summary is to boil the proposal down to a text that can be read in minutes. In one to three pages, the executive summary goes over the current situation, the plan, the qualifications, and even the costs. It provides an overall snapshot of the proposal, so your readers can quickly determine the proposal's major points and claims.

Executive summaries can be organized many different ways, but they tend to mirror the structure of the proposal itself. The first paragraph in the summary identifies the purpose, subject, and main point of the proposal. The body paragraphs summarize the situation, plan, qualifications, and costs. The conclusion of the executive summary might mention a few benefits of the plan.

The importance of the executive summary should not be underestimated. Decision makers in most companies are typically short on time, so they often rely on executive summaries to help them to cut down the pile of competing proposals to a few proposals that will be read in depth. Also, readers often use the executive summary at meetings to help them quickly refresh their understanding of the proposal's main points. In some cases, the decision makers may end up reading the executive summary more closely and frequently than the proposal itself. So, it needs to be well written.

FIGURE 12.3
An Ineffective Table of Contents

Table of Contents
Executive Summary..iii
Introduction...1
Situation..1
Plan...2
Qualifications 6
Costs...7
Conclusion 8
Appendix: Budget 9

Table of Contents

A table of contents is a standard feature in most proposals over ten pages. It provides the readers with an overview of the contents of the proposal, helping them determine the most efficient way to read the text. It also forecasts the structure of the proposal, providing the readers with a mental framework into which the content of the proposal will be placed.

Ineffective tables of contents tend to use headings that lack meaning. For example, Figure 12.3 shows a table of contents that relies too heavily on nonspecific headings. This table of contents does not provide the readers with a solid understanding of the contents of the proposal. It also signals that the headings used in the proposal are not particularly descriptive or helpful.

An effective table of contents provides the readers with a meaningful outline of the contents of the proposal. Each title in the table of contents should be distinctive, specific, and long enough to give the readers a clear sense of what is in each section. To avoid a table of contents that lacks meaning, use meaningful headings that are found in the proposal itself. List out these headings in the table of contents in a way that highlights the structure of the proposal (see Figure 12.4).

FIGURE 12.4
A More Effective Table of Contents

Table of Contents
Executive Summary iii
Introduction 1
The Office Space Needs at Earl Grey....................................1
Our Plan: Maintaining Flexibility 2
Qualifications of Insight Systems...6
The Plan's Benefits and Project Costs 7
Appendix: Budget Rationale 9

Overall, the changes from Figure 12.3 to Figure 12.4 are small, but the revised table of contents offers more description of the contents of the proposal. The readers can now better anticipate the topics that will be discussed.

Inventing Back Matter

Back matter includes additional materials that support the information in the body of the proposal. Often called the *appendices,* the back matter in a proposal becomes a reference tool for the readers. It can include any or all of the following items related to the subject of the proposal:

- Itemized budget and budget rationale
- Resumes of management and key personnel
- Analytical reports or white papers
- News or magazine articles
- Prior proposals
- Formulas and calculations
- Glossary of terms
- Bibliography
- Personal or corporate references

Each appendix should be labeled with a number or letter, so it can be referred to in the body of the proposal. For example, in the body of the proposal, the readers might see the note, "The geothermal formulas and calculations used to determine these figures can be found in Appendix D." If the readers want to check those figures, they will know that they can then turn to that appendix in the back of the proposal.

In each appendix, an opening paragraph should introduce the contents that follow. For instance, if you decide to include copies of some magazine articles you collected on the subject, the appendix's opening paragraph might explain that you have included the articles to show the importance of the subject to the public. You might also briefly discuss how these articles reinforce the argument you are making in the body of the proposal. Even a glossary of terms should include some kind of short opening paragraph to help the readers understand the purpose of the glossary.

The most important form of back matter, the budget rationale, was discussed in Chapter 8. Let us look at some other kinds of back matter.

Resumes of Management and Key Personnel

It is becoming increasingly common to include the resumes of managers and key personnel in an appendix to the proposal. Though your Qualifications section may have included biographies of the executives involved with the project, the readers may want to know more about the backgrounds of people involved in the project. One- to two-page resumes for each executive will help the readers gather this additional information.

A typical resume in the appendix will include the following information on each manager and key person on the project:

- Employment history
- Education
- Special training or skills
- Awards
- Memberships in professional groups

The appendix should also include an introduction that states the purpose of the appendix (i.e., to provide resumes of managers and key personnel) and lists out the people whose resumes follow.

Glossary of Terms and Symbols

As much as we try to avoid it, proposals often include jargon words and symbols that are unfamiliar to the readers. In these cases, an appendix that includes an alphabetical listing of terms and symbols with definitions can help the readers work through the complex terminology of the proposal. Glossaries are especially helpful for readers who are not familiar with the technical aspects of the project.

Each item in a glossary should be written as a sentence definition. A sentence definition has three parts: (1) the name of the item, (2) the class to which the item belongs, and (3) the features that distinguish the item from its class. For example, here are a few items that might appear in a glossary.

cathode ray tube: a vacuum tube in which electrons are projected onto a fluorescent screen.

cyclotron: a particle accelerator in which charged particles (e.g., protons) are propelled in a circular motion by a magnetic field.

direct labor: the body of workers who are directly used in the production of goods and services.

Σ **(sigma):** the total number of electrons measured after one minute of testing.

Each of these definitions starts out with the name of the item being defined. Then, it names the class to which the item belongs (e.g., particle accelerator, vacuum tube, body of workers, total amount of electrons). The remainder of the definition tells how the item can be distinguished from its class.

Bibliography

The bibliography should include a list of printed sources, interviews, and other outside materials that were cited in the proposal or consulted during its development. The bibliography should list out the sources of any quotations, graphics, data, or ideas that you took from another document. Also, if you conducted interviews, the dates and times of these interviews should be placed into the bibliography.

The format of a bibliography should follow guidelines found in style manuals, like those offered by the American Psychological Association (APA) or the Modern Language Association (MLA). The APA style is widely used in scientific and technical proposals. The MLA style is typically used in nontechnical proposals. Many reference books include examples of these styles. However, it is always helpful to consult the style guides themselves. Here are their official titles so you can track them down in a library or at a local bookstore:

- *Publication Manual of the American Psychological Association*
- *MLA Handbook for Writers of Research Papers*

Corporations and government bodies often develop their own style guides, which define specific rules for citations. In the end, the style chosen is usually not important (unless the clients specify a specific style). Consistency in your citations, however, is important. Each item in your bibliography list should follow a predictable format.

Formulas and Calculations

In the body of a proposal, the inclusion of formulas and calculations can be a momentum killer. And yet, these numerical tools are critical if the readers are going to assess the soundness of your proposal.

You may consider moving your formulas and calculations to an appendix, especially when you are addressing an audience that includes nontechnical readers. In the appendix, each formula and calculation should be properly labeled in a way that explains exactly how it is used. In some cases, an explanatory narrative should be included that leads the readers through any derivations of formulas or any calculations. Try to avoid dumping the readers into a rat's nest of symbols and numbers. After all, if the clients or their experts cannot follow your derivations or calculations, they are not going to trust the conclusions you draw from them.

Related Reports, Prior Proposals, FYI Information

In some cases, you might decide to include copies of documents that are discussed in the proposal. For example, a scientist may include an article or white paper that supports an important argument in the proposal, or a business proposal writer may include a recent magazine article that praises his company. Also, you may want to include prior proposals related to the subject.

Essentially, an appendix can include any number of additional documents as long as the readers aren't overburdened with unnecessary information. For each document you include, though, make sure you also include a small paragraph that identifies the context for the document. Tell the readers why the document is important, when it was written, who it was written for, and where it was used or appeared.

This explanatory information is important, because you should not expect the readers to figure out why you decided to include additional documents in the appendix.

Revising the Proposal

In Chapter 1, you learned that writing a proposal involves a *process*. Even the best proposal writers cannot consistently sit down and crank out a proposal in one try—though you will certainly hear corporate myths about the person who could write proposals without any revision. In reality, though, proposals usually require at least a few drafts before they are complete. To be successful, you should plan to devote significant time to revising and editing your proposals.

Most writers revise their work as they finish each section of a proposal—always a good idea—but you should also rethink and revise the proposal as a whole text. Why? Because often writing a proposal causes you to think more deeply about your subject. While writing, your original ideas about the situation, the plan, or the needs of the readers have almost certainly evolved or changed. During the revision phase of the writing process, it is time to rework all the sections of the proposal so they tell a consistent story.

The Rhetorical Situation

Start out the revision process by looking closely over your notes about the rhetorical situation. Ask yourself the following questions, looking at each section in the proposal separately:

Subject

Is the subject of the proposal still the same? Does any content in the proposal drift outside the boundaries of the subject? Is the subject defined at the beginning of the proposal the same as the subject at the end?

Purpose

Does the proposal achieve the stated purpose? Do you need to refine or broaden the purpose statement to suit a deeper understanding of the situation?

Readers

Does the proposal address the motives, values, attitudes, and emotions of the primary readers? Will the secondary and gatekeeper readers be satisfied with the proposal? Does the proposal contain any information that hostile tertiary readers could use to damage you, your team, or your company?

Context

Is the proposal appropriate for the physical, economic, political, and ethical situations in which it might be used? Can you make any changes to the format or design to make it more usable? Are any parts of your proposal politically or ethically vulnerable?

Objectives

Besides the purpose, does the proposal meet the objectives of you, your team, and your corporation? Will the proposal still meet some other important objectives, even if it is turned down?

You need to be honest with yourself when looking over the rhetorical situation. Certainly, there is a tendency to ignore problems with the proposal now that you are reaching the end. But you should keep reminding yourself that the readers will not ignore these problems. The extra time and effort you spend rethinking the rhetorical situation will help you make the final adjustments needed to help you win the contract or receive the funding you need.

Rethinking the Problem or Opportunity

After reconsidering the rhetorical situation, look closely at your notes in which you identified the problem or opportunity that the proposal was written to address. Often, especially in larger proposals, a writer's original understanding of the problem or opportunity changed somewhat during the drafting and revision phases. As a result, the proposal is now handling a much more complex issue than was first defined. If so, perhaps you need to scale back the proposal to handle a smaller problem or opportunity. Or, perhaps you need to rewrite parts of the proposal to suit that larger problem.

Reconsider the question, "What changed?" as you study the problem or opportunity defined in the proposal. Proposals, as mentioned in Chapter 1, are tools for managing change. While revising the proposal, you should ask yourself whether your proposal is addressing the elements of change in the current situation. Are you shaping change to the advantage of your company or organization? Are there any elements of change that you are *not* addressing in your proposal?

Then, think about the type of proposal you were asked to write. Were you supposed to write a research proposal, planning proposal, implementation proposal, estimate proposal, or a combination of two of these kinds of proposals? Often, during the proposal writing process, the project will experience a certain amount of "mission creep." For example, a research proposal will tend to creep ahead and start offering a strategic plan. Or, a planning proposal will begin describing implementation, offering details like schedules and personnel that would be typically found in an implementation proposal.

To avoid mission creep, give the clients exactly what they asked for—nothing more and nothing less. Clients usually want to handle a project one step at a time. If they asked for an assessment of their facilities' production capacity, they don't want you to also tell them that you will be showing up with the heavy equipment in a month to start rebuilding their factory. If they asked for a cost estimate for recycling some post-production materials, they don't want a planning proposal that shows how you might restructure their factory to reduce waste.

Another reason for giving the readers exactly what they asked for is the simple fact that you do not want to give your ideas away for free. If you provide them a detailed implementation plan in addition to the strategic plan they asked for, you just gave them a blueprint for solving their problem without your help.

Rethinking the Rhetorical Elements

Finally, reconsider the rhetorical elements of your document, separately considering the content, organization, style, and design.

Content

Is the proposal's content complete? Is there any information missing that would help you make your case? Are there any digressions in the proposal where you have included details that go beyond "need to know" information?

Organization

Does the proposal follow a logical order, or the order specified by the client? Does it tell a story, leading the readers from the current situation, through a plan, to a beneficial conclusion? Does the introduction set an effective context for the body of the proposal by highlighting the subject, purpose, and main point while offering any helpful background information, stressing the importance of the subject, and forecasting the body of the proposal? Do the opening paragraphs of each section identify the purpose and point of their respective parts of the proposal?

Style

Does the proposal reflect an appropriate tone/persona for the readers and subject? Is the style plain where the proposal is instructing the readers and persuasive where you are trying to influence them? Can you use any stylistic devices like similes, analogies, or metaphors to make the text clearer or more powerful?

Design

Does the proposal follow an appropriate, consistent page design? Are the pages balanced? Does the proposal appropriately use alignment, grouping, and consistency? Have you used bulleted or numbered lists, where appropriate? Does data appear in tables or charts? Are the graphics properly placed and labeled? Would more graphics help illustrate difficult points?

As the deadline looms and you grow tired of working on a proposal, it is tempting to cut revision time to a minimum. Sometimes you can actually convince yourself that the readers don't care whether the proposal is polished or not. But in reality, readers do care very much about the final form of the proposal. Often the difference between the successful proposal and the runner-ups was the added time the winners put into revising the final document. Proverbs such as "The devil is in the details," and "Quality is found at the edges," are very true of proposals. You should always set aside a significant block of time for revising the proposal. Often, the additional time spent on revising can be the difference between winning and losing the contract or funding.

Last Word

A proposal is the beginning of a relationship. Essentially, the readers are interviewing you and your company, trying to determine whether a basis for a positive, constructive alliance exists. Your proposal is the face you are presenting to the client. If they feel comfortable with your proposal, they will feel comfortable with you and your company. If something feels wrong about your proposal, they will tend to accept another proposal that "just feels right."

In this chapter, we went over the endgame of the proposal-writing process. Once you finish with the proposal, you should be able to conceptualize the document as a whole. It should be complete, organized, easy to read, and well designed. If you feel comfortable with the proposal in its final form, with no regrets, chances are good your readers will feel comfortable with the proposal too.

CASE STUDY: Revising and Polishing

When John, Karen, Thomas, and Sally finally pulled the proposal together, it looked a bit rough. While writing the proposal, some of their ideas about the rhetorical situation had evolved, and they needed to make adjustments to suit Sally's decisions about style and Thomas's decisions about the layout of the proposal. With a draft of the proposal completed, they also felt they had developed a sharper understanding of the problem, their readers, and the contexts in which their proposal might be used.

As a result, many of the things they wrote in the Situation section of their proposal would need to be modified. Meanwhile, they would need to include the step "Hire an accountant" somewhere in their Plan section. Nevertheless, for the most part, the proposal seemed to hold together well. John and Sally agreed to handle the revision phase of the proposal, leaving final editing and proofreading to Karen and Thomas.

John and Sally began revising by looking over their notes about the rhetorical situation. They both read through the proposal, checking for places where they might have strayed from the subject or purpose. They made sure they were addressing the concerns of their primary readers, the other business owners, and their secondary, tertiary and gatekeeper readers such as the city government, the media, and the Elmdale Hill

Neighborhood Association. They made adjustments to Thomas's page layout and Karen's graphics to fit the physical contexts in which the proposal might be read. And, to address the political issues involved in the proposal, they tried to soften any criticism of city officials or the media. Finally, they checked to see if the proposal was meeting their other objectives, besides the purpose.

As they looked over their original definition of the problem, they noticed how their understanding of the current situation had evolved. Their Situation section defined the problem as "real or perceived lack of convenience" in the Elmdale Hill business district. Yet their Plan section talked about building unity by creating an Elmdale Hill Merchants Association.

"So, is the problem really a lack of unity among the merchants, not a lack of convenience?" asked Sally.

After a moment of thought, John said, "I think the two go hand-in-hand. Our lack of unity has fostered the perception that Elmdale Hill is not convenient for customers."

As they revised the Situation section they tried to better link the lack of convenience with the lack of unity. As they reworked the Plan section, they tried to show that more unity would lead to better customer convenience. They also tried to work this connection into the proposal's introduction, the Qualifications section, and the discussion of the benefits in the conclusion.

When Karen and Thomas received the revised proposal from John and Sally, they were pleasantly surprised by the changes. The revisions had turned the document into something that looked like an actual proposal.

Before editing and proofreading the proposal, Karen and Thomas reviewed their notes on the content, organization, style, and design of the proposal. They began editing the content by crossing out any sentences that did not include "need to know" information. Then, they added some of Karen's survey data into the Situation section to reinforce their claims about the decline of sales.

While revising the organization, they paid special attention to the transition points between larger sections. They tried to better weave together the closing of each section with the opening of the following sections.

When revising for style and design, they found themselves mostly making small corrections to wording and format. Here or there, they discovered that they had used different terms to describe the same things, forcing them to make adjustments to some of the sentences.

Meanwhile, design features of the text like headings, rules, and lists needed to be corrected for consistency. When their editing was completed, they proofread the whole text from front to back and back to front, correcting any typos or grammar mistakes.

Finally, Karen gave preliminary copies of the proposal to their "gatekeeper" readers to solicit some reactions and final suggestions for improvement. A copy of the proposal went to Gail Smithson at Sanders and Associates, so she could check over any financial claims. Karen also gave a copy to the president of the Elmdale Hill Neighborhood Association. When they received comments back from their gatekeepers, Karen and Thomas made some minor revisions to address the suggestions offered by Gail and the neighborhood association president.

The whole proposal writing process had taken a month. John, Karen, Thomas, and Sally met in the Elmdale Café one last time to look over the final copy.

"We're finished," said Thomas.

Sally agreed, "It looks great. If this won't convince them to start a merchants association, nothing will."

"Even if this goes nowhere, I'm pretty happy we did it." said Karen. "I have learned a lot about Elmdale Hill, nonprofit organizations, local politics, and many other things over the last month. I'm already feeling better about our future in Elmdale Hill. I believe this proposal will also get others thinking about how we can improve this area of town."

"I hope this proposal is just the beginning of better times and better relationships," said John. "After we finish our coffee, let's go over to the copy place. We can start handing out these proposals tomorrow morning."

A copy of their final proposal for the Elmdale Hill Merchants Association follows the Questions and Exercises for this chapter. A copy of Lisa Miller's final proposal to Earl Grey Design from Insight Systems is also included at the end of this chapter.

Questions and Exercises

1. Look over the two proposals included at the end of this chapter. How do they meet the purpose and the needs of their readers? Are there any further revisions you might make to these proposals? How could they be improved?

2. Find a proposal on the Internet or at your workplace. Write an analysis of the proposal in which you discuss the content, organization, style, and design of the document. In your analysis, point out examples of the proposal's strengths, then make some suggestions for improvement.

3. Write a letter or memo of transmittal for a real or practice proposal of your own. What information do you believe belongs in this letter or memo? What information should be saved for the proposal itself? How can you write the letter with a positive, personal tone that puts the readers at ease?

4. Using a proposal from the Internet or your workplace, write a one-page executive summary that describes what is in the proposal. Your summary should cover all the major sections in the proposal. What did you decide to include? What did you leave out? How did you decide what to keep and what to leave out?

5. Using a proposal of your own, work through the revision process described in this chapter. Revise your work by reconsidering the subject, purpose, readers, context, and objectives of the proposal. Then, check whether your understanding of the problem or opportunity changed as you wrote the proposal. And finally, edit the proposal by paying special attention to its content, organization, style, and design.

Example Proposals

Example Proposal: "A Proposal to Start a Merchants Association in Elmdale Hill"

Example Proposal: "Managing Office Growth: A Proposal to Earl Grey Design from Insight Systems"

Milano's

Why Not Dine Italian Tonight?

Dear Elmdale Hill Business Owner,

We ask you to give the enclosed proposal serious consideration. This proposal is the first step toward forming an Elmdale Hill Merchants Association, which we believe will help our businesses collectively strengthen our sales and reputation. By forming a merchants association, we hope to turn around the recent decline in sales that most businesses in Elmdale Hill have experienced over the past few years.

The proposal describes a process for organizing the Elmdale Hill Merchants Association. The first step will involve a survey, in which we will ask you for some basic demographic information. Then, a townhall meeting will be held at the Star Catcher Theater on **September 15 at 7:00 p.m.** You are invited to attend the meeting and express your ideas and opinions. At the townhall meeting, the attendees will nominate a steering committee, charging them with the task of forming the merchants association.

There are numerous benefits to organizing ourselves. Together, we will compete better, wield more political power, and strengthen our public image. Other business districts that have started merchants associations report substantial increases in sales due to their collective efforts.

Please look over this proposal. If you have any comments or questions, you may contact any of the four people listed below. We will be happy to answer any questions.

Sincerely,

John Legler   *Karen Sanchez*   *Thomas Lee*   *Sally Johnson*

John Legler,   Karen Sanchez,   Thomas Lee   Sally Johnson
Owner, Milano's   Owner, New Fashions   Owner, Star Catcher Owner, Dust Jacket
555-4144   555-6982   555-1189   555-0928

Elmdale Hill Merchants Association

A Proposal to Start a Merchants Association in Elmdale Hill

Elmdale Hill has always been a great place to own a business. Our unique shops and services attract customers who expect quality products, good food, and satisfying entertainment. But times are growing increasingly difficult for some businesses in our area. We now face competition from the Wheatmill Mall and chain stores, which have recently moved into our area. In fact, eight out of ten businesses in Elmdale Hill, according to an informal survey, saw a decline in sales last year (See Figure A). This decline in sales is an urgent signal that we now need to compete harder than ever to keep our customers.

One way to stand up to our competition is to pull together as a family of businesses. Our aim in this proposal is to take the first step toward forming a *merchants association* that can help us build and maintain business relationships in Elmdale Hill. After all, as separate businesses, we will never compete well against malls and chain stores. But together, we can strengthen our public relations, speak with more authority at City Hall, and improve social conditions in the Elmdale Hill area.

Town Hall Meeting at the Star Catcher, September 15 at 7:00 P.M. A $10 donation is requested to help fund a steering committee. Refreshments will be served.

In this proposal, we lay out the first steps toward forming an Elmdale Hill Merchants Association. On Monday, September 15, at 7:00 p.m., a townhall meeting on this subject will be held at the Star Catcher Theater on Central Avenue. You are invited to join us to talk about this proposal and, if we agree to go forward, begin the process of forming the Elmdale Hill Merchants Association.

Reasons For the Decline in Sales

The reasons behind our decline in sales are complex. One reason, mentioned by several local merchants, is the recent opening of the Wheatmill Mall and chain stores in the area. But we believe our problem is not simply new competition. Our main problem is the way we compete against this new competition. Customers view the mall and chain stores as places for convenient one-stop shopping, often spending the whole afternoon browsing from store to store or aisle to aisle. Quite the opposite, they consider each business in Elmdale Hill a separate entity. As a result, they tend to visit only one shop, one theater, or one restaurant per trip to Elmdale Hill. They do not see Elmdale Hill as a convenient place to do all their shopping. Why? There are a few reasons:

First, Elmdale Hill is not prominent in the public eye. Our businesses tend to advertise individually on a very limited basis—unlike the stores at the mall, which pool their advertising dollars or rely on national chains to buy advertising on television or radio. Advertising individually, we cannot afford to reach the television viewers who make up the majority of the customer base in this city. Moreover, our use of individual advertising does not foster a unified sense of Elmdale Hill; therefore, customers view us as a group of single shops rather than a place where they can meet all their shopping needs.

Second, we do not actively project a positive image to the public. As a result, the local news

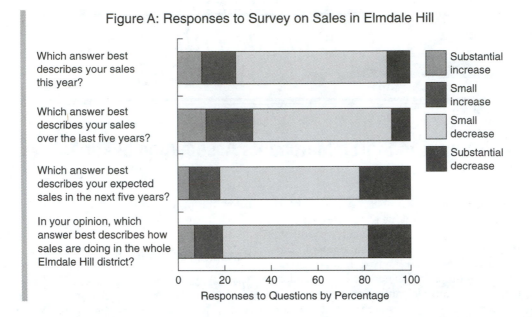

Figure A: Responses to Survey on Sales in Elmdale Hill

Which answer best describes your sales this year?

Which answer best describes your sales over the last five years?

Which answer best describes your expected sales in the next five years?

In your opinion, which answer best describes how sales are doing in the whole Elmdale Hill district?

Substantial increase

Small increase

Small decrease

Substantial decrease

Responses to Questions by Percentage

outlets tend to only report negative stories about Elmdale Hill, giving our customers a bad impression of this part of the city. Positive stories about Elmdale Hill, meanwhile, are rare because we do not have a source for keeping reporters informed about the people and events that make Elmdale Hill a fun place to live, work, and shop.

Third, parking and public transportation have become severe problems in the Elmdale Hill area. When customers drive down here to shop, they discover that parking spaces are hard to find. And even when they are lucky enough to find a spot, they need to shorten their shopping time because the parking meters limit them to a one-hour visit. Under these conditions, window-shopping is out of the question. Seeing a movie, or dining at a restaurant is just about impossible. Customers who take public transportation find bus service sporadic at best. The buses tend to run once an hour, leaving customers waiting in the heat or cold.

Finally, many of our customers believe that crime has increased in the Elmdale Hill area, despite the fact that it has actually decreased (see Figure B).

We must concede, though, that we have experienced a rise in activities that are usually associated with an unsafe neighborhood. For instance, the amount of graffiti on our walls and litter in

our streets seems to have increased dramatically over the last year. Also, there are more street people than ever in our area, hanging out in doorways and asking for change. Our customers are beginning to believe that Elmdale Hill is not a "nice" neighborhood anymore.

Of course, our problems with parking, public transportation, and crime could be the responsibility of City Hall and police. But, like our customers, the people at City Hall and the police tend to also view us as separate entities, meaning each of us alone has very little political influence. As a result, our individual concerns rarely catch their interest.

Unfortunately, if we choose to ignore these pressing issues, they will only become worse over time. As our sales further decline, existing businesses will be replaced by more marginal businesses, causing the reputation of the Elmdale Hill business district to further degrade in the minds of the public. We need to take action now to solve these smaller problems. Only by taking action now can we avoid larger problems in the future.

> "I love having my Business in Elmdale Hill. If we could just pull together, I think we could create something special here." Ben Hanson, Owner of Elmdale Drugs

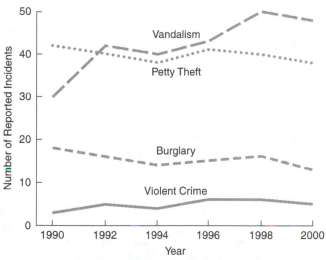

Figure B: Elmdale Hill Crime Trends Since 1990

Source: 2001 Elmdale Hill Neighborhood Watch Report

Our Plan: Organizing a Merchants Association

We believe the best way to turn around our current situation is to begin pulling together to strengthen our businesses and community. Specifically, we believe the businesses in Elmdale Hill should form a merchants association that would pool our resources and help us take unified action when we address City Hall, the police, and the media.

An Elmdale Hill Merchants Association would achieve some important goals. It would—

✔ heighten the public's awareness of shopping opportunities in Elmdale Hill.

✔ restore and promote a positive image of the Elmdale Hill shopping district.

✔ help us devise ways to make our businesses more accessible to the public.

✔ increase sales by helping Elmdale Hill businesses recapture previous customers and bring in new customers.

To create an Elmdale Hill Merchants Association, we propose the following four-step plan:

Step One: Gather Information

An important first step will be to gather demographic information from businesses in the Elmdale Hill district. Through a blind survey, merchants will be asked about their needs, their concerns, and their level of interest in starting a merchants association. The survey will also allow each business owner to offer feedback on this proposal and provide written advice about how we should proceed.

> **"Things have definitely improved since we created a merchants association."** Valerie Thompkins, **President, Market Square Merchants Association**

The survey will meet a few different purposes. First, it will provide us with some baseline data that we could use toward deciding what kind of merchants association is appropriate for Elmdale Hill's needs. Second, the survey will introduce business owners to the idea of a merchants association, raising their awareness that we are trying to create a unified business community. Third, once this data has been collected, we will possess baseline figures to measure our progress toward improving sales.

When the surveys are returned, we will send each merchant a small report that presents and analyzes the findings.

Step Two: Hold a Town-Hall Meeting

A town-hall meeting will be held to discuss whether we should move ahead to form a merchants association in Elmdale Hill. At the meeting, local business owners and residents will have an opportunity to express their ideas on the subject. Also, Sanders and Associates, a local accounting firm, has offered to discuss the steps needed to incorporate the merchants association as a nonprofit organization.

We would like to invite people from City Hall (including the mayor, city council, and police chief) and the news media to attend this meeting. The people at City Hall need to know that we are concerned about our loss of sales, lack of adequate parking and public transportation, and the perception of crime in our area. By inviting the news media, we can notify them that we are working to improve the Elmdale Hill area.

Step Three: Create a Steering Committee

At the meeting, we will ask for volunteers to form a "steering committee." The steering committee will research the economic health of Elmdale Hill and look at options for creating merchant associations. Then, they will write a business plan that—

✔ includes a mission statement that defines the objectives and responsibilities of the merchant association.

✔ describes an organizational structure for the merchants association that is suited to the needs of the Elmdale Hill district.

✔ includes a budget that predicts the associations' revenues and expenses, including estimates of membership costs.

✔ sets association bylaws that lay out the procedures and guidelines by which the association will act.

The business plan will be sent to each merchant in the Elmdale Hill area to solicit comments and revisions. Then, after the business plan is revised, the committee will send out final drafts to merchants, residents, and City Hall.

Funds for the committee's activities will be provided by the donations collected at the first townhall meeting. An estimate of the committee's budget is attached to this proposal.

Step Four: Form the Merchants Association

Another town-hall meeting will then be scheduled to begin turning the business plan into a reality. At this meeting, we will discuss and vote on the business plan and bylaws of the association. We will also discuss the hiring of an accounting firm to handle the process of incorporating the merchants association as a nonprofit organization. After the meeting, if all goes well, we will celebrate the new Elmdale Hill Merchants Association.

With the merchants association in place, we can begin raising the profile of Elmdale Hill by advertising collectively and projecting a consistent public image. We can begin wielding more influence at City Hall to handle our parking and public transportation problems. And, we can start cleaning up the graffiti and litter problems in our area by working more closely with the police. In the end, we will better compete by making Elmdale Hill a convenient, fun place to shop again.

Hiring an Accounting Firm to Help

While collecting information about merchant associations, it became apparent to us that incorporating a nonprofit organization is a complicated process. A local accounting firm, Sanders and Associates, has agreed to help us work through the process. This accounting firm has a long history working with nonprofit groups, and they have successfully helped several business districts like Elmdale Hill organize into merchants associations. The firm has agreed to work with us at no cost until the second townhall meeting.

Gail Smithson, an accountant at Sanders and Associates, has been assigned to handle the incorporation process. She received her CPA in 1985 after graduating from Northwestern University. She has fifteen years of experience as a CPA, and she considers nonprofits an area of expertise. From our discussions with Gail, we feel she would be an asset to our efforts to organize. She can handle all the paperwork and taxes, and she can give us helpful advice about how to organize the merchants association itself.

At the second town-hall meeting, we may choose to hire Sanders and Associates to improve our chances of placing the merchants association on a solid foundation.

Final Comments

The businesses in Elmdale Hill face an important decision—one we should make together. To survive in today's competitive environment, we believe we should organize ourselves into a merchants association. The costs to form and maintain a merchants association would be minimal, but the benefits would be substantial.

Here are just a few of those benefits. First, a merchants association would allow us to work collectively on issues that concern the Elmdale Hill community. We would have more power at City Hall and with the police. Also, we would be able to present a positive image to the press and the public. Most important, however, our sales would increase as we enhanced our competitiveness against the Wheatmill Mall and chain stores

that have recently moved into our area. Figure C shows the increase in sales experienced by the businesses in Market Square after they formed a merchants association. We believe we could experience a similar rise in sales if we were more unified.

The benefits of a merchants association also relate to our quality of life. We all take pride and satisfaction in our businesses and our community. By pulling together, we could stand up to our mega-competitors, who sacrifice quality and customer service for profit. We could continue to provide our customers with the kinds of unique products, services, and entertainment that make Elmdale Hill a special place to work and visit.

Elmdale Hill is a great place to own a business. Together, we can grow established businesses and nurture young businesses in the area. Customers will see Elmdale Hill as a place where they can enjoy shopping, meet friends, and relax. Moreover, as business owners, we will feel more like a family. Together, we can look out for each other's interests.

Thank you for your time and interest. If you plan to attend the townhall meeting, John Legler, owner of Milano's, will take your RSVP. He can also answer any questions you may have. Please call John at 555-4144.

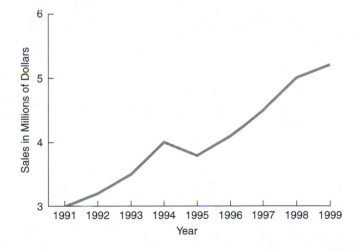

Figure C: Market Square's Increase in Sales after Starting Merchants Association

Operating Budget for the Steering Committee

At this point, we can only predict the expenses for the Steering Committee. The committee's initial expenses should be modest, as shown in Table 1. It needs funds to print surveys, reports, ballots, and posters. It will also need postage to send out those materials and some funds to cover any long-distance calls to other merchants associations. Refreshments at the two organizational meetings will be paid for out of the Steering Committee's budget.

To create a working budget for the Steering Committee, we are asking attendees at the initial organizational meeting on September 15 to donate $10.00. Any additional donations toward this effort will be accepted gratefully at that time also.

The overall costs of incorporating a merchants association, according to Gail Smithson at Sanders & Associates, will run from $2000 to $4000, depending on the kind of merchants association we choose to create. We estimate that charter membership in the Elmdale Hill Merchant Association will cost each business about $150, but the actual cost will depend on the decisions of the Steering Committee and the number of business owners who are willing to participate.

TABLE 1
Steering Committee Budget

ITEM	COST
Printing	
Survey	20.00
Report (Survey Results)	30.00
Report (Steering Committee)	30.00
Ballots	20.00
Posters	50.00
Communications	
Postage (Surveys, Reports, Ballots)	280.00
Long-Distance Calls	100.00
Refreshments	
Drinks (2 organizational meetings)	40.00
Snacks (2 organizational meetings)	70.00
Travel	
By Car	100.00
Total Costs	$740.00

Managing Office Growth

I

A Proposal to Earl Grey Design from

Insight Systems

April 21, 2001

Table of Contents

Executive Summary

This pre-proposal was written to help Earl Grey manage its office growth. In this pre-proposal, Insight Systems proposes to develop a telecommuting network that would allow selected employees at Earl Grey to work from home. We believe this approach would provide Earl Grey with adequate space to grow while avoiding expensive commitments to new facilities. Moreover, a telecommuting network will avoid any disruptions to Earl Grey's current projects.

Earl Grey's success is the main reason why it needs to develop a plan for managing its limited office space. Since 1982, when Earl Grey moved into its current office, business at the firm has grown exponentially. With this growth, more employees and equipment were needed. As a result, the current office space has started to feel a little snug.

Our plan to free up space at Earl Grey's current office is simple. In four phases, we would build a telecommunication local area network (LAN) that allows selected employees to work outside the office. Here is our plan:

Phase One: We will study Earl Grey's telecommuting options.

Phase Two: We will design a local area network (LAN) that will allow selected employees to telecommute from a home office.

Phase Three: We will train Earl Grey's employees in telecommuting basics.

Phase Four: We will assess the success of the telecommuting program after it has been implemented.

The advantages of our plan are its flexibility and low cost. First, a telecommuting network would allow Earl Grey to retain its current office space, avoiding a costly and disruptive move to other facilities. Second, employees at Earl Grey would prefer the flexibility to work at home or from a project site. Third, the investment in a telecommuting network would be minimal, allowing Earl Grey to react quickly to the volatile architectural market in Chicago.

Insight Systems is uniquely qualified to handle this project. Since 1975, we have been providing flexible, low-cost telecommuting solutions to progressive companies like Earl Grey. Our managers, engineers, and staff are all top people in this area. Our background and experience give us the ability to help Earl Grey manage its needs for a more efficient, dynamic office space. Our key to success is innovation, flexibility, and efficiency.

Thank you for the opportunity to write a pre-proposal for this project. We look forward to working with Earl Grey in the near future.

Proposal to Earl Grey Design: Growth and Flexibility Through Telecommuting

Founded in 1979, Earl Grey Design is one of the classic entrepreneurial success stories in the architectural field. Starting the firm with only a thousand dollars in the bank, Susan James and Thomas Weber began designing functional buildings for the Wrigleyville business community. Five years later, Earl Grey cleared its first million dollars in revenue. Today, Earl Grey is one of the leading architectural firms in the Chicago market with over 50 million dollars in annual revenue. The *Chicago Business Journal* has consistently rated Earl Grey one of the top-five architectural firms in the city, citing the company's continued innovation and growth in the industry.

With growth, however, comes growing pains. Earl Grey now faces an important decision about how it will manage its growth in the near future. The right decision could lead to more market share, increased sales, and even more prominence in the architectural field. However, Earl Grey also needs to safeguard itself against over-extension in case the Chicago construction market unexpectedly begins to recede.

To help Earl Grey make the right decision, this proposal suggests an innovative strategy that will support the firm's growth while maintaining its flexibility. Specifically, we propose Earl Grey implement a telecommuting network that allows selected employees to work a few days each week at home. Telecommuting will provide Earl Grey with the office space it needs to continue growing. Meanwhile, this approach will avoid a large investment in new facilities and disruption to the company's current operations.

In this proposal, we will first discuss the results of our research into Earl Grey's office space needs. Second, we will offer a plan for using a telecommuting network to free up more space at Earl Grey's current office. Third, we will review Insight Systems' qualifications to assist Earl Grey with its move into the world of telecommuting. And finally, we will go over some of the costs and advantages of our plan. Our aim is to show you how telecommuting can help Earl Grey grow while maintaining the innovative spirit that launched this firm two decades ago.

The Office Space Needs at Earl Grey

Before describing our plan, let us first highlight some of the factors that created the current office space shortage at Earl Grey.

In 1982, Earl Grey moved into its current office on Michigan Avenue. At the time, the firm employed five architects and fifteen staff members. The office was roomy and flexible, because Susan James designed it with functionality and growth in mind. The original architects at the firm each had a couple drafting tables and a large desk. Meanwhile, desks for staff members were placed strategically throughout the office to maximize the efficiency of the workspace. The design of Earl Grey's office won accolades and awards as a masterpiece of modernist design. In a 1983 interview with *Architectural Review,* James explained that the workspace was designed to be "both aesthetic and pragmatic, a balance of form and function." She also pointed out that she wanted the office to demonstrate the advantages of the modernist design for clients.

Almost two decades later, the office is still considered a modernist masterpiece, but Earl Grey's growth has made the workspace feel a bit cramped. This growth in business began in 1992 when the economy rebounded from recession. Soon, downtown businesses began renovating their neoclassical offices, adopting the modernist style. As a result, Earl Grey found itself one of the firms leading a movement that the

Chicago Tribune dubbed the "Downtown Renaissance." The firm's revenues doubled from 1992-1995 and doubled again from 1995 to 2000. To meet this increased demand, Earl Grey added ten architects and twenty new staff members during the 1990s. As a result, an office that once seemed roomy was becoming increasingly snug. More architects and staff also meant more drafting tables, more desks, and more equipment. Meanwhile, new kinds of equipment, like CAD systems, plotters, and large-format copiers, also began using up precious floor space, further restricting the limited area available.

The office space shortage faced by Earl Grey is simply a symptom of the firm's success and growing influence in the Chicago market. Now, the challenge faced by Earl Grey is to free up office space without disrupting current projects or jeopardizing future growth. Left unaddressed, however, this lack of office space may create some further problems in the near future. One problem is that a restrictive office tends to undermine employee morale, leading to lower productivity and overall employee discomfort (Spenser Institute Study, 1999). Another problem is that the workspace will also become increasingly inefficient, wasting employees' time, while causing minor injuries to personnel and damage to equipment. A cramped office also presents a bad image to clients, especially since Earl Grey prides itself on designing functional workspaces that enhance business activities.

Our Plan: Maintaining Flexibility through Telecommuting

Managing Earl Grey's limited office space requires a solution that allows the company to grow but does not sacrifice financial flexibility. Therefore, we believe a successful solution must meet the following objectives:

- Minimize disruption to Earl Grey's current operations
- Minimize costs, preserving Earl Grey's financial flexibility
- Retain Earl Grey's current office on Michigan Avenue
- Foster a dynamic workplace that will be appealing to Earl Grey's architects and staff

To meet these objectives, Insight Systems proposes to collaborate with Earl Grey to develop a telecommunication network that allows selected employees to work at home. The primary advantage of telecommuting is that it frees up office space for the remaining employees who need to work in the main office. Telecommuting will also avoid overextending Earl Grey's financial resources, so the firm can quickly react to the crests and valleys of the market.

Our plan will be implemented in four major phases. First, we will study Earl Grey's telecommuting options. Second, we will design a local area network (LAN) that will allow selected employees to telecommute from a home office. Third, we will train Earl Grey's employees in telecommuting basics. And finally, we will assess the success of the telecommuting program after it has been implemented.

Phase One: Analyze Earl Grey's Telecommuting Needs

We will start out by analyzing the specific workplace requirements of Earl Grey's employees and management. The results of this analysis will allow us to work closely with Earl Grey's management to develop a telecommuting program that fits the unique demands of a dynamic architecture firm.

In this phase, our goal will be to collect as much information as possible, so the transition to telecommunication will be smooth and hassle-free.

- First, we will conduct surveys of your employees to determine which people might be willing and able to telecommute. These surveys will tell us about their work habits and the way in which a telecommuting network could be adapted to their individual needs.
- Second, we will interview Earl Grey's management. These interviews will help us tailor the telecommuting network to your corporate culture and your managers' specific needs.
- Third, we will conduct empirical studies to help us understand the office dynamics at Earl Grey. These empirical studies will allow us to replicate those office dynamics in a virtual environment.

We estimate this phase will require thirty days. At the end of that time period, we will submit a report to you in which we discuss the findings of our surveys, interviews, and empirical studies. In this report, we will also describe the various telecommuting options available and recommend the option that best suits your needs.

Phase Two: Designing a Computer Network for Telecommuting

Using our findings from Phase One, we will then work with Earl Grey's management to design a telecommuting program that fits the specific needs of the firm.

The telecommunication network would be designed for maximum flexibility. We would begin by creating a LAN that would be connected to a main server and a back-up server at Earl Grey's main office (see Figure 1). These servers would be connected through an ethernet to all in-office workstations and peripherals (plotters, CAD systems, copiers, fax machines, etc.). The ethernet would allow each workstation to communicate with the main server, other workstations, and peripherals.

Using cable modems, employees working at home or remote sites will connect to Earl Grey's LAN through a communication server and a router (Figure 1). The communication server will manage the modem connections. The router, meanwhile, will allow your telecommuting employees to access peripherals, like the plotters and copiers, through the ethernet. The router will also allow Earl Grey's main office to connect easily with future branch offices and remote clients.

To ensure the security of the LAN, we will equip the network with the most advanced security hardware and software available. The router (hardware) will be programmed to serve as a "firewall" against intruders. We will also install the most advanced encryption and virus detection software available to protect your employees' transmissions.

Overall, the advantage of this LAN design is that Earl Grey's telecommuting employees will have access to all the equipment and services available in the main office. Meanwhile, even traveling employees who are visiting clients will be able to easily tap into the LAN from their laptop computers.

Phase Three: Training Earl Grey's Employees

Experience has shown us that employees adapt quickly to telecommuting. Initially, though, we would need to train them how to access and use the LAN from workstations inside and outside the office.

To fully train your employees in telecommuting basics, we would need two afternoons (eight hours). We will show them how to communicate through the network and access peripherals at the main office. The training will also include time management strategies to help your employees adjust to working outside the office. We have

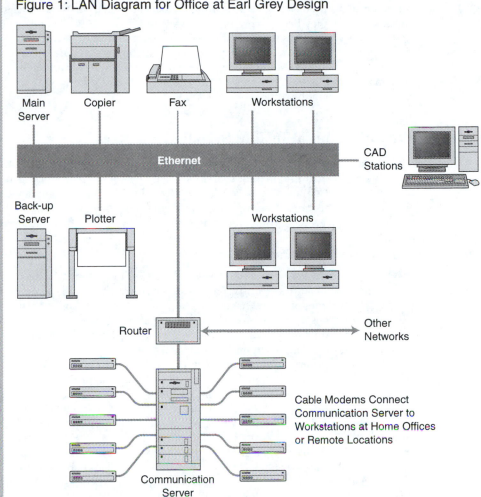

Figure 1: LAN Diagram for Office at Earl Grey Design

found that time management training helps employees work more efficiently at home—often more efficiently than they work in the office.

Insight Systems maintains a 24-hour helpline that your employees can call if they have any questions about using the LAN. Also, our Web site contains helpful information on improving efficiency through telecommuting.

Phase Four: Assessing the Telecommuting Program

To ensure the effectiveness of the telecommuting network, we will regularly survey and interview your managers and employees to solicit their reactions and suggestions for improvements. These surveys and interviews will be conducted every three months for two years.

We will be particularly interested in measuring employee satisfaction with telecommuting, and we will measure whether they believe their efficiency has increased since they began working at home through the LAN. The results of these assessments will help us fine tune the LAN to your employees' needs.

After each three-month survey, we will submit a progress report to Earl Grey that discusses our findings. At the end of the two-year period, we will submit a full report that analyzes our overall findings and makes suggestions for improving the telecommuting program in the future.

Qualifications at Insight Systems

At Insight Systems, we know this moment is a pivotal one for Earl Grey Design. To preserve and expand its market share, Earl Grey needs to grow, but it cannot risk overextending itself financially. For these reasons, Insight Systems is uniquely qualified to handle this project, because we provide flexible, low-cost telecommuting networks that help growing companies stay responsive to shifts in their industry.

Management and Labor

With more than seventy combined years in the industry, our management team offers the insight and responsiveness required to handle your complex growth needs. (The resumes of our management team are included in Appendix B).

Hanna Gibbons, our CEO, has been working in the telecommuting industry for over 20 years. After she graduated from MIT with a Ph.D. in computer science, she worked at Krayson International as a systems designer. Ten years later, she had worked her way up to vice president in charge of Krayson's Telecommuting Division. In 1993, Dr. Gibbons took over as CEO of Insight Systems. Since then, Dr. Gibbons has built this company into a major industry leader with gross sales of $15 million per year. Excited about the new innovations in telecommuting, Dr. Gibbons believes we are seeing a whole new workplace dynamic evolve before of our eyes.

Frank Roberts, chief engineer at Insight Systems, has thirty years of experience in the networked computer field. He began his career at Brindle Labs, where he worked on artificial intelligence systems using analog computer networks. In 1985, he joined the Insight Systems team, bringing his unique understanding of networking to our team. Frank is very detail oriented, often working long hours to ensure that each computer network meets each client's exact specifications and needs.

Lisa Miller, Insight Systems' senior computer engineer, has successfully led the implementation of thirty-three telecommuting systems in companies throughout the United States. Earning her computer engineering degree at Iowa State, Lisa has won numerous awards for her innovative approach to computer networking. She believes that clear communication is the best way to meet her clients' needs.

Our management is supported by one of most advanced teams of high technology employees. Insight Systems employs twenty of the brightest engineers and technicians in the telecommunications industry. We have aggressively recruited our employees from the most advanced universities in the United States, including Stanford, MIT, Illinois, Iowa State, New Mexico, and Syracuse. Several of our engineers have been with Insight Systems since it was founded. Also, we have forged an ongoing training relationship with Simmons Technical Institute to ensure that our employees stay at the forefront of their fields.

Corporate History and Facilities

Insight Systems has been a leader in the telecommuting industry from the beginning. In 1975, the company was founded by John Temple, a pioneer in the networking field. Since then, Insight Systems has followed Dr. Temple's simple belief that computer-age workplaces should give people the freedom to be creative.

Recently, Insight Systems earned the coveted "100 Companies to Watch" designation from *Business Outlook* magazine (May 2001). The company has worked with large and small companies, from Vedder Aerospace to the Cedar Rapids Museum of Fine Arts, to create telecommuting options for companies that want to keep costs down and productivity high.

Insight Systems' Naperville office has been called "a prototype workspace for the information age." (*Gibson's Computer Weekly,* May 2000). With advanced LAN systems in place, only ten of Insight Systems' fifty employees actually work in the office. Most of Insight Systems' employees telecommute from home or on the road.

Experience You Can Trust

Our background and experience gives us the ability to help Earl Grey manage its needs for a more efficient, dynamic office space. Our key to success is innovation, flexibility, and efficiency.

The Plan's Benefits and Project Costs

To conclude, let us summarize the advantages of our plan and discuss the costs. Our preliminary research shows us that Earl Grey Design will continue to be a leader in the Chicago market. The strong economy, coupled with Earl Grey's award-winning designs, will only increase the demand for your services. At Insight Systems, we believe the best way to manage Earl Grey's growth is to implement a telecommuting network that will allow some of the company's employees to telecommute from home or on-site.

Cost is the most significant advantage of our plan. As shown in Appendix A, implementation of our plan would cost an estimated $97,311. We believe this investment in Earl Grey's infrastructure will preserve your company's financial flexibility, allowing you to react quickly to the market's crests and valleys. But the advantages of our plan go beyond simple costs:

- *First, a telecommuting system will allow your current operations to continue without disruption.* When the telecommuting network is ready to go online, your employees will simply need to attend two four-hour training sessions on using the LAN. At these training sessions, we will also teach them time-tested strategies for successful telecommuting from home. Your management can then gradually convert selected employees into telecommuters.

- *Second, employee morale will benefit from using the telecommuting network.* With fewer employees at the office, there will be more space available for the employees who need to be in the office each day. Also, studies have shown that telecommuting employees not only report more job satisfaction, they also increase their productivity. Improved employee morale is especially important in your field, because architects often feel more comfortable working in less formal environments. The flexibility of telecommuting will allow Earl Grey to recruit and retain some of the best people in the industry.

When the telecommuting system is in place, Earl Grey will be positioned for continued growth and leadership in the Chicago architectural market. The key to Earl Grey's success has always been its flexibility in a field that seems to change overnight. Telecommuting will open up space at your current downtown office while maintaining the morale and productivity of your employees as your business continues to grow.

Thank you for giving Insight Systems the opportunity to work with you on this project. We look forward to submitting a full proposal that describes our plan in greater depth. Our CEO, Dr. Hanna Gibbons, will contact you on May 15 to discuss this pre-proposal with you.

If you have any suggestions for improving our plan or you would like further information about our services, please call Lisa Miller, our Senior Computer Engineer, at 1-800-555-3864. Or, you can e-mail her at lmiller@insight_ systems.com.

Appendix A: Budget

At Insight Systems, we pride ourselves on developing low-cost solutions for managing limited office space. In this appendix, we would like to go over some of the major costs of the telecommuting plan discussed in this proposal. These figures are estimates, as you requested in your RFP. We will provide a fully itemized budget with the formal proposal. Table A offers a summary of our estimated costs for the Earl Grey project.

As shown in Table A, management and labor are our primary costs. These costs represent two full-time managers, three computer engineers, two carpenters, and an electrician. These employees will be committed full time to the Earl Grey project.

Hardware and software make up the other significant expense in our budget. Where possible, we will utilize Earl Grey's existing computer infrastructure. However, additional hardware and software will be needed to upgrade your current infrastructure and create a LAN system.

Finally, our estimates for materials are dependent on the amount of carpentry required to hardwire the LAN system into your current operations. Our materials estimate in Table A is based on similarly sized projects we have handled in the past.

Overall, you should find that these costs are a small investment in your company's infrastructure. This investment will help you manage your limited office space while allowing you to maintain financial flexibility. If you have any questions about these figures, please call Lisa Miller at 1-800-555-3864 or e-mail her at lmiller@insight_ systems.com

TABLE A
Budget Summary

ITEM	COST
Management and Labor	$35,982
Equipment Rental and Purchase	5,250
Hardware and Software	30,482
Materials	10,340
Travel	1,298
Communicatons	700
Costs Before Profit	$84,052
Profit (10% of before-profit costs)	8,405
Taxes (Gross Receipts)	4.854
Total Costs	$97,311

References

Aristotle. (1991). *On rhetoric.* G. Kennedy (trans.) New York: Oxford UP.

Arnheim, Rudolph (1964). *Art and visual perception.* Berkeley: University of California Press.

Bernhardt, Stephan (1986). Seeing the text. *College Composition and Communication, 30,* 66–78.

Burke, Kenneth (1954). *A grammar of motives.* Berkeley: U of California P.

Burton, D. (1998). *Technical writing style.* Boston: Allyn and Bacon.

Cicero. (1986). *On oratory and orators.* J. Watson (trans.) Carbondale, IL: Southern Illinois UP.

Donnelly, R. (1984). *Guidebook to planning.* New York: Van Norstrand Reinhold.

Eastman, R. (1978) *Style.* New York: Oxford UP.

Haviland, S. and Clark, H. (1974). What's new? Acquiring new information as a process in comprehension. *Journal of Verbal Learning and Verbal Behavior, 13,* 512-521.

Koffka, K. (1935). *Principles of gestalt psychology.* New York: Harcourt.

Kostelnick, C., and Roberts, D. (1998). *Designing visual language.* Boston: Allyn and Bacon.

Laib, N. (1993). *Rhetoric and style.* Englewood Cliffs, NJ: Prentice Hall.

Lanham, R. (1991). *Revising business prose.* Boston: Allyn and Bacon.

Mathes, J. C., and Stevenson, D. W. (1976). *Designing technical reports.* Indianapolis: Bobbs-Merrill Educational Publishing.

Moore, P., and Fitz, C. (1993). Using gestalt theory to teach document design and graphics. *Technical Communication Quarterly, 2,* 389–410.

Penrose, A., and Katz, S. (1998). *Writing in the sciences.* New York: St. Martin's.

Ramsey, J., and Ramsey, I. (1985). *Budgeting basics.* New York: Franklin Watts.

Swales, J. (1984). Research into the structure of introductions to journal articles and its applications to the teaching of academic writing. In R. Williams, J. Swales, J. Kirkman, (eds.), *Common ground: Shared interests in ESP and communication studies.* (pp. 77–86). New York: Pergamon.

Tufte, E. (1983). *The visual display of quantitative information.* Cheshire, MA: Graphics Press.

Vande Kopple, W. (1989). *Clear and coherent prose.* Boston: Scott, Foresman.

White, J. (1988). *Graphic design for the electronic age.* New York: Watson-Guptill.

Williams, J. (1990). *Style.* Chicago: U of Chicago P.

Williams, R. (1994). *Nondesigners design book.* Berkeley, CA: Peachpit.

Index